CULTURAL ANTHROPOLOGY

A PROBLEM-BASED APPROACH

CULTURAL ANTHROPOLOGY
A PROBLEM-BASED APPROACH

RICHARD H. ROBBINS

DEPARTMENT OF ANTHROPOLOGY
STATE UNIVERSITY OF NEW YORK—PLATTSBURGH

F.E. PEACOCK PUBLISHERS
ITASCA, ILLINOIS 60143

New ways of thinking!
Judging others, deciding
(my dosies (see appendix
(.2)

Copyright © 1993
F. E. Peacock Publishers, Inc.
All rights reserved
Library of Congress Catalog Card No. 92-061963
ISBN 0-87581-375-5
Printed in the United States of America
Printing: 10   9   8   7   6   5   4   3   2   1
Year: 97   96   95   94   93

C O N T E N T S

ACKNOWLEDGMENTS

It is characteristic of the individualist emphasis in American society that a project such as this book, to which so many have contributed, is attributed to a single author. A book is truly a collaborative effort. Among the many whose contributions have made this book possible are James Clifton, Leo Weigman, Dan Spinella, Gloria Reardon, Ali Pomponio, Jon McGee, Pat Hoffmann, James Armstrong, Phil Devita, Mark Cohen, Pat Higgins, Ted Peacock, Tom Moran, Joyce Waite, Deborah Light, Christine L. Fry, Susan Abbott-Jamieson, Charles O. Ellenbaum, Alice Pomponio, Stanley M. Newman, R. Jon McGee, Myrdene Anderson, Thomas Hakansson, Jeffery Hopkins, Tracy Hopkins, Lesiak/Crampton Design, Inc., Cheryl Kucharzak, and Kim Vander Steen. The students in my introductory anthropology course who used and commented on various drafts of the book also contributed heavily. Responsible also are the researchers whose studies of human behavior and belief provided the substance for the text and the people from cultures around the world whose cooporation has helped enrich our understanding of them and of our common humanity. Finally, I wish to acknowledge the patience and help of my family—Amy, Rebecca, and Michael—and my parents—Al and Yetta—to whom the book is dedicated.

F O R E W O R D

In 30-some years of college teaching, I never managed to lay hands on an introduction to a cultural anthropology textbook I found satisfactory for very long. Texts I personally admired commonly repelled most students, while texts students deemed highly satisfactory I often thought unpalatable. And then there was the nearly insurmountable problem of integrating the contents of a textbook with what happened in the classroom, and—an even more serious matter—what went on inside students' heads.

I wish Richard Robbins had written this book decades ago. Had he done so, he would have made my life as teacher far more agreeable and effective, and he would have helped me get more of the core of cultural anthropology into the minds of many more students.

Robbins is one of that rarest breed of academics, a dedicated, seasoned, and thoughtful teacher as well as an experienced practicing anthropologist. Of greater importance, following years of thinking and testing, he brings to this book a clear understanding of how young people best learn and a solid view of pedagogy—a theory of how to go about casting light into the unilluminated recesses of someone else's mind. This is no standard, average anthropology text. It is not an omnibus compilation of conventional topics, simplified definitions, and amusing or startling graphics. It is not a textbookish text.

It is a book that works at getting students into a situation where they can grasp what modern cultural anthropology is all about at its center. Long after their short-term memories will have lost the particulars—the short definitions of *kula* ring or gender role—they will firmly retain deep knowledge of the styles, approaches, and core issues of the cultural anthropology of today. This is a book, properly used by students and teachers, that will affect lives and living for decades to come.

This sort of persistent learning Robbins facilitates with layers of structure. Seven large problems represent the ribs of the book, but these are tied to one another with salient queries that form part of its connective tissue. All, together, illustrate just some of the ways anthropologists go about knowing about humankind. These problems and approaches are supplemented by a selection of diverse exercises. Some of these can be accomplished by solo efforts, in the solitude of a student's late-night hours. Others, and I think these the strongest, demand active learning—interactive learning—in small and large groups. Always, Robbins encourages creative participation—reactive thoughtfulness. This will surely lead to the greatest thrill humans ever experience, the discovery of new insights and understanding.

What these will consist of I cannot say. Neither can Robbins nor anyone else. For one vital lesson of cultural anthropology is that ours is an unfinished quest. Only this new generation, and generations to come, can push the edges of our understanding along. Anthropology is not a selection of fixed questions and pat answers, as students will learn from using this book. Only they can make it work and grow.

In writing this book I think Robbins has gone well beyond performing as an anthropologist-teacher. Here he serves as a mentor, in the fullest sense of that word. He tells you where he is going. He shows you part of the way and some of what you need to move along. He describes some way stations and intermediate goals. But he does not lead you by the hand. He must do it this way because much of the human condition remains a puzzle, no matter how well we may now think we can see some of the pieces and designs. Discovering more parts and patterns will be the task of those who profit from reading and using this book. I envy them their quest, and their opportunity.

James A. Clifton
Scholar-in-Residence, Department of Anthropology
Western Michigan University

For anthropologists, learning and teaching form part of a cultural process that is affected by a host of social, cultural, individual, and situational factors. A college classroom constitutes but one of many learning environments that influence the kinds of learning that occur within its boundaries. This is why I initially undertook the writing of *Cultural Anthropology: A Problem-Based Approach.* My underlying purpose was to help instructors in introductory courses in cultural anthropology develop a classroom culture that, regardless of class size or instructional technique, promotes active learning and critical thinking and impresses on students that they, along with other peoples and cultures of the world, are cultural animals who are worthy of anthropological study.

The organization of the text by problems and questions rather than topics actively involves students in the learning process. Each of the first seven chapters focuses on a specific problem of anthropological as well as general concern. These problems, listed in the Contents, include such controversies as: How can people begin to understand beliefs and behaviors that are different from their own? Why do different peoples believe different things, and why are they so certain that their view of the world is correct and others' views are wrong? Why are modern societies characterized by social, political, and economic inequalities? These kinds of comprehensive problems may have no definitive solutions, but they are what drive much intellectual inquiry.

From each problem specific questions were derived that are amenable to study and research, and about which more-or-less definitive conclusions can be reached. These questions provide the structure for examining the comprehensive problems, as indicated by their use as subheads for Chapters 1–7. The final chapter has a different format; it presents examples of actual applications of anthropology to the solution of problems reflecting cultural diversity.

It would be impossible in an introductory-level textbook in cultural anthropology to present all questions of relevance to cultural anthropologists. In selecting the content, therefore, I looked for problems and questions that are central to anthropological concerns and that allow discussion of subjects and works typically covered in introductory courses in cultural anthropology. The Topic-Questions Correspondence Chart, which links these topics to the problems and questions considered in this text, can be used as a guide for using the material in a different course sequence.

TOPIC-QUESTIONS CORRESPONDENCE CHART

The following guide indicates the chapters or questions in which topics treated in the typical cultural anthropology textbook are addressed.

TOPIC	CORRESPONDING QUESTIONS OR CHAPTERS
Applied anthropology	Chapter 8
Art	Question 3.2
Caste	Question 6.1
Colonialism	Questions 2.3, 2.5
Cultural evolution	Question 2.1
Culture change	Chapters 2, 8
Culture concept	Chapter 1
Education	Questions 3.2, 5.3; Application 8.3
Family organization	Chapter 4
Feud	Questions 7.1, 7.3
Food production	Questions 2.2, 2.3
Gender roles	Chapter 4; Questions 5.2, 5.3, 6.3
Gift giving	Questions 4.3, 5.4, 5.5
Kinship	Chapter 4; Question 5.2
Language and culture	Questions 1.4, 3.1, 3.3, 5.3, 7.5
Marriage rules	Question 4.2
Medical anthropology	Question 2.4; Application 8.1
Peasants	Chapter 4; Question 2.3; Application 8.2
Political organization and control	Questions 5.5, 6.2, 6.5, 7.3, 7.4; Application 8.5
Racial stratification	Question 6.3
Religion	Questions 1.1, 3.1, 3.2, 3.5, 6.3, 6.5, 7.1
Revolution	Questions 6.3, 7.3
Ritual	Questions 1.4, 1.5, 2.4, 3.2, 3.3, 4.2, 5.3, 5.4
Sexual stratification	Questions 5.3, 6.1, 6.3, 7.3
Sexuality	Questions 4.3, 5.2, 5.3, 6.3, 7.3
Social stratification	Chapter 6
Socialization	Question 5.1, 5.2, 5.3
Status and rank	Chapter 6
Subsistence techniques	Questions 2.1, 2.2, 2.3; Application 8.2

TOPIC	CORRESPONDING QUESTIONS OR CHAPTERS
Symbolism	Questions 1.1, 1.4, 1.5, 3.1, 3.2, 3.3
Systems of exchange	Questions 4.1, 4.3, 5.4, 5.5
Urbanism	Question 6.4
War	Chapter 7

The sources used to explore answers to the questions posed were selected to present a balanced viewpoint that invites students to formulate their own informed responses. They also represent both the classical studies typically used in introductory-level courses and new or less-well-known works that bear on contemporary concerns. Instead of footnotes, each chapter concludes with an annotated section of references and suggested readings that cites the works used in response to each question and suggests additional readings. A bibliography and a glossary of terms are included at the end of the text.

Cultural Anthropology: A Problem-Based Approach also promotes active learning with the exercises, application problems, and simulations included in the text or in the Instructor's Handbook available with it. These are designed to help students realize some of the implications of the problems or questions for their own lives as well as the lives of others. They can serve as discussion questions, writing exercises, or topics of group inquiry or cooperative learning. In my experience, these exercises convey to students the positive value, the enjoyment, and the necessity of intellectual exchange. The Handbook includes suggestions on using the exercises and information on what to expect in the way of student response. There is also a list of film and video materials to accompany each question raised in the text.

Finally, I do not believe that students learning about the cultures of others can fully appreciate them without first understanding something of their own cultural perspectives. That is, to appreciate the fact that different peoples construct their own worlds, students must appreciate that they, as cultural animals, do the same. For that reason, the text contains numerous comparisons of world cultures with American culture, and many of the exercises invite students to apply what they have learned to the analysis of their own behaviors and beliefs.

Implicit in the text and the Handbook materials is my conviction that the culture of the classroom should foster cooperation. However, I do not believe that cooperation precludes conflict and critique. I would be grateful for comments from instructors and students about the text, the problems and questions, and the general approach, as well as for suggestions for additional exercises, videos or films, or other materials that would enhance its use. I also would be happy to distribute such suggestions to instructors who have adopted the text. I can be contacted at the Department of Anthropology, SUNY at Plattsburgh, Plattsburgh, NY 12901, or through electronic mail at Robbins@SNYPLAVA.Bitnet.

Richard H. Robbins

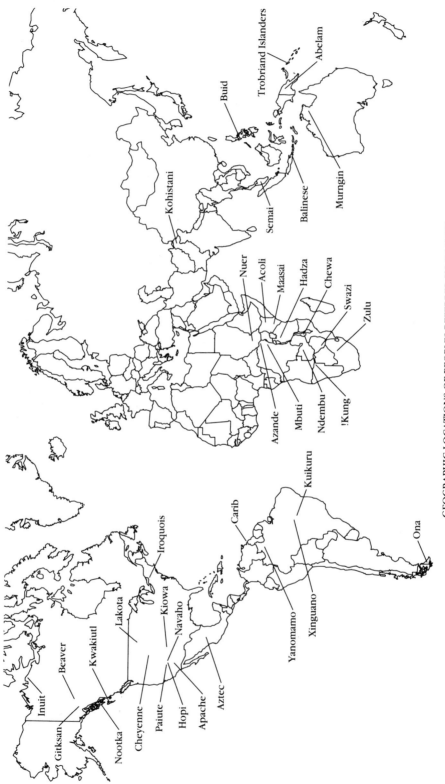

GEOGRAPHIC LOCATIONS OF PEOPLES REFERRED TO IN TEXT.

C H A P T E R   1

CULTURE AND MEANING

PROBLEM 1: HOW CAN PEOPLE BEGIN TO UNDERSTAND BELIEFS AND
BEHAVIORS THAT ARE DIFFERENT FROM THEIR OWN?

[W]e have come to think of our social and cultural world as a series of sign systems, comparable to languages. What we live among and relate to are not physical objects and events; they are objects and events with meaning; not just complicated wooden constructions but chairs and tables; not just physical gestures but acts of courtesy or hostility. If we are able to understand our social and cultural world, we must think not of independent objects but of symbolic structures, systems of relations which by enabling objects and actions to have meaning, create a human universe.

Jonathan Culler

INTRODUCTION: *The Problem of Us and Them*

Traveling through Europe in 1867, the American author Mark Twain recorded his impressions of the people he met. Here is how he described the people of the Azores that he encountered at his first stop: "The people lie, and cheat the stranger, and are desperately ignorant, and have hardly any reverence for their dead. The latter trait shows how little better they are than the donkeys they eat and sleep with."

Here is what Twain had to say about the Greeks:

Every body lies and cheats—every body who is in business, at any rate. Even foreigners soon have to come down to the custom of the country, and they do not buy and sell long in Constantinople till they lie and cheat like a Greek.

He didn't spare Italian farmers either:

They were not respectable people—they were not worthy people—they were not learned and wise people—but in their breasts, all their stupid lives long, resteth a peace that passeth understanding! How can men calling themselves men, consent to be so degraded and happy?

Twain, who often was equally harsh on his fellow Americans, also had many complimentary things to say about the people he met on this travels. But his reactions to his first confrontations with different cultures were probably no different from those of thousands of travelers and explorers who preceded and followed him. Twain was comparing (unfavorably, in this case) *us* with *them*.

Of course, people who confront American customs for the first time also find them a bit odd. Visitors from Thailand think it strange that Americans can just say hello to others and then turn away; people from the Middle East think it odd that American women can walk around unescorted without covering their faces. Richard Scaglion is fond of telling the story of his friend, a member of the Abelam tribe of Papua New Guinea, who was looking through an issue of *Sports Illustrated* magazine. The friend, dressed in full ceremonial regalia with a feather through his nose, was laughing uncontrollably at a woman shown in a liquor advertisement. When he managed to stop laughing long enough to explain what he thought was so funny, he said, "This white woman has made holes in her ears and stuck things in them." When Scaglion

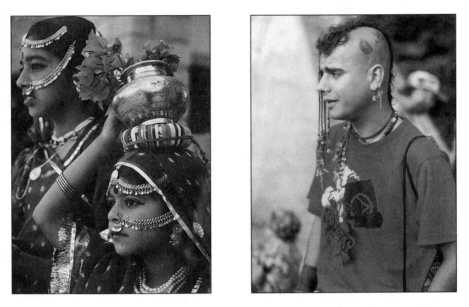

An American devotee of punk rock at Woodstock, New York, and a young East Indian girl taking part in a welcoming ceremony demonstrate certain similarities in ideas about bodily ornamentation, though there are varying standards for appropriate attire in either society.

pointed out that his friend had an ornament in his nose, the reply was, "That's different. That's for beauty and has ceremonial significance. But I didn't know that white people mutilated themselves."

In culturally diverse societies such as the United States, people no longer need to explore, travel, or reside in different countries in order to confront different ways of believing and acting. The multicultural character of urban society, the varied social backgrounds of students in schools and at colleges and universities, the internationalization of business, and the ease of communication across national boundaries all have increased the likelihood of confronting different ways of looking at the world. How people react to these confrontations is largely determined by their understanding of the reasons for cultural variety. Explaining the varieties of human belief and behavior and making sense of the meanings that peoples from different societies ascribe to their experiences are the goals of **cultural anthropology**.

This book is organized around seven general problems that arise from the human condition, problems such as how to understand people with different beliefs and behaviors, how to explain why ways of life change, how societies justify violence, and whether there is any solution to problems of social inequality. These are problems that concern not only cultural anthropologists but all of us. None of the problems considered has a definitive answer; the best we can do is try to reach a better understanding of why the problem exists and consider some of the things that might be done about it. To do this, we can ask certain questions concerning these problems that anthropologists have studied and sought answers for. At various points you will be asked to supply your own answers to these questions and perhaps to discuss your solutions with others. Furthermore, understanding other peoples requires you to recognize that your behaviors and beliefs, as well as those found in other societies, are socially patterned and constructed. For that reason, you will find many comparisons between American life and life in other societies. The final chapter presents some applications of anthropological knowledge to actual problems for which you may provide your own solutions.

In considering the principal problem of how we can begin to understand beliefs and behaviors that are different from our own, this chapter focuses on five questions. The first and most basic is why human beings differ in their beliefs and behaviors; that is, what is it about human nature that produces such a variety of ways of believing and behaving? The second question is one of values. More often than not, people react to different ways of life with shock, scorn, or disapproval. Are such reactions warranted, and, if they aren't, how do we judge the beliefs and behaviors of others? The third question is critical to anthropological inquiry. Is it possible to set aside the meanings that we ascribe to experience and see the world through the eyes of others? Fourth, assuming that it is possible to come to some understanding of how others see the world, how can the meanings that others find in experience be interpreted and described? The final question concerns what learning about other peoples can tell us about ourselves.

QUESTIONS

1.1 Why do human beings differ in their beliefs and behaviors?
1.2 How do people judge the beliefs and behaviors of others?
1.3 Is it possible to see the world through the eyes of others?
1.4 How can the meanings that others find in experience be interpreted and described?
1.5 What can learning about other peoples tell Americans about themselves?

QUESTION 1.1 *Why Do Human Beings Differ in Their Beliefs and Behaviors?*

From an anthropological perspective, members of a society view the world in a *similar* way because they share the same **culture**; people *differ* in how they view the world because their cultures differ. A good place to start to understand the concept of culture is with the fact that members of all human societies experience specific life events such as birth, death, and the quest for food, water, and shelter. All societies have what are for them appropriate rules for courtship, ideas about child rearing, procedures for exchanging goods, methods of food production, techniques for building shelters, and so on. But from society to society, the meanings people give to such events differ.

Take death, as one example. For some people, death marks the passage of a person from one world to another. For others, death is an ending, the final event of a life cycle, while still others consider death a part of a never-ending cycle of birth, death, and rebirth. The Kwakiutl of British Columbia, for example, believe that at a person's death the soul leaves the body and enters the body of a salmon. When a salmon is caught and eaten, a soul is released and is free to enter the body of another person.

Some societies fear the dead; others revere them. In traditional China, each household contained a shrine to the family ancestors. Before any major family decision, the head of the household addressed the shrine to ask the ancestor's advice, thus making the dead part of the world of the living. In southern Italy, however, funeral customs were designed to discourage the dead from returning. Relatives placed useful objects such as matches and small change near the body to placate the soul of the deceased and ensure that it did not return to disturb the living.

Members of some societies accept death as a natural and inevitable occurrence, while others always attribute death to the malevolent act of some person, often through sorcery. In these societies every death elicits suspicion and a demand for vengeance. Members of other societies require great demonstrations of grief and mourning for a deceased. Some, such as the Dani of New Guinea, require a close female relative of a recently deceased person to sacrifice part of a finger. In southern Europe widows were required to shave their heads, while in traditional India, widows were cremated at their husbands' funerals. In the United States, survivors of the deceased are expected to restrain their grief almost as if it were a contagious disease. To Americans, the sight of southern Italian women pulling their hair and being restrained from flinging themselves into an open grave is as bewildering as their own restraint of grief would be to traditional Italians.

Of all the some two million species of living organisms that inhabit the earth, only humans dwell largely in worlds that they themselves create by giving meanings to things. This creation is what anthropologists mean by the term *culture*. Human beings are cultural animals; they ascribe meanings of their own creation to objects, persons, behaviors, emotions, and events and proceed to act as though those meanings are real. All facets of their lives—death, birth, courtship, mating, food acquisition and consumption—are cloaked with meanings.

Clifford Geertz suggests that human beings are compelled to impose meaning on their experiences because without these meanings to help them comprehend experience and impose an order on the universe, the world would seem a jumble, "a chaos of pointless acts and exploding emotions." Geertz says that human beings are "incomplete or unfinished animals who complete themselves through culture—not culture in general, but specific forms of it: Balinese, Italian, Ilongot, Chinese, Kwakiutl, American, and so on." When people share the meanings they give to experiences, they share and participate in the same culture.

Differences in culture arise in part from the fact that different groups of human beings, for various reasons, create, share, and participate in different realities—different meanings for death, for birth, for marriage, for food. Objects, persons, behaviors, emotions, and events in a human world have the meanings ascribed to them by those who share, use, or experience them. The clothes people wear, the way they wear them, the food they eat (or refuse to eat), and even their gender are defined through the meanings people give them.

EXERCISE 1.1 ────────────────────────────────

Food is a cultural creation; that is, human beings define what is and what is not food. Consider, for example, the items listed below, all of which serve as food among one group of people or another. Which of these would you eat, and which would you not eat? If there are any you would not eat, ask yourself why.

	Yes	No
eel		
kangaroo tail		
dog		
guinea pig		
raw squid		
sea urchin (sea slugs)		
ants		
monkey brains		
grubs		
possum		
rattlesnake		
iguana		
horse		
dolphin		
pickled pig's feet		
haggis (stuffed intestines)		
cow brains		
blood sausage		
raw steak		
rotten meat		
armadillo		

One of the problems that cultural anthropologists address is understanding why different groups of human beings have different cultures. Why does one group assign one set of meanings to what they experience, while another group assigns it another set of distinct meanings? Many of the questions to be addressed in later chapters concern how these differences can be explained. We may be able to explain our initial shock or bewilderment upon confronting different cultures if we understand something of why cultural differences exist. But how should we react if the meanings that others ascribe to experience differ from our own? Since human groups create different, often seemingly incompatible worlds, it is often necessary, though difficult, to accommodate the alternative meanings others ascribe to objects, persons, behaviors, emotions, and events.

QUESTION 1.2 *How Do People Judge the Beliefs and Behaviors of Others?*

There are so many versions of what the world is like, how do we go about trying to understand each of them without making positive or negative judg-

Depiction by a European artist in 1723 of a sacrificial ceremony by Mexican aborigines in the southeastern Mexican state of Tabasco. Behaviors such as human sacrifice can test the limits of cultural tolerance.

ments? *Which version is correct?* Are there any we can reject or condemn? Can we say, as so many have, that one culture is superior to another?

In the catalog of human behaviors and beliefs, it is not difficult to find practices or ideas that may seem bizarre or shocking even to trained anthropologists. Cultural anthropologists have described the beliefs of the Ilongots of the Philippines, who must kill an enemy to obtain a head they can throw away in order to diminish the grief and rage they feel at the death of a kinsman or kinswoman. They have studied the historical records of the Aztecs of Mexico who, when contacted by Cortes in 1519, believed that the universe underwent periodic destruction, and that the only way to ward off disaster was to pluck the hearts from live sacrificial victims to offer to the gods. They have reported on the circumcision practices of the people in the Nile Valley of the Sudan where, in order to ensure a young girl's chastity and virginity, her genitalia are mutilated to close the vaginal opening so completely that additional surgery is often required to allow intercourse and childbirth later in life. The question is, how should we react to practices and beliefs such as these? Should we condemn them or accept them?

The Ethnocentric Fallacy and the Relativistic Fallacy

If we do condemn or reject the beliefs or behaviors of others, we may be committing the **ethnocentric fallacy**, the idea that our beliefs and behaviors are right and true, while those of other peoples are wrong or misguided. Cultural anthropologists have long fought against such **ethnocentrism**. They try to show that what often appears on the surface to be an odd belief or a bizarre bit of behavior is functional and logical in the context of a particular culture. They find the ethnocentric fallacy *intellectually* intolerable; if everyone everywhere thinks that they are right and others must be wrong, we can only reach an intellectual and social dead end. Furthermore, if we assume that we have all the right answers, our study of other cultures becomes simply the study of other people's mistakes.

EXERCISE 1.2 *WATCH SPECIFIC WORDS!!*

operational defs

Individually write down whether you "agree" or "disagree" with each statement that follows. Then see if anyone disagrees with each statement being considered. If even one person disagrees, change the wording so that the statement is acceptable to *all*. You may not simply "agree to disagree."

STATEMENTS:

better v. different

what you mean

1. The fact that the United States was able to place people on the moon proves its technological superiority.
2. Foreigners coming to live here should give up their foreign ways and adapt to the new country as quickly as possible.

what does this mean?

3. Many of the world's populations do not take enough initiative to develop themselves; therefore they remain "underdeveloped."
4. Minority members of any population should be expected to conform to the customs and values of the majority.

Because of the intellectual implications of enthnocentrism, cultural anthropologists emphatically reject this position. But the alternative to ethnocentrism, **relativism**, is equally problematic. Relativism, simply stated, holds that no behavior or belief can be judged to be odd or wrong simply because it is different from our own. Instead, we must try to understand a culture in its own terms and to understand behaviors or beliefs for the purpose, function, or meaning they have to people in the societies in which we find them. In other words, a specific belief or behavior can only be understood in relation to the culture—the system of meanings—in which it is embedded.

For example, according to Renato Rosaldo, the ceremonies and rituals accompanying a successful headhunting expedition psychologically help the Ilongot manage their grief over the death of a kinsperson. Rose Oldfield-Hayes explains that even to the women of the northern Sudan, the genital mutilations of young girls makes perfect sense. Since family honor is determined in part by the sexual modesty of female family members, the operation, by preventing intercourse, protects the honor of the family, protects girls from sexual assault, and protects the honor and reputation of the girl herself. Moreover, says Oldfield-Hayes, the practice serves as a means of population control.

However, relativism poses a *moral* predicament. We may concede that it is permissible to rip hearts out of living human beings, provided you believe this is necessary in order to save the world, or that it is permissible to subject young girls to painful mutilation to protect family reputations or control population growth. But this quickly leads us into the **relativistic fallacy**, the idea that it is impossible to make moral judgments about the beliefs and behaviors of others. This, of course, seems morally intolerable because it implies that there is no belief or behavior that can be condemned as wrong. So we are left with two untenable positions: the ethnocentric alternative, which is intellectually unsatisfactory, and the relativistic alternative, which is morally unsatisfactory. How do we solve this problem?

Clifford Geertz says that "the aim of anthropology is the enlargement of the universe of human discourse." Encountering other cultures enhances our understanding by presenting us with puzzles, particularly puzzles about ourselves, that might not otherwise occur to us. The predicaments created for us by our confrontations with other cultures provide us with one way out of our anthropological dilemma. We can avoid judging as wrong all cultures that are different from our own, or, at the other extreme, claiming that we can make no judgment about the rightness or wrongness of others' behaviors and beliefs. Then we can proceed by treating human differences and similarities as puzzles through which we can enlarge our understandings of ourselves as well as others. That is, confronting what at first seems strange, bizarre, absurd, or just different in other peoples should lead us to examine what it is about ourselves that makes others seem so different.

Ideally, our attempts to understand what at first seemed puzzling in some culture, and our arrival at some solution to that puzzle, should result in questioning what it was about us that made the behavior or belief seem puzzling in the first place. In addition, we need to understand that if each culture orders the world in a certain way for its members, it also blocks or masks other ways of viewing things. We need to appreciate that there are perspectives different from our own, and that our ethnocentric biases may blind us to those alternatives. In other words, while culture provides us with certain meanings to give to objects, persons, behaviors, emotions, and events, it also shields us from alternative meanings. What our culture hides from us may be more important than what it reveals.

QUESTION 1.3 *Is It Possible to See the World Through the Eyes of Others?*

This question lies at the heart of the anthropological enterprise. The task of the cultural anthropologist is to learn one culture and then relate what she or he learns to members of another culture, to translate the meanings of one world into the meanings of another. The unique feature of cultural anthropology is the application of the **ethnographic method**, the immersion of investigators in the lives and cultures of the people they are trying to understand in order to comprehend the meanings these people ascribe to their experience. This process utilizes the techniques of anthropological fieldwork, especially

participant observation, the active participation of the observer in the lives of those being studied.

The ethnographic method is only part of the anthropological enterprise, however. The anthropologist also seeks to explain why peoples view the world as they do and to contribute to the understanding of human behavior in general. But the fieldwork used in the ethnographic method is the beginning of the enterprise. Fieldwork involves the meeting of at least two cultures: that of the researcher and that of the culture and the people the researcher is trying to understand. Anthropological researchers must set aside their own views of things and attempt to see the world in a new way. In many respects, they must assume the demeanor and status of children who must be taught by their elders the proper view of the world. And like children making their way in a world they do not fully comprehend, anthropologists often find themselves in awkward or embarrassing situations and must be prepared to learn from these experiences.

The Honest Anthropologist

When Susan Dwyer-Shick traveled to Turkey to study folklore, her husband and not quite two-year-old daughter stayed behind in the United States. In the field, anthropologists are often asked as many questions about their personal lives as they ask of others. Dwyer-Shick resolved in advance that she would be completely "honest" in answering questions, so when some Turkish women asked about her marital and parenting life, she responded by telling about her husband and daughter. Then the women asked her with whom she had left her daughter, and she explained that her husband was looking after the child. Thinking that the anthropologist had perhaps misunderstood their language, the women asked her again. When they got the same response, they asked a schoolboy to interpret for them; they thought she still had not understood the question.

At this point the anthropologist realized that her response to the question might determine the way the women viewed her and whether they would trust her. She was learning from an awkward moment something about being a woman in Turkey, and so, to answer "correctly," she lied. Dwyer-Shick realized from the questions and the reluctance of the women to accept her initial answer that for Turkish women it was inappropriate to leave a child in the care of a husband, and indeed for the husband to be left without a woman to care for him. She then told the women that her mother was looking after her daughter, and they accepted that.

The Embarrassed Anthropologist

Awkwardness and embarrassment are a part of fieldwork, as well as a part of the process through which the fieldworker learns about another culture. Richard Scaglion spent over a year with the Abelam of Papua New Guinea. Shortly after he arrived in the field, he observed and photographed an Abelam pig hunt in which the men set out nets and waited while the women and children made lots of noise to drive the pigs into the nets. Soon after, he was invited by the Abelam to participate in a pig hunt, and he took this as a sign of acceptance, that the people "liked him." He started to go with the men, but they told him they wanted him to go with the women and children to beat the bush, explaining, "We've never seen anyone who makes as much noise in the jungle as you." Later, wanting to redeem himself, Scaglion offered to help an Abelam who was planting crops with a digging stick. A crowd gathered to watch as Scaglion used a shovel to try to dig a demonstration hole. After he had struggled for several minutes to get the shovel into the hard-packed soil, someone handed him a digging stick, and he was amazed at how easy it was to use. Later he found out that several Abelam had shovels but rarely used them because they didn't work.

After months of answering Scaglion's questions about their view of the natural world, such as the moon, sun, and stars, some Abelam asked him about his views of the universe. Feeling on safe ground, he gave the usual grade school lecture about the shape of the earth and its daily rotation and travels around the sun. He used a coconut to show them the relative positions on the earth of New Guinea, Australia, Europe, and the United States. Everyone listened intently, and Scaglion thought it went well until about a week later, when he overheard some elders wondering how it was that Americans walked upside down!

Beginning again, Scaglion used the coconut to explain how, as the earth rotates, sometimes the United States would be upright and New Guinea would be on the bottom. The Abelam rejected this because they could see that they were *not* upside down, and no one, not even some of the old people in the community, remembered ever having walked upside down. Scaglion began to draw on the physics he had studied in college, and as he tried to explain Newton's law of gravity (or "grabity," as his friends pronounced it), he realized that he didn't understand "grabity" either. It was something he had accepted since third grade, a concept that even physicists take for granted as a convenient theoretical concept.

Awkward or embarrassing moments in the field may help anthropologists to understand a culture, or even to question their own view of the world. But the possibility of seeing the world through the eyes of others remains a subject of contention among anthropologists. Obviously, to communicate with anyone, even members of their own society, people must share some of the meanings they ascribe to objects, persons, behaviors, emotions, and events. But what happens when views of the world are completely different?

EXERCISE 1.3

Think of some awkward or embarrassing situation created by something you did or didn't do, said or didn't say. What was inappropriate about your behavior, and why did it lead to misunderstanding or embarrassment? What did you learn from the experience about the meaning of your or others' behavior?

Confronting Witchcraft in Mexico

When Michael Kearney traveled to the town of Santa Catarina Ixtepeji in the valley of Oaxaca, Mexico, he intended to study the relationship between the people's view of the world and their social arrangements and environment. He began his work secure in his knowledge of the scientific and materialist view of the world in which he was reared, but he was often fascinated by the differences between his view and that of the people of Santa Catarina Ixtepeji. Theirs was a world controlled by mystic notions of "fate," the will of God, and malevolent witches and other harmful and sometimes lethal spiritual forces. He became familiar with the Ixtepejanos view of the world, never doubting that it was "unscientific" but justified, perhaps, by a life in which suffering, disease, and death were common.

Kearney's faith in his own view of the world was momentarily shattered by an incident that began innocently enough. Walking to an appointment, he came upon an obviously distressed woman, Doña Delfina. She was known as a witch, and Kearney had been trying unsuccessfully to interview her. When they met she explained that her sister-in-law had a "very bad disease in her arms," and she wanted him to help. Kearney accompanied Doña Delfina to her house, where he found that the sister-in-law's arms were ulcerated with deep, oozing lesions that looked to him like infected burns. They rejected his offer to take the sick woman to a doctor for medical treatment, so Kearney said he had some ointment that might help, and they eagerly agreed that he should use it. He got the ointment, which contained an anesthetic, and daubed it on the woman's sores. Much to the amazement of Doña Delfina, her sister-in-law immediately felt better. By that afternoon, her arms had greatly improved, the next morning scabs had formed, and the day after she had completely recovered.

Kearney was credited with a "miraculous cure." But the same day, when an Ixtepejanos friend asked Kearney what he had done and he proudly explained, the friend replied, "Why did you do that? It was not a good thing to do." The sick woman, he said, had been the victim of black magic; another woman, Gregoria, was trying to take Delfina's brother away from his wife and was using black magic to make Delfina's sister-in-law sick. Delfina was using *her* magic to keep her brother in the household, but Gregoria was winning. Now, the friend explained to Kearney, he had intervened, tipping the balance of power back to Delfina but creating a powerful enemy in Gregoria. "Maybe you should leave town for a while until Gregoria calms down," Kearney's friend suggested. But Kearney did not take the danger seriously and may never have done so were it not for two incidents that occurred soon afterward.

A young doctor in town asked Kearney, who came from a medical background, to assist in an autopsy of a man who had died in a fall off a truck. It was a particularly long and gory autopsy accomplished only with rusty carpenter's tools in a dimly lit room; images of the scene and the cadaver disturbed Kearney's sleep over the next few days. One night, about a week later, as the wind beat cornstalks against his house, Kearney felt an itching on his arm. Rolling up his sleeve, he discovered several angry welts that seemed to be growing as he watched them. Immediately he thought of the chancrous arms of Delfina's sister-in-law, realizing at the same time that Gregoria's house was only 50 yards from his and she could be trying to kill him. "She got me!"

he thought. The image of the cadaver on the table jumped into his mind, followed by a wish that he had gotten out of town while there was time. As Kearney put it, he was witnessing the disintegration of his scientific, materialist view of the world and grappling with forces with which he was unprepared to deal.

Kearney is not sure how long his initial terror lasted—seconds, perhaps minutes. As he struggled against it, he realized that he was suspended between two worlds, that of the Ixtepejanos and his own. He was questioning a world of meanings that he had until then taken for granted. He was able to truly believe that the world was as the Ixtepejanos saw it for only a while, but as he retrieved his own view, the Ixtepejano worldview, filled with witchcraft and magic, ceased to be only intellectually interesting. It acquired a reality and a sense of legitimacy for him that it did not have before he experienced the real fear that he had been bewitched.

The experiences of these three anthropologists—Dwyer-Shick, Kearney, and Scaglion—highlight certain features of the ethnographic method. They especially illustrate the attempt of anthropologists to appreciate the views of others while at the same time questioning their own views of the world. The tension created by attempting to enter the lives of others and at the same time to maintain one's own emotional and cognitive balance is what makes the ethnographic method unique.

Claude Levi-Strauss, one of the leading anthropologists of the twentieth century, says that fieldwork, and the attempts of anthropologists to immerse themselves in the world of others, makes them "marginal" men or women. They are never completely native because they cannot totally shed their own cultural perceptions, but they are never the same again after having glimpsed alternative visions of the world. Anthropologists are, as Roger Keesing put it, outsiders who know something of what it is to be insiders.

QUESTION 1.4 *How Can the Meanings That Others Find in Experience Be Interpreted and Described?*

In one Sherlock Holmes detective story, Dr. Watson, Holmes's assistant, decides to teach the great detective a lesson in humility. He hands Holmes a pocket watch owned by Watson's late brother and challenges Holmes to infer from the watch the character of its owner. Holmes's interpretation: "[Your brother] was a man of untidy habits—very untidy and careless. He was left with good prospects, but he threw away his chances and finally, taking to drink, he died."

Watson, astounded at the accuracy of Holmes's description of his late brother, asks if it was guesswork. "I never guess," replies Holmes:

> I began by stating that your brother was careless. When you observe the lower part of the watch case, you notice that it is not only dented in two places, but it is cut and marked all over from the habit of keeping other hard objects, such as coins or keys, in the same pocket. Surely it is no great feat to assume that a man who treats [an expensive] watch so cavalierly must be a careless man. Neither is it a very far-fetched inference that a man who inherits one article of such value is pretty well provided for in other respects.

"But what about his drinking habits?" asks Watson. Holmes responds:

Look at the innerplate which contains the keyhole [where the watch is wound]. Look at the thousands of scratches all around the hole—marks where the key has slipped. What sober man's key could have scored those grooves? But you will never see a drunkard's watch without them. He winds it at night, and he leaves these traces of his unsteady hand. Where is the mystery in all this?

Had Sherlock Holmes been an anthropologist, he might have been tempted also to draw some inferences about the society in which the watch was manufactured. The people must be preoccupied with time, and they must have both the need and the means to measure it. Activities in their society must be carefully scheduled, since they need to carry timepieces. They must have an exact technology to be able to produce an object that small and that precise, and they must have an elaborate system of occupational specialization, as well as a system of mass production. Watson's brother's watch was a product of Western society, part of its culture. Holmes "read" the watch as if it were a collection of symbols or words, a text that revealed the character of its owner. He could have as easily viewed it as a text inscribed with the symbols that revealed the character of the civilization that produced it.

One way to think about culture is as a text of significant symbols—words, gestures, drawings, natural objects—anything, in fact, that carries meaning. To understand another culture we must be able, as Holmes was with a watch, to decipher the meaning of the symbols that comprise a **cultural text.** We must be able to interpret the meanings embedded in the language, objects, gestures, and activities that are shared by members of a society. Fortunately, the ability to decipher a cultural text is part of being human; in our everyday lives we both read and maintain the text that makes up our own culture. We have learned the meanings behind the symbols that frame our lives, and we share those meanings with others. To understand other cultures, we must take the abilities that have enabled us to dwell in our own culture and apply them to the cultures of others.

Deciphering the Balinese Cockfight

To illustrate how an anthropologist might decipher a cultural text, imagine yourself coming upon a cockfight on the island of Bali. You see a ring in which two roosters with sharpened metal spurs attached to their legs are set at each other until one kills the other. Surrounding the fighting cocks are men shouting encouragement to their favorites, each having placed a wager that his favorite will kill its opponent.

What do you make of this? Your first reaction might be one of shock or disgust at the spectacle of the crowd urging the cocks to bloody combat. After a while you might begin to find similarities to events that are meaningful to you, such as some American sport. But what if, like Sherlock Holmes (or like Clifford Geertz, from whom this example is taken), you want to understand the meaning of what is happening and what that meaning tells you about the ways the Balinese view their world? If you assume that the cockfight is a feature of Balinese culture, a Balinese text filled with symbols that

Malaysian men prepare to release their birds at a cockfight, a major sporting event in their society that helps the people assign meanings to their lives.

carry meaning about what it is to be Balinese, how might you proceed to read this text?

You might begin by finding out the language the Balinese use to talk about the cockfight. You would no doubt discover that the double entendre of *cock* both as a synonym for *rooster* and as a euphemism for *penis* is the same for the Balinese as it is for Americans. The double entendre even produces the same jokes, puns, and obscenities in Bali as it does in the United States. You would discover that *sabung,* the Balinese word for cock, has numerous other meanings and is used metaphorically to mean the same as *hero, warrior, champion, political candidate, bachelor, dandy, lady-killer,* or *tough guy.* Court trials, wars, political contests, inheritance disputes, and street arguments are compared with cockfights. Even the island of Bali is thought of as being cock-shaped. You would also find that men give their fowls inordinate attention, spending most of their time grooming them and even feeding them a special diet. As one of Geertz's Balinese informants put it, "We're all cock crazy."

Having discovered the importance of cockfights to the Balinese and the connection they make between cocks and men, you next examine the cockfight itself. You learn that cockfights are public events held in arenas of about 50 square feet from late afternoon until after sundown. Handlers, expert in the task, attach sharp spurs to the cocks' legs; if a cock is thought to be superior to its opponent, the spurs are adjusted in a slightly disadvantageous position. The cocks are released in the center of the ring and fly at each other, fighting until one kills the other. The owner of the winning cock takes the carcass of the loser home to eat, and the losing owner is sometimes driven in despair to wreck family shrines. You discover that the Balinese contrast heaven and hell by comparing them to the mood of a man whose cock has just won and the mood of a man whose cock has just lost.

You find out that while the Balinese place odds on cockfights, there are strict social conventions that dictate the wagering. For example, a man will never bet against a cock that is owned by someone of his family group or village or a friend's family group or village, but he will place large bets against a cock owned by an enemy or the friend of an enemy. Rarely is a cockfight without social significance (e.g., between two outsiders), and rarely do cocks owned by members of the same family or village fight each other. Moreover, the owners of the cocks, especially in important matches, are usually among the leaders of their communities. You might learn that cockfights come close to encouraging an open expression of aggression between village and kin-group rivals, but not quite, because the cockfight is, as the Balinese put it, "only a cockfight."

Given the social rules for betting and the ways odds are set, you might reason, as Geertz did, that the Balinese rarely make a profit betting on cockfights. Geertz says, in fact, that most bettors just want to break even. Consequently, the meaning of the cockfight for a Balinese has little to do with economics. The question is, what meaning might you suppose the cockfight does have for the Balinese? What is the cockfight really about, if it is not about money?

Geertz concludes that the Balinese cockfight is above all about status, about the ranking of people vis-à-vis one other. The Balinese cockfight is a text filled with meaning about status as the Balinese see it. Cocks represent men, or, more specifically, their owners; the fate of the cock in the ring is linked, if only temporarily, to the social fate of its owner. Each cock has a following consisting of the owner, the owner's family, and members of the owner's village, and these followers "risk" their status by betting on the cockfight. Furthermore, Geertz maintains that the more a match is between near equals, personal enemies, or high-status individuals, the more the match is about status. And the more the match is about status, the closer the identification of cock and man, the finer the cocks, and the more exactly they will be matched. The match will inspire greater emotion and absorption, and the gambling will be more about status and less about economic gain.

For Geertz, the cockfight is like any art form; it takes a highly abstract and difficult concept—status—and depicts it in a way that makes it comprehensible to the participants. The cockfight is meaningful to the Balinese because it tells them something real about their own lives, but in a way that does not directly affect their lives. They see the struggle for status that is part of everyday life vividly portrayed, even though, in the cockfight itself, no one really gains or loses status in any permanent sense.

A few words of caution are necessary concerning what we might learn about the Balinese from this particular cultural text. First, it would probably be a mistake to assume that the people gain status by being on the winning side or lose it by being on the side of the loser. The status outcomes of the cockfight do not translate into real life any more than the victory of your favorite sports team increases your status. Instead, says Geertz, the cockfight illustrates what status is about for the Balinese. *The cockfight is a story the Balinese tell themselves about themselves.* It would also be a mistake to assume that the character of the Balinese could be read directly from the cockfight; that is, a conclusion that the cockfight is indicative of an aggressive, competitive, violent national character would quickly be dispelled. The Balinese are shy about competition and avoid open conflict. The slaughter in the cockfight is not how things are literally, but as they could be. Finally, the cockfight reveals only a segment of the Balinese character, as Watson's brother's watch revealed only a segment of its owner's character. The culture of a people, like the possessions of a person, is an ensemble of texts—collections of symbols and meanings—that must be viewed together for a full understanding.

They express these things thru the medium of the cock fight

QUESTION 1.5 *What Can Learning about Other Peoples Tell Americans about Themselves?*

Anthropologists do not limit themselves to the study of cultures that are different from their own. Rather, they often apply concepts and techniques that are useful in understanding and interpreting other cultures to understand and interpret their own. One of the objectives of studying other cultures is to help us recognize the meanings we impose on our experiences. When Renato Rosaldo asked the Ilongots why they cut off human heads, they replied that rage, born of grief, drives them to kill others; by severing the heads of their victims, they are able to throw away the anger born of bereavement. Rosaldo found it difficult to accept the ideas that the death of a kinsperson could cause anger or rage and that such rage in itself could drive a person to kill another. He questioned the Ilongots further but could obtain no other reason for their head-hunting; he devised other theories to explain it, but none were satisfactory. Only his own experience of grief and anger at the accidental death of his wife, Michelle, while both were doing fieldwork among the Ilongots helped him realize how grief can generate rage and how grief drove the Ilongots to hunt the heads of their enemies. At the same time that he began to understand the Ilongots, he began to understand his own grief and reaction to death.

Whether we approach other cultures as anthropologists, as travelers, or as professionals who need to communicate with people of other cultures, the confrontation with other ways of believing and behaving should cause us to reflect on our way of viewing the world. To illustrate, try to step outside yourself and objectify an experience whose meaning you take for granted. Pretend you are a Balinese anthropologist who suddenly comes upon a spectacle as important in its way to Americans as the cockfight is to the Balinese: a football game.

A Balinese Anthropologist Studies Football

As a Balinese, your first reaction to this American text might be one of horror and revulsion to see men violently attacking one other while thousands cheer them on to even more violent conflict. As you settle in, however, you would soon find some obvious similarities between the football game and the cockfight you are familiar with at home. Both are spectator sports in which the spectators sort themselves into supporters of one side or the other. In fact, in football, the sorting is even more carefully arranged, since supporters of one

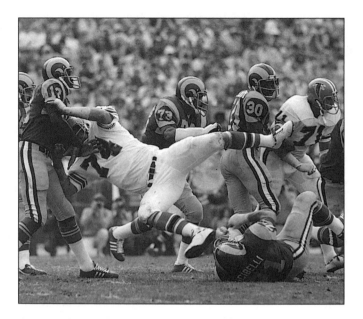

One way Americans try to understand such concepts as war, gender differences, and success is by interpreting the sport of football in similar terms.

team are seated on one side of the arena and fans of the other team are seated opposite them.

Your next step (as in interpreting the cockfight) would be to examine the language Americans use to refer to the football game. You discover that they use similar expressions in talking about football and war: *defensive line, blitz, bomb.* Coaches talk about getting "revenge" for defeats, as generals might talk about getting revenge on the battlefields. You conclude that Americans seem to feel the same way about football as they do about war.

One of the words Americans use to refer to players is *jock,* a term also applied to an athletic supporter worn only by men. Since you see only men attacking one another, you might assume that the gender meanings of cockfights and football games are also similar. *Cocks* stand for men; football players are men. Moreover, football players dress to emphasize their maleness: large shoulders, narrow hips, big heads, pronounced genitals. You might test your interpretation with an American spectator who would argue that football gear is simply protective but, if pressed, would have to admit that it is used offensively as much as defensively. Furthermore, you see young women participating in the spectacle as cheerleaders, dressed to highlight their femininity in the same way the players dress to accent their masculinity. This contrast between between male and female in American society leads you to conclude that football is also a story about the meanings that Americans ascribe to gender differences.

You soon discover that winning and losing football games is as important to Americans as winning and losing cockfights is to Balinese. Winners of football games engage in frenzied celebrations called *victory parties,* and losers are often despondent in defeat. As anthropologists know, this is not always the case in other societies. When the Gahuku-Gama of the Highlands of New Guinea started playing soccer, they always played until a committee of elders decided that the score was tied, and then the match was considered completed. So you speculate that football is also about the meanings that Americans give to the idea of success. You learn that success in America (like status in Bali) is a highly abstract idea; because it is abstract, its meaning is embedded in activities whose meanings are shared by members of the society. You need to find answers to certain questions about the meaning of success in American society: How is success defined? How is it obtained? Why doesn't everyone who follows all the rules for gaining success attain it?

The Meaning of Success

Through your fieldwork, you find that Americans believe that "all men are created equal," and every person has (or at least should have) an equal opportunity to succeed. People compete for success, and they ought to compete on an equal footing, on a "level playing field," as some put it. Success, Americans believe, comes from hard work, sacrifice, and self-denial. But you wonder how Americans know that hard work, sacrifice, and self-denial bring success. Aren't there instances where they do not? How do Americans explain why women and minorities succeed less often than white males do? And why do some people achieve more success than others? You conclude that it is, in fact, impossible to prove directly in real life the correctness of this American success model, which maintains that hard work and sacrifice lead to success. Faith in the value of work and self-denial must be generated in other ways. As a Balinese anthropologist studying the American custom of football, you conclude that in addition to its meanings relative to war and gender, the meaning of American football also lies in its demonstration of the American success model as it is supposed to work.

Anthropologists have found that football, like the Balinese cockfight, is carefully controlled by fixed rules so there is only one outcome: Almost always, there is a winner and a loser. As a text that carries meaning about success, *who* wins is unimportant; it is only important that *someone* wins. ("A tie," as one coach said, "is like kissing your sister.") But more than that, football tells Americans what it takes to win or lose. Success in football not only takes hard work and sacrifice but, as one American anthropologist, William Arens, points out, it also requires teamwork, specialization, mechanization, and submission to a dominant authority—the coach. Two other American anthropologists, Susan P. Montague and Robert Morais, note that the football team looks very much like one of the most important settings in which Americans seek success—business corporations. Both football teams and corporations are compartmentalized, hierarchical, and highly sophisticated in the coordinated application of a differentiated, specialized technology, and they both try to turn out a winning product in a competitive market. Football coaches sometimes are hired to deliver inspirational lectures to corporate groups on "winning"; they may draw analogies between football and corporate life or portray the sport as a means of preparing for life in the business world.

Anthropologists therefore can conclude (as did Montague and Morais) that football provides for Americans, as the cockfight does for the Balinese, a small-scale rendering of a concept (status in the case of the Balinese, success in the American case) that is too complex to be directly comprehended. Football is compelling because it is a vivid demonstration of the validity of the value of success, as well as a dramatic set of instructions on how to attain it. Consequently, the audience for a football game is led to believe that if the rules that govern the world of football are equated with the business world, then the principles that govern success on the football field must also apply in the world of work. That is, if hard work, dedication, submission to authority, and teamwork lead to success in a game, they will lead to success in real life. The rules by which success is won in football can also be applied to win success in the real world.

Of course, football is also a game that people enjoy. Analyzing it should not reduce our enjoyment of it but rather should heighten our fascination with it. By looking at football from the same perspective as Geertz viewed the cockfight, we should gain an understanding of why the meaning carried by the game is important. While understanding the cockfight heightens our appreciation of the football game, it also helps us to see similarities between Americans and Balinese. If you were shocked by the cockfight, seeing the similarities to football should lessen that shock, while at the same time making football seem just a bit more exotic.

CONCLUSIONS

This chapter has considered five questions, each having to do with the problem of how to understand ways of life that are different from our own. Why do human beings differ in what they believe and how they behave? One answer is that human beings, unlike other animals (or, at least, to a greater extent than other animals), create their own worlds and ascribe meanings to objects, persons, behaviors, emotions, and events, meanings that together constitute a culture. As Geertz suggests, human beings are compelled to create meanings if only to create some sense of order in their lives.

The judgments we make about the beliefs and behaviors of other people create a dilemma. If, on the one hand, we assume the meanings that others give to their experiences are wrong, silly, or absurd simply because they are different from ours, we are committing the ethnocentric fallacy. Ethnocentrism is intellectually awkward because it allows everyone to believe that their views are correct, and the views of others are wrong. This would make any kind of intercultural understanding virtually impossible. If, on the other hand, we conclude that the beliefs and behaviors of others can be judged only in the context of their cultures, we are confronted with the relativistic fallacy, which implies that any belief or behavior is acceptable, provided it makes sense to the people of the society in which it occurs. This places us in a moral dilemma because we must then accept virtually any belief or behavior.

Whether it is possible to set aside the meanings we ascribe to experience and see the world through the eyes of others is another question. Anthropologists conclude that the understandings that they reach of other cultures can be at best limited. Furthermore, in many ways, the ethnographic method transforms the fieldworker into a "marginal" person, an outsider who knows only something of what it is to be an insider.

One way we describe and interpret the meanings other people find in their experiences is to consider a culture as a text inscribed with symbols whose meaning can be deciphered. We can examine virtually any cultural activity this way and find in it a portion of the overall view of the world of a people. If we approach our own culture in the same way we approach other cultures, we should gain a better understanding of the meanings we give objects, persons, and events. If we objectify our own beliefs and behavior in the same way we objectify the beliefs and behaviors of others, our own culture should become more exotic, while the cultures of others become less strange, shocking, or bizarre.

REFERENCES AND SUGGESTED READINGS

INTRODUCTION: THE PROBLEM OF US AND THEM   The epigrath comes from Jonathan Culler's article, "In Pursuit of Signs," in *Daedalus,* vol. 106 (1977), pp. 95–112. The selections from Mark Twain come from *The Complete Travel Books of Mark Twain,* edited by Charles Neider (Doubleday, 1966). Richard Scaglion tells about his experiences doing fieldwork with the Abelam in "Ethnocentrism and the Abelam," in *The Humbled Anthropologist: Tales from the Pacific,* edited by Philip Devita (Wadsworth Publishing, 1990), pp. 29–34. An excellent work on how other professional social scientists view American culture can be found in *Distant Mirrors,* edited by Philip Devita and James Armstrong (Wadsworth Publishing, 1992).

WHY DO HUMAN BEINGS DIFFER IN THEIR BELIEFS AND BEHAVIORS?   The information on concepts of death is derived from Stanley Walens's account of Kwakiutl ritual and belief, *Feasting with Cannibals: An Essay on Kwakiutl Cosmology* (Princeton University Press, 1981); Daniel David Cowell's article, "Funerals, Family, and Forefathers: A View of Italian-American Funeral Practices," *Omega,* vol. 16 (1985–86), pp. 69–85; and Renato Rosaldo, *Culture and Truth: The Remaking of Social Analysis* (Beacon Press, 1989). A comprehensive review of beliefs about death can be found in "Death: A Cross-Cultural Perspective," by Phyllis Palgi and Henry Abramovitch, in *Annual Review of Anthropology,* vol. 13 (1984), pp. 385–417. Clifford Geertz's treatment of the concept of culture is from his essay, "The Impact of Culture on the Concept of Man," in *The Interpretation of Cultures* (Basic Books, 1973).

HOW DO PEOPLE JUDGE THE BELIEFS AND BEHAVIORS OF OTHERS?   The example of head-hunting among the Ilongot comes from Rosaldo's *Culture and Truth,* cited above. A description of Aztec ritual sacrifice is found in Marvin Harris's *Cannibals and Kings: The Origins of Culture* (Vintage Books, 1977). The account of female circumcision comes from Rose Oldfield-Hayes, "Female Genital Mutilation, Fertility Control, Women's Roles, and the Patrilineage in Modern Sudan: A Functional Analysis," *American Ethnologist,* vol. 2 (1975), pp. 617–633. An excellent treatment of the different perspectives a person can take when looking at other cultures may also be found in Richard A. Shweder and Edmund J. Bourne's article, "Does the Concept of the Person

Vary Cross-Culturally?" in *Cultural Conceptions of Mental Health and Therapy,* edited by A. J. Marsella and G. M. White (D. Reidel Publishing, 1984).

IS IT POSSIBLE TO SEE THE WORLD THROUGH THE EYES OF OTHERS? Susan Dwyer-Shick describes her experiences in Turkey in "Some Consequences of a Fieldworker's Gender for Doing Cross-Cultural Research," in *The Naked Anthropologist: Tales from Around the World,* edited by Philip Devita (Wadsworth Publishing, 1991), pp. 253–263. Richard Scaglion's tale of his experiences among the Abelam is told in his article "Ethnocentrism and the Abelam," cited above. Michael Kearney describes his brush with witchcraft in "A Very Bad Disease of the Arms," in *The Naked Anthropologist,* pp. 47–57. Claude Levi-Strauss's observations about the role of the anthropologist are from *Triste Tropiques* (Atheneum Publishers, 1974). Roger Keesing's observations come from his article "Not a Real Fish" in *The Naked Anthropologist,* pp. 73–78. Three classic accounts of fieldwork experiences are Richard Lee's paper, "Eating Christmas in the Kalihari," first published in *Natural History Magazine,* December 1969; Jean L. Briggs's account of her fieldwork among the Eskimo in *Never in Anger* (Harvard University Press, 1970); and Laura Bohannan's account of her experience translating *Hamlet* to the Tiv, "Shakespeare in the Bush," originally published in *Natural History Magazine,* August/September, 1966.

HOW CAN THE MEANINGS THAT OTHERS FIND IN EXPERIENCE BE INTERPRETED? Sir Arthur Conan Doyle's Sherlock Holmes story "The Sign of the Four" from *The Complete Sherlock Holmes,* vol. 1 (Doubleday, 1930) was used to illustrate the deciphering of a text by Manfred F. R. Kets de Vries and Danny Miller in "Interpreting Organizational Texts," in *Journal of Management Studies,* vol. 24 (1987), pp. 233–247. The approach to culture as a text is best formulated by Clifford Geertz in his 1973 book, *The Interpretation of Cultures.* Geertz's analysis of the Balinese cockfight, "Deep Play: Notes on the Balinese Cockfight," first appeared in *Daedalus,* vol. 101 (1972), pp. 1–37.

WHAT CAN LEARNING ABOUT OTHER PEOPLES TELL AMERICANS ABOUT THEMSELVES? Renato Rosaldo speaks candidly about his struggle to come to grips with his wife's death in *Culture and Truth,* cited above, which also explores the issues of how we learn of other cultures and what we can expect to understand about them. The analysis of the meaning of American football comes from William Arens's article, "Professional Football: An American Symbol and Ritual," and the article by Susan P. Montague and William Morais, "Football Games and Rock Concerts: The Ritual Enactment of American Success Models," both in *The American Dimension: Cultural Myths and Social Realities,* edited by William Arens and Susan P. Montague (Alfred Publishing, 1976). A more recent view of the importance of football to American communities in the Southwest can be found in Douglas E. Foley's *Learning Capitalist Culture: Deep in the Heart of Tejas* (University of Pennsylvania Press, 1990). The account of how the Gahuku-Gama of the New Guinea Highlands adapted soccer to their own needs is based on Kenneth E. Read's *The High Valley,* originally published in 1965 by Columbia University Press and reprinted in 1980. An excellent review of anthropological studies of American culture can be found in George and Louise Spindler, "Anthropologists View American Culture," in *Annual Review of Anthropology,* vol. 12 (1983), pp. 49–78.

C H A P T E R 2

The Meaning of Progress

PROBLEM 2: How can the transformation of human societies from small-scale, nomadic bands of hunters and gatherers to large-scale, urban-industrial states be explained?

My position is, that if we have anything to learn from the Noble Savage, it is what to avoid. His virtues are a fable; his happiness is a delusion; his nobility nonsense.

Charles Dickens, upon viewing an exhibit of life
among the Bushmen of southern Africa in 1847

INTRODUCTION: *The Death of a Way of Life*

We live in an era in which we will witness (if we have not already) the extinction of a way of life that is over 100,000 years old. We know that just 10,000 years ago virtually all human beings lived in small-scale, nomadic groups of 30 to 100, gathering wild vegetable foods and hunting large and small game, as they had for thousands of years. Today, virtually no human beings anywhere in the world live by hunting and gathering, although every society in existence is descended from those groups. Their people are the common ancestors of us all.

The extinction over the course of 10,000 years or so of a type of society that had flourished for at least 100,000 years poses both a riddle and a moral predicament. The riddle is why, approximately 10,000 years ago, after thousands of years of living as hunters and gatherers, some of these societies began to abandon their way of life. Why did they begin to domesticate plants and animals and exchange their nomadic existence for sedentary dwelling in villages and towns? The moral predicament is how we can relate to the few remaining small-scale, tribal societies that exist in the world today. Do we assume, as many have and still do, that human beings chose to abandon a nomadic, gathering and hunting life because they discovered better ways of living? Do we assume that the few existing small-scale tribal societies are remnants of an inferior way of life, and that, given the opportunity, their members also will choose to progress, to adopt modern farming, wage labor, or urban life? Or is the concept of **progress**—the idea that human history is the story of a steady advance from a life dependent on the whims of nature to a life of control and domination over natural forces—a fabrication of contemporary societies based on ethnocentric notions of technological superiority?

A thumbnail sketch of what we know about the course of cultural history and evolution will be useful before we examine this problem. If we combine what we have learned about human history from the work of archaeologists and historians with the information of cultural anthropologists who have worked among hunting-gathering and tribal societies, we get a relatively clear picture of **culture change.** Until approximately 10,000 years ago, earth's inhabitants were scattered in small-scale, nomadic bands, gathering wild plants and hunting game. With groups that were small and mobile, simple economic, social, and political arrangements sufficed; there were no formal leaders and little occupational specialization. Any specialist was likely to be a person who was believed to have special spiritual powers that could be used to cure illness or (if used malevolently) to cause illness or death. Kinship served as the main organizing principle of these societies, and social differences among people were based largely on age and gender. With little occupational specialization or differences in individual wealth or possessions, relations among persons were likely of an egalitarian nature.

At some point in history, certain hunters and gatherers began to plant crops and domesticate wild animals. These groups became **sedentary,** living in permanent or semipermanent settlements of 200 to 2,000 people. They practiced **slash-and-burn,** or **swidden, agriculture;** forests were cleared by burning the trees and brush, and crops were planted among the ashes of the cleared ground. This land would be cultivated for one or two years, and then another plot of land would be burned and planted. Since larger, more sedentary groups required more formal leadership, certain members assumed the role of chief or elder, with the authority to make decisions or resolve disputes. Villages consisted of **extended family** groups, organized into **clans** of 200 to 500 people claiming descent from a common ancestor. As a result of the development of leadership and occupational roles, members of some groups were ranked in importance. Later, perhaps because of a need for defense against other groups, several settlements might combine under common leaders to form a **state** consisting of many thousands of persons. The development of agriculture intensified, and slash-and-burn techniques were replaced by **plow** or **irrigation agriculture.** Table 2.1 summarizes the development of societies from hunter-gatherer groups to agricultural states.

Then leaders began to organize labor for the purpose of constructing public works—roads, defensive fortifications, or religious structures such as the pyramids in Mexico or the churches of medieval Europe. Competition between groups over available resources contributed to the development of standing armies; hereditary leaders emerged; settlements grew into cities. As technological complexity increased, people began to develop specific skills and to specialize in occupational tasks (e.g., herder, baker, butcher, warrior, potter), and occupational specialization led to increased trade and the evolution of a class of merchants. Some 300 years ago, some of these ranked state societies began to develop into large-scale, industrialized states, which now are found all over the world; the United States is one.

One simple explanation for the transformation of societies from nomadic bands to industrial states is that human inventions created better ways of doing things; human culture progressed. However, in the past 30 years, anthropologists have begun to question the idea that the life of hunters and gatherers was harsh and difficult. They propose instead that in many ways this way of life was superior to that of groups maintained by sedentary agriculture.

Some have proposed further that tribal societies of slash-and-burn agriculturists were more efficient and less wasteful than modern food producers are. But, if that is true, what other explanations are there for why groups abandoned hunting and gathering for sedentary agriculture and later developed industrialized societies? Moreover, if life in small-scale, tribal societies is not inferior to modern life, why are people in such societies, without advanced agriculture and industry, starving and dying of disease? And why are

TABLE 2.1   SUMMARY OF THE DEVELOPMENT OF SOCIETIES FROM GATHERERS AND
HUNTERS TO AGRICULTURAL STATES

	Hunters & Gatherers	*Agriculturists*	*State Societies*
POPULATION DENSITY	Approximately 1 per square mile.	Approximately 10 to 15 per square mile.	Approximately 300 per square mile.
SUBSISTENCE	Hunting, gathering, and fishing.	Slash-and-burn agriculture with mixed livestock herding.	Plow or irrigation agriculture.
WORK, LABOR, AND PRODUCTION	Very high yield relative to labor expended.	High yield relative to labor expended.	High labor needs relative to yield. High degree of occupational specialization.
POLITICAL ORGANIZATION	Informal political organization. Few, if any, formal leaders. Conflict controlled by limiting group size, mobility, and flexibility of group membership. Little intergroup conflict.	More formalized political organization, often with well-established leaders or chiefs. Increased population density and wealth result in increased potential for conflict. Intergroup warfare, motivated by desire for wealth, prestige, or women, common.	Highly developed state organization, with a clear hierarchy of authority. Often a two-class society with rulers (landowners) and peasants. Authority of the elite backed by organized use of force (police or army). Warfare for purpose of conquest common. Well-established mechanisms for resolving conflict (e.g., courts) exist side by side with informal mechanisms.
SOCIAL ORGANIZATION	Small family groups. Major purpose economic cooperation. Few status distinctions other than those of gender and age. Marriage for economic partnership and interfamily alliance.	Emphasis on extended family groups. Descent important for the distribution of wealth and property. Status distinctions based on wealth common, but status mobility usually possible.	Emphasis on nuclear family. Family is strongly patriarchal, with women holding low status. Strong bonds of intergenerational dependence built on inheritance needs. Social distinctions between people emphasized, sometimes based on occupations. Little or no status mobility.

small-scale, tribal societies disappearing? Answers to these questions might explain the transformation of human societies that is the problem considered in this chapter.

QUESTIONS

2.1 Why did hunter-gatherer societies switch to sedentary agriculture?
2.2 If the idea of progress is rejected, how can the transformation of human societies from hunting and gathering to sedentary agriculture be explained?
2.3 Why are hunger and famine prevalent in some less modern or unindustrialized countries?
2.4 How do modern standards of health and medical treatment compare with those of traditional societies?
2.5 Why are simpler societies disappearing?

QUESTION 2.1 *Why Did Hunter-Gatherer Societies Switch to Sedentary Agriculture?*

The simplest explanation of why hunters and gatherers chose at some point to settle down and domesticate plants and animals is that sedentary agriculture was an easier, less dangerous, and more productive way to get food. People who discovered they could plant and harvest crops and domesticate animals rather than having to search for their food began to do so. They had progressed.

The idea that change occurs because of a desire to progress is well entrenched in Western societies. Beginning in the nineteenth century, anthropologists contributed significantly to this view. Lewis Henry Morgan, a Rochester, New York, attorney who took great interest in the historical evolution of culture, offered his own idea of how humankind had progressed. Morgan first became fascinated with the Iroquois of New York, and later he sent out questionnaires to travelers and missionaries all over the world asking them about the family organization and kinship terminology of cultures they visited. In his book *Ancient Society,* first published in 1877, Morgan postulated a theory of human development in which societies evolved through three stages that he labeled *savagery, barbarism,* and *civilization.* He further divided savagery and barbarism into early, middle, and late stages. Some societies, notably our own, had evolved completely to civilization; others had yet to complete their transformation and remained in the stages of savagery or barbarism. The passage of societies from one stage to the next, Morgan reasoned, required some major technological invention. Thus the advance from early to middle savagery was marked by the invention of fire; from middle to late savagery by the invention of the bow and arrow; from late savagery through late barbarism by the invention of pottery, agriculture, and animal domestication, and so on, until certain societies had progressed to civilization. Other writers (including many anthropologists) have elaborated on the scheme developed by Morgan, assuming, as he did, that humankind was progressing and would continue to do so.

EXERCISE 2.1

Make lists of what you think are the advantages and disadvantages of civilization, and the advantages and disadvantages of life 10,000 years ago.

In the mid-twentieth century, an anthropologist, Leslie White, proposed what is probably the most elaborate and influential of these later evolutionary schemes. Like Morgan, White saw technology as the driving force of cultural evolution. From White's perspective, human beings seek to harness energy through technology and to transform that energy into things such as food, clothing, and shelter that are required for survival. By means of technology, energy is put to work, and the amount of food, clothing, or other goods produced by the expenditure of energy is proportional to the efficiency of the technology available. Because hunters and gatherers had only their own muscle power to work with, the amount of energy produced by their work was limited. As technological advances such as the plow, the waterwheel, and the windmill enabled people to grow more crops and to domesticate animals, they became able to transform more and more energy to their use. Later, when new forms of energy in the form of coal, oil, and gas were harnessed by means of steam engines and internal combustion engines, the amount of energy human beings could harness again leaped forward.

Cultural development, from White's perspective, varies directly with the efficiency of the tools employed. More efficient technology allows human societies to transform more energy to their needs and then to produce more food and support larger populations. At some point the increased efficiency in food production allows a few people to produce enough food for everyone, freeing others to develop other skills and occupational specializations. Specialization results in widespread trade and commerce. The increase in population, along with increased contact between groups, ultimately requires the development of a state to coordinate group activities and organize armies to protect the growing wealth of members.

White's view of technology as the driving force in cultural evolution was highly influential in the development of anthropological theory in the twentieth century. But more relevant to us, his theories represent the coalescence of a point of view that is prevalent among many people today—the opinion that technology is the true measure of progress, and the more energy human societies can harness through the development of new power sources, the more social, economic, and political problems they will solve.

The benefits of technological progress remains a popular explanation for the transformation of societies, and many people view the application of technology as the solution to continuing world problems. Nevertheless, the progress theory of cultural transformation began to be seriously questioned by anthropologists in the second half of the twentieth century. These questions were raised in part by studies of hunting and gathering societies that suggested that life as a nomadic hunter and gatherer was not nearly as harsh and dangerous as had been supposed. In fact, some anthropologists suggested that hunting and gathering represented something of a lost paradise.

One of the first suppositions about life in hunting and gathering societies to be challenged had to do with the roles of males and females. Contrary to common belief, studies found that the gathering activities of women produced by far the greater share of food in these societies; men hunted, but, except in areas such as the Arctic and subarctic regions, meat and fish constituted only about one-quarter of the diet. A second supposition, that hunters and gatherers often went hungry, proved to be unfounded. Apparently they had plenty of food. And, contrary to opinion, they did not have to work very hard to get it.

Life among Hunter-Gatherers: The Hadza and !Kung

When they were studied by James Woodburn in the 1960s, the Hadza were a small group of nomadic hunters and gatherers in Tanzania, eastern Africa. Woodburn described their territory as dry, rocky savanna, characterized by one traveler as "barren land" and "desert." Hunters and gatherers are often depicted as living on the verge of starvation, but Woodburn found the Hadza area to be rich in food and resources. Wild game such as elephant, giraffe, zebra, and gazelle was plentiful. Plant foods—roots, berries, and fruit—were also abundant for those who knew where to look and constituted about 80 percent of the Hadza diet. The Hadza spent about two hours a day obtaining food.

Hadza women were responsible for almost all the plant food gathered, and hunting was exclusively a male activity. The men hunted with bows and poisoned arrows; when Woodburn lived among them, they used no guns, spears, or traps. While the Hadza consider only meat as proper food and may say they are hungry when there is no meat, in fact plenty of food was available, and Woodburn found that for a Hadza to go hungry was almost inconceivable. Plant food was so plentiful that the Hadza made no attempt to preserve it. Physicians who examined Hadza children in the 1960s found them in good health by tropical standards. From a nutritional point of view, the Hadza were better off than their agricultural neighbors.

The !Kung peoples of the Kalahari Desert, in Namibia in southwest Africa, are another hunting and gathering society that has contributed extensively to what anthropologists have learned about small-scale societies. Lorna Marshall, assisted by her children Elizabeth and John, began research among the !Kung in the 1950s. Their work, along with later studies by Richard Lee and others, has provided a good description of !Kung hunting and gathering activities. There is some controversy in anthropology over whether the !Kung have always been hunters and gatherers, but that was the way they lived when they were visited by the Marshalls and Lee through the 1960s.

!Kung groups lived around water holes, from which they would wander as far as six miles in search of plant and animal foods. Their groups numbered from 30 to 40 people during the rainy season when water holes were full and plentiful and increased to 100 to 200 during the dry season. Lee found that the food quest was constant among the !Kung, as it was among the Hadza. They did little food processing, so they had to get food supplies every third or fourth day. Vegetable foods constituted 60 to 80 percent of the diet; women gathered most of it, producing two to three times as much food as men.

African women return to their camp after foraging for nuts. !Kung women provide 60 to 80 percent of their families' food this way.

Lee reports that the !Kung never exhausted their food supply. The major food source was the mongongo nut, which is far more nourishing than our own breakfast cereals and contains five times the calories and ten times the protein of cooked cereals. Mongongo nuts provided over 50 percent of the !Kung caloric intake; there are 1,260 calories and 56 grams of protein in 300 nuts. !Kung territory contains more than 80 other species of edible plants, most of which they did not use, though they did eat about 20 species of roots, melons, gums, bulbs, and dried fruits. In addition, meat was provided by an occasional giraffe, antelope, or other large game and the more usual porcupine, hare, or other small game. Their meat intake was between 175 and 200 pounds per person per year, an amount comparable to the meat consumption in developed countries. In other words, Lee found that the environment of the !Kung provided ample, readily accessible food. Their diet consisted of some 2,300 calories a day, with a proper balance of protein, vitamins, and minerals. If the !Kung diet was deficient, it was in carbohydrates, since there was no equivalent to white bread, pasta, rice, or sugar.

The !Kung did not spend much time getting food. Lee conducted a careful study of !Kung work habits. The first week he recorded the amount of time spent getting food, he found that individuals averaged 2.3 days at this work, with an average working day of six hours. Overall, the average time each week spent getting food was 2.4 days, or less than 20 hours of work per week. The most active person Lee observed worked at getting food an average of 32 hours a week. Other time was spent doing housework or mending tools.

Lee concludes that, contrary to the stereotype that hunters and gatherers must struggle with limited technology to obtain the food they need for survival, they do not have to work very hard to make a living. He regards the assumption that hunting and gathering societies struggle for existence as an ethnocentric notion that places our own technologically oriented society at the pinnacle of development. But if Lee and others are correct about the ease of survival of hunters and gatherers, and if their life is not harsh and dangerous, why did those who lived ten thousand years ago begin to domesticate crops and animals and settle in permanent villages and towns?

QUESTION 2.2 *If the Idea of Progress Is Rejected, How Can the Transformation of Human Societies from Hunting and Gathering to Sedentary Agriculture Be Explained?*

There is a perspective on cultural evolution that views the change from hunting and gathering to modern industrial society less as development or progress and more as a necessary evil. This perspective emphasizes the influence of **population growth** and **population density,** or the number of people living in a given area. To understand this point of view you need to examine the transition from hunting and gathering to agriculture and the reasons for the eventual change from relatively simple slash-and-burn agriculture to more complex, labor-intensive irrigation agriculture. A comparison between modern agricultural techniques and less complex methods in the production of potatoes also illustrates the point.

When Mark Cohen set out to explain why individuals or groups abandoned hunting and gathering for agriculture, and why so many did so in a relatively short period of time, he examined their food-gathering strategies. Hunters and gatherers settle in a given area to collect food and, as the resources decline in one spot, enlarge the area within which they travel in search of it. Imagine this area as a series of concentric circles; as the outer circles are approached from the center, the group may decide to move to another area where food is more plentiful in order to reduce the distance members must travel. Cohen suggests that when population density in a given geographical area reached a point where different groups began to bump into each other, or when groups found they had to travel farther and farther to get enough food to feed a growing population, they began to cultivate their own crops. Anthropological and archaeological evidence suggests that they knew how to do this all along but chose instead to gather crops until the labor involved in traveling to new food sources surpassed the labor involved in growing their own crops. In other words, the historical transition from hunting and gathering to simple agriculture was a necessary consequence of population growth, rather than a consequence of a discovery or invention that was adopted because it made life better.

In a limited way, of course, this transition from gathering to cultivating did make life easier; by planting and harvesting crops in a limited area and remaining in villages, groups no longer needed to travel so far. However, Cohen and others argue that agriculture didn't make life better at all; in fact it made life worse. (I'll discuss that claim a little later in this chapter.)

EXERCISE 2.2

Here is the situation: The year is approximately 10,000 B.C. You are a group of elders of a hunting and gathering group similar to the !Kung. Your band numbers some 80 people. For as long as you can remember, you have lived by gathering nuts, roots, fruits, and other foodstuff, and by hunting wild game. Your territory has always been adequate to supply the necessary food for members of the group, but recently people have noticed that they have to travel greater distances to collect food or to find game. Moreover, the territory that you consider your own now overlaps with other hunting and gathering groups.

Like most hunting and gathering peoples, you know how to plant crops and harvest them, and you have come to the realization that there is sufficient wild wheat, yams, maize, or other vegetable foodstuff to support your group as long as you cultivate it (plant it, save seeds for replanting, etc.), harvest it when it is ripe, store it, and settle down next to the stored food. A group of younger members of the band, tired of traveling greater distances in search of food and fearful of conflict with neighboring bands whose territory overlaps yours, advocates settling down and taking advantage of wild crops.

THE PROBLEM:

Should you take the advice of the younger members of the group, begin to harvest and store wild foods, and settle down in relatively permanent villages?

If you say yes, you need to give reasons why this is necessary in order to convince others in the group who are against the move. You must tell them what the consequences of not settling down would be.

If you say no, you need to be able to defend your decision to the younger members of the group and explain to them the consequences of settling down. You also need to tell them the conditions under which you would take their advice.

In most parts of the world, when societies abandoned gathering and hunting, they likely began to utilize slash-and-burn agricultural techniques. Slash-and-burn, or swidden, agriculture can be practiced by relatively small, kinship-based groups. As a form of growing crops, it is highly efficient and productive. The Kuikuru who inhabit the tropical rain forest of central Brazil annually produce about two million calories per acre of land farmed, or enough to feed two people for a year. Moreover, the Kuikuru work only about two hours a day.

However, swidden agriculture requires large tracts of available land, because after a plot is farmed for a couple of years it must lie fallow for 20 to 30 years to allow the brush and trees to grow back so it can be used again. If the population and the amount of land needed to feed it both increase, plots must be used more frequently, perhaps every five or ten years. But when land needs to be used more frequently, the yield per acre declines. Thus swidden agriculture is efficient only as long as the population and the amount of land available both remain constant.

TABLE 2.2   DAYS OF LABOR PER ACRE PER HARVEST, BY TYPE OF
AGRICULTURE

Type of Agriculture	Days of Labor per Acre
Advanced swidden	18–25
Plow cultivation	20
Hoe cultivation	58
Irrigation agriculture	90–178

Source: Data from Eric R. Wolf, *Peasants* (Englewood Cliffs, N.J.: Prentice-Hall, 1966).

Farmland may become scarce not only because of increasing population, but also because of environmental changes or the encroachment of other groups. Then new agricultural techniques must be developed to increase the yield on the available land. The digging stick may be replaced with the plow or irrigation systems may be devised, and each of these developments requires a great deal of labor. In other words, the more food the group needs to produce, the more complex is the technology needed to produce it, and the more complex the technology, the greater is the amount of work.

Relationships among land, labor, population, and methods of agriculture are suggested in Tables 2.2 and 2.3. Table 2.2 indicates that the amount of labor required to produce a harvest increases with the complexity of agricultural techniques. For example, it requires up to ten times more labor to produce a harvest with irrigation agriculture than it does to produce one with swidden agriculture.

Then why abandon swidden agriculture? The answer is because there is not enough land to support the population. Table 2.3 lists the amount of land needed to feed 100 families using different agricultural methods. For example, as little as 90 acres of land are required to feed 100 families if irrigation agriculture is used, while 3,000 acres are needed if swidden agriculture is used. The conclusion is that if a group has enough land, it might as well keep its farming methods simple. Change is necessary only if population increases or the supply of land decreases.

TABLE 2.3   LAND NEEDED TO FEED 100 FAMILIES USING DIFFERENT
AGRICULTURAL METHODS

Agricultural Method	No. of Acres Needed to Feed 100 Families
Swidden agriculture	3,000
Swidden with garden plots	1,600
Irrigation agriculture	90–200

Source: Data from Eric R. Wolf, *Peasants* (Englewood Cliffs, N.J.: Prentice-Hall, 1966).

The history of humankind, however, has in fact been marked by an increase in population and an increase in the ratio of people to land. Robert L. Carneiro has outlined the consequences of population density for cultural development. The increase in the number of people relative to the available land creates two problems. First, if there are more people than there is available land to feed them, conflict may arise between people vying for the available resources. Second, if, to meet the increase in population, a society decides to intensify its efforts to produce food by adopting more labor-intensive methods of growing crops, there is a need for greater societal organization. Irrigation agriculture, for example, requires the digging of ditches, the building of pumps to bring water to the fields and to drain water from them, and the coordination of one and sometimes two harvests a year. Thus whether a society deals with an increasing ratio between land and people by intensifying efforts to produce more food, or it addresses the problem by denying some people access to the necessary resources, the groundwork is laid for the emergence of a stratified society and the need for a state organization.

The views of anthropologists such as Cohen and Carneiro suggest that the historical changes of societies from gathering and hunting to gradually more labor-intensive methods of agriculture were not changes of choice. Slash-and-burn agriculture wasn't easier than gathering and hunting, and plow and irrigation agriculture wasn't more efficient than slash-and-burn agriculture. Instead, the changes in food production techniques represented necessities brought about by population growth or an increase in population density. They in turn created the necessity for more formal, more elaborate political and social institutions, both to organize labor and to maintain order among more and more people.

If we conclude (and not all anthropologists do) that the transition from hunting and gathering to complex agriculture, along with the associated transformations in social, political, and economic institution, does not represent progress, isn't it safe to say, at the very least, that Western society, particularly that of the United States, has agricultural techniques vastly superior to those of small-scale, tribal societies? Those who claim that modern food-producing techniques are far more efficient than any other point out that in American society, only one calorie of human energy is needed to produce 210 calories for human consumption, while hunter-gatherers produce less than ten calories of food for every calorie they use collecting the food. Others argue that these figures are deceptive. At the same time we vastly decreased the amount of human labor required to produce food, they say, we vastly increased the amount of nonhuman energy required for food production. From that perspective, we expend one calorie of nonhuman energy in the form of nonrenewable fossil fuels (e.g., oil and coal) for every eight calories we produce.

Producing Potato Calories

To make this point about energy, John H. Bodley compares the production of sweet potatoes in New Guinea with potato production in the United States. In New Guinea, people cultivate sweet potatoes by slash-and-burn agriculture; plots of land are burned, cleared, and planted with digging sticks. When the crops are ready, sweet potatoes are cooked in pits and eaten. In one New Guinea community of 204 people, sweet potatoes account for 21 percent of the diet. Some of the sweet potatoes are fed to pigs, thus producing protein and accounting for an even larger proportion of the diet. The people use only 10 percent of the arable land, and there is no danger of resource depletion. With their agricultural techniques, the New Guinea farmers can produce about five million calories per acre.

American potato farms produce more than twice as many calories per acre as New Guinea farmers do—about 12 million calories an acre. However, as Bodley points out, in addition to the human energy that goes into American farming, vast amounts of nonhuman energy are expended. Chemicals must be applied to maintain soil conditions and control insects and fungus. For example, in the state of Washington in the 1960s, 60 percent of potato acreage was airplane-sprayed five to nine times each season to control insects; another 40 percent was treated for weeds. American potato farmers need specialized machines to cut, seed, harvest, dig, and plant. In 1969, 36,000 tons of fertilizer was applied to 62,500 acres—over 1,000 pounds per acre. Thus while the Washington system produced more potatoes, the actual energy costs per calorie were far higher than in New Guinea. Moreover, all kinds of hidden costs from such consequences as soil erosion and pollution were incurred in the United States.

Americans must also deal with distribution costs, which are minimal in traditional cultures, where most households consume what they produce. In modern industrial societies, where 95 percent of the population is concentrated in or around urban centers, the energy expended in distributing the food now exceeds the energy expended in producing it. Taking the food-producing process as a whole—the manufacture and distribution of farm machinery, trucks, and fertilizer; irrigation projects; food processing; packaging; transportation; industrial and domestic food preparation; and refrigeration—Americans expend 8 to 12 calories of energy to produce a single calorie of food!

Bodley suggests that the reason Americans expend so much energy to produce food is to make money. He maintains that Western agricultural techniques are wasteful and inefficient. To illustrate his point, consider the potato chip. About half of the potatoes grown in the United States are sold raw; the rest are processed into products such as instant mashed potatoes and potato chips. On the average, each American consumes 4.6 pounds of potato chips each year. All potatoes undergo significant processing after being harvested. They are mechanically washed, chemically sprayed to inhibit sprouting, colored and waxed to increase consumer appeal, and transported and stored under controlled conditions. Potatoes that are sold for potato chips must also be chemically sprayed weeks prior to planting to kill the stems, otherwise the starch buildup would produce unappealing (but otherwise nutritious) dark potato chips. These potatoes also are chemically treated to prevent darkening after they are peeled and sliced; oils, salts, and preservatives are added in the cooking; and, finally, the end product is packaged in special containers and shipped. Then the marketing costs and energy expended by manufacturers to convince consumers to buy the chips must be added in.

Thus the human and nonhuman energy required to convert a potato into potato chips is far greater than the energy expended in New Guinea to produce a more nutritious sweet potato! Moreover, we do not fully appreciate the health risks involved in adding some 2,500 substances to foods to color them, flavor them, or preserve them.

QUESTION 2.3 Why Are Hunger and Famine Prevalent in Some Less Modern or Unindustrialized Countries?

If we conclude that all the changes in food-producing technology, from the development of swidden agriculture to industrial farming techniques, do not constitute progress, then how do we explain the fact that people in some societies, notably our own, have so much food, while people in societies we call underdeveloped are going hungry? Isn't a stroll through a modern supermarket ample proof of how far we have come in our ability to produce food? Aren't our freedom from hunger and the advances in food production made possible by technology proof that we have progressed? When we consider that in Bangladesh in 1974 100,000 people died of starvation, and that hundreds of thousands are starving in Ethiopia, it would seem we could conclude that the lack of modern agriculture is a reason for famine. We might adopt the position that hunger could be eliminated in such countries by controlling population growth, introducing advanced agriculture, and building industry and creating jobs.

The Politics of Hunger

In another view, famine is not caused by either overpopulation or the inefficiency of primitive agricultural techniques. John Bodley suggests some alternative explanations: More than enough food is available to feed everyone in the world; in fact, there is grain alone to ensure every person over 3,000 calories a day. The reason people are starving is that they have been forcibly removed from the land by large landowners or forced into low-wage labor to produce cash crops such as sugar, coffee, and soybeans.

Bangladesh is an excellent example of how small farmers were removed from their land. When the British arrived on the Indian subcontinent in 1757, the area that is now Bangladesh was excellent agricultural land that supported a thriving cotton industry. Farmers tilled collectively owned land to earn money to purchase food or were allowed enough land on which to grow their own. Then the British forcibly introduced cash crops and the private ownership of land. Over the years, through legal and extralegal means, the peasant farmers were deprived of their land, and by 1977 (some 200 years after the British had arrived) less than 10 percent of the land was held by two-thirds of the households. Without land, people could not get enough to eat, even though they required more calories because they were working harder. They lacked the money to buy food.

In traditional China the same situation existed—a small percentage of the population owned most of the land, siphoning off the resources and misusing the land. The result again was periodic famine. Yet today China, with less agricultural land per person than Bangladesh, provides adequate nutrition for 800 million people!

Thousands of acres in Africa, Asia, and Latin America are devoted to satisfying the consumer demands of developed nations for tea, coffee, and chocolate, while their own populations are deprived of the land needed to produce food. Brazil is an example. In the 1960s, the government of Brazil made a conscious decision to industrialize. Industrialization involves the building of factories and the development of power resources to produce goods and transportation systems to distribute them, and this requires capital. Brazil had to borrow this money from the world banks. At first the country became a model of modern industrialization; factories created jobs, and people flocked to the cities for employment. But to pay back its debt to the banks, Brazil needed to encourage landowners to produce crops that could be sold for money, especially crops that could be sold in the United States and Europe.

Since the West already produced more than enough food (American farmers were being paid by the government *not* to grow food crops), Brazilian farmers turned to crops with other uses, such as soybeans, sisal, cocoa, and coffee. To grow more of these products required modern farming techniques and lots of land. Small farmers, forced off their land, had to find farm employment growing cash crops or migrate to the cities in search of jobs that, for most, didn't exist. Moreover, the pay of those who found jobs on the large farms was insufficient to purchase the food that they had previously grown themselves on their small plots. Brazil did increase production of some food crops, notably beef, but because poor Brazilians could not pay as much for it as many Americans and Europeans could, most Brazilian beef is exported.

As a result of industrialization and the introduction of modern farming techniques, it is estimated that over 20 percent of Brazil's population is hungry. And Brazil is not unique; most of Central and South America followed the same formula for development, and in most cases these countries achieved the same result—increased poverty and hunger for their people.

Thus, according to Bodley and others, famine and hunger are caused by neither overpopulation nor inefficient agriculture. Rather, they are the result of poverty and the practice of treating food as a commodity whose availability is subject to the market demands of those who have the wealth to purchase it.

What does this conclusion say about our concept of progress? Discussion of Questions 2.1 and 2.2 has suggested that hunters and gatherers lived well, and slash-and-burn agriculture is in some way more efficient than modern agricultural techniques. If the answer to Question 2.3 is that people are starving not because they are *backward* but because of economic exploitation—that is, because of their participation in the modern world—is there any sense in saying that throughout the world today, people live better than their tribal ancestors did?

QUESTION 2.4 *How Do Modern Standards of Health and Medical Treatment Compare with Those of Traditional Societies?*

The arguments of some anthropologists that human societies have not progressed and that, on a global scale, life on earth generally was more secure 10,000 years ago than it is today have not been accepted without question. From the perspective of Americans, whose per capita income is considerably higher than that of the rest of the world's population, it is difficult to accept the idea that, on the whole, people are worse off today than they were 10,000 years ago. Even if we cannot claim to have progressed in solving the problems of food production and hunger, can't we claim to be on the way to eradicating disease? Aren't simpler, less technologically sophisticated societies (such as the Hadza and the !Kung) who lack the advantages of modern medicine more at the mercy of infectious disease?

The differences between primitive and modern societies in health and medical care are not always clearly evident. Of the 466 !Kung studied by Lee in the 1960s, 46 (10 percent) were over 60 years of age. This compares to 13.2 percent of Americans in 1960 and 16.8 percent in 1989.

Another measure is infant mortality. Among the !Kung, 20 out of every 100 infants born die before they reach one year of age. While this is a high percentage, 70 to 80 percent of infant deaths are caused by diseases such as tuberculosis and malaria that are likely to be far more serious now than in the past. The general infant mortality rates in Third World societies are approximately 10 to 20 per 100. Official infant mortality rates in American society are much lower; in 1990 there was about one infant death for every 100 live births. However, our infant mortality rates among minorities and the poor are anywhere from four to ten times higher than the national average. Moreover, in 1990, the United States lagged behind 22 other nations in preventing infant death.

Civilization and Infectious Disease

To evaluate the impact of infectious disease on different societies, you need to understand two things. First, the most common form of disease is infection caused by microscopic parasites such as viruses, bacteria, and protozoa that can enter into the human body, survive in human tissues, and spread by growing and finding a new host outside the body.

The second thing you need to understand about infectious disease is that human behavior, itself a product of culture, determines in most cases the incidence and spread of disease. The AIDS epidemic, for example, is a consequence of human actions related in most cases to recreational drugs or sexual behavior. In other words, the ways people live greatly influence whether they will come into contact with or spread infectious disease. If a human population is small and scattered over a large area, the likelihood of the spread of infection is smaller than if the population is large and concentrated in a small area. Cholera, for example, is caused by microorganisms that spread through human feces; poor sanitation that results in the runoff of human waste into drinking water is likely to increase the incidence of this disease. Populations that either dispose of human excrement or change their habitat frequently are less likely to come into contact with the organisms that cause the infection.

Bubonic plague existed for years among small populations in Asia. The virus that causes plague survived in fleas that infected rodents. When trade between Asia and Europe increased in the fourteenth and fifteenth centuries, the rodents that carried the fleas that carried the virus that causes the plague spread to Europe. In this case, trade, a trait of more advanced societies, increased the spread of disease.

Warfare and conquest also spread disease. The Europeans who led the invasion of North and South America brought with them diseases unknown in the New World. As a consequence, some 90 percent of the indigenous populations of North and South America died in the century after the European invasion.

In his study of the relationship between civilization and disease, Mark Cohen concludes that as societies become more complex, the incidence of infectious disease increases. This is not to say that infectious diseases did not occur in the hunting-gathering societies that inhabited the world 10,000 years ago. But analysis of existing societies and the evidence of skeletal remains from thousands of years ago indicate that the incidence was less, simply because the life-styles of these societies were not as hospitable to the survival and spread of disease-causing organisms.

More complex societies create conditions that encourage not only the spread of disease but also the survival of microorganisms. Large, permanent settlements attract and sustain vermin such as rats and fleas that serve as hosts to microorganisms and ensure their survival and spread. Permanent settlements also result in the buildup of human wastes. With sedentary agriculture, the landscape must be altered in ways that can further increase the incidence of disease. Schistosomiasis, for example, is a disease caused by worms or snails that thrive in the irrigation ditches constructed to support agriculture. The domestication of animals such as dogs, cats, cattle, and pigs, another characteristic of advanced societies, increases contact between people and disease-causing microorganisms. The requirements of large populations for the storage and processing of food also increases the likelihood of the survival and spread of disease-causing agents.

In short, according to Cohen and other researchers, the course of history and societal development from simple societies to large industrial states has been marked, not by a decrease in the incidence of disease, but by an increase.

The Meaning of Illness

Even if we conclude that modern societies are more susceptible to contagious disease, haven't they at least improved the techniques for curing illness? To examine this question you need to understand that the meanings members of different societies give to illness vary as much as the meanings they give to other aspects of their lives. In American society, illness is most often viewed as an intrusion by microorganisms—germs, bacteria, or viruses. Our curing techniques emphasize the destruction or elimination of these agents. Death can occur, we believe, when we have failed to eliminate them.

In many other societies, the interpretation of illness is different. Illness may be said to be caused by witchcraft, sorcery, soul loss, or spirit possession. Belief in witchcraft or sorcery involves a claim that a witch or sorcerer can use mystical or magical power to inflict illness on another person. Belief in soul loss assumes that illness results from the soul leaving the body. Spirit intrusion or possession is based on the idea that a foreign spirit enters the patient and causes illness. These explanations are not mutually exclusive; the soul, for example, may flee the body as the result of witchcraft or sorcery.

Americans sometimes have difficulty appreciating the meanings others place on events, and the meaning of illness is no exception. We fail to recognize that beliefs in illness or death by witchcraft, sorcery, soul loss, or spirit possession involve an additional belief that the illness has social as well as supernatural causes. For members of societies that believe in spiritual or magical causes for illness, the witch or sorcerer does not strike at random, the soul does not leave the body without cause, and the spirit does not possess just anyone. There must also be a social reason for the witch to act or the soul to flee. Witchcraft involves moral relationships between people; the witch voluntarily or involuntarily afflicts someone who has offended it or has breached a rule of conduct. Likewise, in cases of soul loss or spirit possession, the soul leaves the body of a person who is having difficulty with others, or the spirit possesses a person who has created social problems or who has not honored social obligations.

The Chewa of Malawi in southeast Africa claim that illness and death are caused by sorcery. Max Marwick points out that sorcery-induced illness or death does not strike randomly; it occurs when there is a conflict over judicial rights and claims or when someone fails to observe some social norm. We react to illness or death by seeking the disease or accident responsible; the Chewa ask, what wrong has the victim committed, with whom has the victim quarreled, or who is jealous of the victim? They recognize explicitly the connection between sorcery and social tension, saying that people who have quarreled are likely to practice sorcery against each other.

A Chewa who becomes ill consults a diviner to discover the cause of the illness. During the consultation the patient and the diviner discuss the social roots of the illness. The diviner needs to know about the patient's relationships with kin, and, if ancestral spirits may be responsible, the genealogy of the patient. Thus Chewa medical theory, while couched in the idiom of sorcery, is a social theory of illness, not simply a supernatural one. Someone gets ill because of a breach in social relations, not solely because of some magical act.

There is a disease syndrome in Latin America called *susto.* There are other terms for it—*pasmo, espanto, perdida de la somba*—but all are based on the belief that the soul has detached itself from the body. Symptoms of *susto* include restlessness, listlessness, loss of appetite, disinterest in dress or bodily appearance, loss of strength, and introversion. The onset of the illness is said to follow a fright brought on by a sudden encounter or accident, and the cure begins with a diagnostic session between the patient and a healer. After deciding what brought on the disorder, the healer coaxes the soul back into the body. The patient is then sweated, massaged, and rubbed with some object to remove the illness.

Arthur Rubel, who analyzed specific cases of *susto,* found that all the cases share two characteristics: *Susto* occurs only when the patient perceives some situation as stressful, and the stress results from difficulties in social relations with specific persons. In one case of *susto* a father was afflicted when he discovered he could no longer provide for his family, and in another a mother was stricken when she was not able to take proper care of her child. A wife lost her soul as a result of not honoring her obligations to her husband,

By painting an image of the universe with colored sand on the earthen floor, a Navaho doctor hopes to effect a cure by helping the patient regain a proper place in the world.

while a young boy lost his after he refused to act in a way his peers thought appropriate. In every case, *susto* resulted when a person did not or could not fulfill an expected social obligation. In other words, *susto*, like witchcraft or sorcery, is a statement about social tensions, not simply a description of a magical event.

These traditional theories of illness—soul loss, spirit possession, sorcery, and witchcraft—all have one thing in common. They are all expressions of an **interpersonal theory of disease,** in which it is assumed that illness is caused not by microorganisms but by tensions or conflicts in social relations. So-called "natural" explanations for illness fail to take into account that witches, spirits, and souls are mediating concepts; they are theoretical entities that, like germs, provide a link between a social cause—tension and conflict—and a physical result—illness or death.

If giving meaning to an instance of illness involves the attribution of illness to social causes, then it follows that the cure must also be, at least in part, social. Therefore a curer attempts not only to remove a spell, return the soul to the body, or remove a spiritual object that is causing the symptoms of illness but also to repair the social problem that initiated the episode of illness. To illustrate, Victor Turner provides a look at one society, the Ndembu, an agricultural society in northwestern Zambia.

The Ndembu believe that a persistent or severe illness is caused either by the punitive action of some ancestral ghost or the secret malevolence of a sorcerer or witch. The ghosts punish people when they forget to make a ritual offering to their ancestors, or because, as the Ndembu put it, "kin are not living well together." Explicit in Ndembu interpretations of illness is the idea that illness results either from personal failure to fulfill social obligations or from social conflict.

To effect a cure, the Ndembu patient consults a native doctor, who first inquires about the patient's social relations: Has he or she quarreled with anyone? What is the state of the patient's marital relations? Is anyone jealous of the patient? The doctor asks those the patient has quarreled with or insulted to participate in the ceremony, a dramatic affair with chanting and drumming, sometimes lasting for hours. People who have complaints about the patient's social behavior may come forward, and the patient may report grudges against neighbors. At the climax the doctor may dramatically extract from the patient's body some object that could have been causing the illness. In one case Turner followed closely, the doctor did indeed succeed in patching up a patient's social relations, along with his physical complaints.

The Ndembu recognize, at least implicitly, that social strain and stress may produce physical illness, and one way to treat illness is to treat the sources of social strain. Western medical practice has been slow to recognize the impact of stress on physical health, but there is significant evidence that certain life events can increase the likelihood of becoming ill. Such events as the death of a spouse, the loss of a job, relocation to a new home, even holidays such as Christmas can increase the chances of illness. These are the same kinds of events that can trigger the need for ceremonial cures in traditional societies.

Traditional cures not only can be beneficial, they are also affordable. One of the consequences of medical advances is the increasing dependence on technology—and medical technology is expensive. Consequently, while significant advances have been made in medicine, the cost to the patient of many such advances has made them unavailable to all but a small percentage of the world's population. Indeed, they are unavailable to many Americans. But in traditional societies, when healing arts are lost or discouraged by Western-educated government officials who consider them backward, members are left with virtually no medical treatment.

QUESTION 2.5 *Why Are Simpler Societies Disappearing?*

Modern societies have not been kind to traditional groups that have retained or tried to retain a way of life that is thousands of years old. Societies such as the !Kung, the Inuit of Alaska and the Canadian Arctic (the proper term for the people we call Eskimos), and the people of the New Guinea Highlands have not fared well when contacted by more complex civilizations. Living in small, scattered groups with little need for complex political structures or technology, they were no match for the well-armed, organized, acquisitive people and governments who coveted their land or labor. Even hunting-and-gathering peoples in isolated, seemingly inhospitable locations were susceptible to cultural extermination or genocide.

The Last Ona

The Ona inhabited the island of Tierra del Fuego just off the southern tip of South America, whose climate was described by an early settler as 65 days of unpleasant weather and 300 days of rain and storms. After their first encounters with Europeans in the 1870s and 1880s, the Ona were exposed to deadly diseases to which they had no resistance, such as syphilis, measles, and tuberculosis. They were systematically hunted and killed by European sheepherders and miners and were captured by Argentine soldiers and sent to mission stations or kept by the soldiers as servants. Those that survived on the island were pushed farther inland, and the animals on which they depended for food were systematically depleted by European hunters. Having little food on which to survive, they began to raid sheep ranches and were shot by hunters or ranchers who were paid a bounty for every Ona killed. At the turn of the century, Europeans built lumber camps in the last forests in which the Ona could live without being in permanent contact with Europeans. Finally, in 1973, 100 years after the first European settlement was built on Tierra del Fuego, the last full-blooded Ona died.

The extermination of the Ona was not an isolated event. Native groups were systematically exterminated by representatives of modern societies all over the world. The Spanish, for example, totally exterminated the natives of the Florida peninsula. The Indians of the American plains, who lived by gathering and hunting as late as the 1860s, were first decimated by disease and then systematically driven from their land by miners and ranchers and isolated by government decree on reservations. Today Native American unemployment approaches 90 percent on some reservations, and the infant mortality rate is five times the national average. In areas of Brazil that are now being entered by Europeans, members of the native population, many of whom still live by gathering and hunting or small-scale agriculture, are being hunted and killed, much as the Ona were some 100 years ago.

EXERCISE 2.3

It is the year 1967. You are members of a task force of the Botswana government that has been asked to evaluate the living conditions of the !Kung. Another group of government officials, distressed over the primitive ways of the !Kung, had recommended that they should begin to enjoy the benefits of civilization. Specifically, the group had recommended that the government should settle the !Kung in permanent villages, dig wells to ensure a steady water supply, distribute domesticated animals to ensure a ready food supply, and introduce modern health services. The group had also recommended that jobs be found for the !Kung.

You have toured the area and spoken to some of the !Kung. Your specific job is to evaluate the recommendations of the previous government task force and then make your own recommendations to the government on how the lives of the !Kung could be improved. You may agree or disagree with the previous panel, but you must give reasons for your recommendations.

Attempts to assimilate hunting and gathering peoples into Western life have more often than not destroyed the native culture and created populations of rural slums whose people are dependent upon occasional wage labor or government handouts. Nowhere is this more apparent than among the Ju/wasi, a group of Bushmen in Namibia closely related to the !Kung.

Tourists and the Ju/wasi

The Ju/wasi were the last independent, self-sufficient hunters and gatherers in southwest Africa. Until recently they were still practicing their ancient way of life. Over the past 20 to 25 years, however, they have lost over 70 percent of the land they had occupied for at least 100 and perhaps as many as 20,000 years and have been crowded into rural slums around administrative, police, and army posts. Dependent on handouts, the Ju/wasi have seen their society disintegrate. John Marshall reported in 1984 that the livelihood of many consists of begging from the few who are employed by the administrators or army. They are riddled by tuberculosis and other diseases and subsist on a diet that consists mainly of cereal, alcohol, and sugar. Their death rate exceeds their birth rate, and they do not receive sufficient education to allow them to compete for jobs in modern Namibia. Annual per capita income for the 2,300 Ju/wasi in Bushmanland is 360 rand, or $190 per year, and this average is weighted by the comparatively huge income made by Ju/wasi soldiers (R600, or $300 per month). Thus a great deal of money passes through the hands of a few young men who use it to buy such things as tape decks and cars. As Marshall describes them, "Ju/wasi are a society of haves and have-nots in which most people have nothing to do and not enough to eat."

However, one group of Ju/wasi, numbering some 200 persons, has adapted by herding cattle around the permanent water holes in Bushmanland. The products of husbandry for these tribal people account for 15–30 percent of their diet, family gardens account for 10 percent, and gathering accounts for about 20 percent. Another 30 percent comes from salaries paid to sons in the army or working for the government, and 10 percent comes from other sources such as welfare and army rations. The survival of these Ju/wasi therefore depends on the kind of mixed economy common in countries with low income, high unemployment, and few industries.

This way of life became threatened in June of 1984, when a proposal was submitted by the Department of Nature Conservation to the administrator general of Namibia to form a nature reserve on land inhabited by the Ju/wasi that includes all the remaining natural water holes. If the reserve were set aside, the Ju/wasi would be forbidden to graze the cattle they keep for subsistence. The communities would be evicted and forced to move west to boreholes (as opposed to natural water holes) that they cannot afford to maintain. Their lives would depend on government handouts, and they would have to live on land they are not familiar with, that has little game, and that is inadequate to support their mixed economy.

The government justifies plans for the nature reserve by claiming that Ju/wasi will be allowed to hunt with bows and arrows and gather with digging sticks "forever" in the reserve. According to Marshall, however:

Since children no longer know how to hunt and gather, these activities are to be taught in school. The reserve is designed for a "special class" of tourists who will be flown into selected campsites and taken on nature walks. Only 8 of the 34 guides will be Ju/wasi. Ju/wasi, presumably in skins, will be the main attraction. The nature reserve will "protect" the Bushmen so their land will not be taken from them by other people. (Marshall 1984:16)

Marshall notes that the government does not indicate who would take their land, apart from the government itself. In effect, he concludes, the Ju/wasi are to be evicted to provide a nature preserve for the benefit of white tourists.

The dilemmas of the Ona and the Ju/wasi in trying to maintain their way of life, despite increased pressure from more modern societies, are shared by hundreds of other societies around the world, peoples such as the Batak of the Philippines, the Mbuti (Pygmies) of Zaire, and the Ache of Paraguay, to name just a few. Equally involved are the so-called civilized societies that are responsible for driving such peoples to the edge of extinction or forcing them to enter civilization through its dark side of poverty, disease, and forced labor. We might well assess the values embedded in modern urban-industrial societies that permit such treatment of the tribal, pristine societies that, until recently, have remained in the world. What image is cast on the civilized world by the shadows of those extinct or near extinct cultures? More important, if we conclude that progress and the change from simple hunter and gatherer societies to modern industrial states is not all positive, we may be short-changing ourselves. By the systematic destruction of the remnants of these early societies, we may be eliminating societies whose systems of meaning hold solutions to compelling current world problems, such as environmental destruction, intergroup and intragroup conflict, poverty, and sickness.

CONCLUSIONS

This chapter began by noting that in a period of 10,000 years, human societies have abandoned a way of life that had survived for some 100,000 years. How do we explain why societies of hunters and gatherers changed into societies of sedentary agriculturists? The idea of a need to progress and develop better ways of living might explain the change. However, studies of hunter-gatherer societies have revealed that the people live quite comfortably and with minimum effort.

If we reject the idea of progress, how do we explain the transformation of human societies over the past 10,000 years? An increase in population or population density may have fueled the transition of societies from hunting and gathering to swidden agriculture, and from there to plow or irrigation agriculture. It is also possible that modern agricultural technology is simply better and more efficient, but Bodley's analysis of the energy expenditures of modern agriculture suggests that this is difficult to conclude.

If modern agricultural techniques are not better, why are peoples around the world who lack advanced agricultural technology suffering from starvation and famine? Famine, it has been suggested, is not so much due to a lack of modern agriculture as it is a consequence of poverty and attempts to industrialize. The need to repay bank loans secured for industrialization has led countries such as Brazil to encourage the development of large farms that grow primarily cash crops for export. Their people are dispossessed of their land and left without enough money to buy food.

But modern societies may have an advantage in health care and methods of medical treatment. Aren't Western standards higher than those of less modern societies? In fact, researchers have concluded that infectious disease is more common in modern societies and that human behaviors associated with industrialization and modernization often promote the spread and incidence of contagious diseases. Moreover, traditional theories of illness and curing ceremonies can be effective in the diagnosis and treatment of illness or disease.

Then why, in spite of all they have to offer, are simpler societies disappearing? The answer is that most are not disappearing because of the choice of their members, but rather because of the actions of so-called civilized countries. The idea of progress may simply be a convenient rationale for one society imposing its economic and political will on others.

REFERENCES AND SUGGESTED READINGS

INTRODUCTION: THE DEATH OF A WAY OF LIFE   The epigraph comes from Carmel Schrire's article, "Wild Surmises on Savage Thoughts," in *Past and Present in Hunter Gatherer Studies,* edited by Carmel Schrire (Academic Press, 1984). A general up-to-date discussion of the issues of cultural evolution and a comprehensive bibliography are provided in William H. Durham's article, "Advances in Evolutionary Culture Theory," in *Annual Review of Anthropology,* vol. 19 (1990), pp. 187–210. A classic account of cultural history is Alfred L. Kroeber's *Anthropology* (Harcourt, Brace, 1948). A more recent comprehensive work is Eric R. Wolf, *Europe and the People without History* (University of California Press, 1982).

WHY DID HUNTER-GATHERER SOCIETIES SWITCH TO SEDENTARY AGRICULTURE?   An excellent account of the history of anthropological theory is John J. Honigmann, *The Development of Anthropological Ideas* (Dorsey Press, 1976). Lewis Henry Morgan's *Ancient Society* was originally published in 1879 and reissued by the Belknap Press in 1964. Leslie White's theories of cultural evolution are summarized in *The Science of Culture* (Farrar, Straus & Giroux, 1949) and elaborated in *The Evolution of Culture* (McGraw-Hill, 1959). The description of the Hadza comes from James Woodburn, "An Introduction to Hadza Ecology," in *Man the Hunter,* edited by Richard Lee and Irven DeVore (Aldine Publishing, 1968). Elizabeth Thomas's most noted account of her work among the !Kung is *The Harmless People* (Alfred A. Knopf, 1959). Lorna Marshall's work is described in *The !Kung of Nyae Nyae* (Harvard University Press, 1976). Richard Marshall is best known for his films about the !Kung, including *The Hunters, Bushmen of the Kalahari* and *Ni: Story of a !Kung Woman.* The description of the !Kung by Richard Lee is found in *The Dobe !Kung* (Holt, Rinehart and Winston, 1984).

For some dissenting views on the lives of gatherers and hunters, see Carmel Schrire's article "Wild Surmises on Savage Thoughts," cited above. See also Edwin N. Wilmsen and James R. Denbow, "Paradigmatic History of San-speaking Peoples and Current Attempts at Revision," *Current Anthropology,* vol. 31 (1990), pp. 489–512. A comprehensive review of the literature on hunter-gatherers is available in Fred R. Myer, "Critical Trends in the Study of Hunters-Gatherers," in *Annual Review of Anthropology,* vol. 17 (1988), pp. 261–282.

HOW CAN THE TRANSFORMATION OF HUMAN SOCIETIES BE EXPLAINED? Mark Cohen's *The Food Crisis in Prehistory* (Yale University Press, 1977) contains one of the best explorations of the reasons for the adoption of agriculture. Another view is provided by David Rindos in *The Origins of Agriculture* (Academic Press, 1984). Marvin Harris provides an account, also, in *Cannibals and Kings* (Vintage Books, 1977). The analysis of slash-and-burn agriculture comes from Robert L. Carneiro, "Slash-and-Burn Cultivation among the Kuikuru and Its Implication for Cultural Development in the Amazon Basin," in *The Evolution of Horticultural Systems in Native South America: Causes and Consequences, Anthropologica* Supplement 2 (1979), edited by J. Wilbert. Information in the tables on land, labor, and agriculture was adapted from Eric Wolf, *Peasants* (Prentice-Hall, 1966). The material on modern potato farming and the potato chip comes from John Bodley, *Anthropology and Contemporary Problems,* 2nd edition (Mayfield Publishing, 1985). The *Statistical Abstract of the United States* (U.S. Bureau of the Census, 1990) provided the information on how many potato chips Americans consume.

WHY ARE HUNGER AND FAMINE PREVALENT IN SOME UNINDUSTRIALIZED COUNTRIES? The analysis of modern agriculture and its impact on traditional societies comes from John Bodley's *Anthropology and Contemporary Problems,* cited above. Additional information on the impacts of the introduction of cash crops and industrialization can be found in Frances Moore Lappe and Joseph Collins, *Food First: Beyond the Myth of Scarcity* (Random House, 1977). See also Parker Shipton's review, "African Famines and Food Security," in *Annual Review of Anthropology,* vol. 19 (1990), pp. 353–394. An excellent overview of the problem of, and reasons for, world hunger can be found in *Hunger and Public Action,* by Jean Drèze and Amartya Sen (Cambridge University Press, 1991).

HOW DO MODERN STANDARDS OF MEDICAL TREATMENT COMPARE WITH THOSE OF TRADITIONAL SOCIETIES? The discussion of infectious disease is based largely on Mark Cohen's *Health and the Rise of Civilization* (Yale University Press, 1989). Additional material can be found in Ann McElroy and Patricia Townsend, *Medical Anthropology* (Duxbury Press, 1979), and Marcia C. Inhorn and Peter J. Brown, "The Anthropology of Infectious Disease," in *Annual Review of Anthropology,* vol. 19 (1990), pp. 89–117. Information on traditional curing techniques can be found in Peter Worsley's article, "Non-Western Medical Systems," and Allan Young's article, "The Anthropologies of Illness and Sickness," both in *Annual Review of Anthropology,* vol. 11 (1982), pp. 315–348 and 257–285. The account of Chewa beliefs about illness and curing is based on *Sorcery in Its Social Setting,* by Max Marwick (University of Manchester Press, 1965). An analysis of *susto* is found in Arthur Rubel, "The Epidemiology of a Folk Illness: *Susto* in Hispanic America," *Ethnology,* vol. 3 (1964), pp. 268–283. Victor Turner provides a brilliant analysis of Ndembu cures in *The Forest of Symbols: Aspects of Ndembu Ritual* (Cornell University Press, 1967). A review of the role of stress in illness can be found in an article by James S. House, Karl R. Landis, and Debra Umberson, "Social Relationships and Health," in *Science,* vol. 241 (1988), pp. 540–545.

WHY ARE SIMPLER SOCIETIES DISAPPEARING? The account of the Ona comes from Jason W. Clay, "Yahgan and Ona—The Road to Extinction," *Cultural Survival Quarterly,* vol. 8 (1984), pp. 5–8. The material on the Ju/wasi comes from John Marshall, "Death Blow to the Bushmen," *Cultural Survival Quarterly,* vol. 8 (1984), pp. 13–17. An excellent popular account of the implications of the disappearance of tribal societies can be found in "Lost Tribes, Lost Knowledge" by Eugene Linden in *Time,* September 23, 1991, pp. 46–56. Cultural Survival, Inc., is an organization whose purpose is to assist tribal societies to resist extinction and exploitation. Information about the services, products, and publications of Cultural Survival can be obtained by writing to 53–A Church Street, Cambridge, Mass. 02138.

C H A P T E R   3

THE SOCIAL CONSTRUCTION OF REALITY

PROBLEM 3: WHY DO DIFFERENT PEOPLES BELIEVE DIFFERENT THINGS, AND WHY ARE THEY SO CERTAIN THAT THEIR VIEW OF THE WORLD IS CORRECT AND OTHERS' VIEWS ARE WRONG?

There is an obvious rightness about our own world view. It seems, in some way, to mirror reality so straightforwardly that it must be a consequence of direct apprehension rather than effort and imagination. Conversely, alternative beliefs possess an obvious wrongness. The more natural our own perspective becomes, the more puzzling become the strange propositions of ancestors, aliens and eccentrics. How did such mistaken ideas come to be held? However have they remained uncorrected for so long?

Barry Barnes

INTRODUCTION: *The Problem of Belief*

Most people would probably say that they gained their knowledge of the world through observation, through their senses. On reflection, however, we should realize that this cannot be right. How could we reconcile the fact that we think we experience the world directly with our senses with the fact that others, with the same senses, living in the same world, experience it so differently? Moreover, our senses are bombarded with thousands of sensations each minute, and it is impossible to see, hear, or feel every one of them.

more on agreement reality

Obviously, then, our knowledge of the world is not constructed solely from the direct experience of our senses. It must be somehow mediated, controlled, or filtered through other mediums. And, since we share our view of the world with some people but not with others, those who have the same views must share the same mediums. In other words, the mediums must have social origins. So while we think of ourselves as individuals with eyes and ears to give us knowledge of the world, we must also think of the social groupings we belong to as having a set of controls that filters experience for us. And social groupings for other peoples also have their own sets of controls to filter experiences for their members.

Some of these social controls are easy to identify. Since language is one of the mediums we use to make our knowledge concrete and to communicate to others, it must play a major role in selecting or emphasizing certain experiences over others. **Symbolic action**—the rituals, myths, arts, literature, and music that we enjoy or participate in—also plays a role in organizing and making concrete a particular view of the world. And there must be some way—humor, perhaps—to help us deal with the doubts and uncertainties all people face about their views of the world at one time or another. Certainly the fact that others agree or disagree with us about the nature of the world will influence what we believe is true or not true and determine how we react to experiences that challenge a particular view. The questions we must address are how to ascertain how such things as language, ritual, humor, and the opinions of others determine our view of the world, how they work to convince us that a particular view of the world is correct (and others are wrong), and how and why we change what we believe.

QUESTIONS ─────────────────────────

3.1 How does language affect the meanings people assign to experience?

3.2 How does symbolic action reinforce a particular view of the world?

3.3 Can humor be used to resolve the contradictions inherent in language and metaphor?

3.4 How do people collectively defend beliefs that are threatened?

3.5 How can people reorder their view of the world if it becomes unsatisfactory?

QUESTION 3.1 *How Does Language Affect the Meanings People Assign to Experience?*

Language is one medium through which we make contact with the world. We tend to take it for granted, to assume that it is only a medium for the transmission of thought, a tool for communication. Edward Sapir challenged this view of language, suggesting that specific languages serve not only as a medium of communication but also to define and guide our perception of experience. That is, specific languages—French, English, Navajo, Chinese, Tupi, or any of the other thousands of languages that human beings speak—somehow order the experiences of those who speak them. Benjamin Lee Whorf later elaborated on Sapir's ideas and suggested that each language constitutes a frame of reference that orders a particular people's views of the world. — *language paradigm*

The Sapir-Whorf Hypothesis

The relationship between language and thought can exist at various levels. The most obvious is at the level of vocabulary. According to Sapir and Whorf, vocabulary reflects the social and physical environment of a people. Whorf noticed, for example, that the Inuit have a variety of words for different kinds of snow, while we have only one, and that the Aztecs of Mexico used the same word for cold, ice, and snow. Sapir noted how the vocabulary of the Nootka of the northwest coast of North America precisely defined the variety of marine animals on which they subsisted, and how the vocabulary of the Paiute, living in the desert regions of southern Utah and northern Arizona where complex directions for finding water were necessary, contained detailed descriptions of the landscape. Our own rich vocabulary for expressing units of time is linked to our concern for the temporal ordering of activities. Sapir suggests that the vocabulary of a language not only reveals what is important to its speakers but also cues them to be more sensitive to the named features of their environment.

Sapir and Whorf also explored the relationship between the grammar of a language and the modes of thought characteristic of its speakers. In English, Whorf points out, there are two dominant types of sentences: the subject-predicate type, such as "The book is green," and the actor-action type, such as "Sally runs." In both cases, the subject of the sentence—the book in the first case, Sally in the second—is spoken of as if it were an enduring object, something stable through time that acts or is acted on by something else. Whorf maintains that this indicates a pervasive tendency in English to view the world as being made up of objects, so that experiences described in English lose the fluidity of passing experience. For example, we speak of time as if it were an object or thing, as if we could isolate a piece of it ("I'll study for three hours"), the same way we select food ("I'll take three hamburgers"). In English grammar, time occupies the same grammatical space as food. In this sense our grammar reflects, reinforces, and perhaps determines our general view of the world as consisting of objects or substances, with everything perceived as an attribute of some object.

Other grammars, such as that of the Hopi, convey a different view of the world. For the Hopi, events rather than objects seem to be the stuff of experience. For example, where our view of time as an object allows us to speak of it as an aggregate (e.g., "ten days"), in the same way we speak of an aggregate of concrete things (e.g., "ten books"), the Hopi would say "until the eleventh day" or "after the tenth day." Instead of being an object, for the Hopi time is a state of becoming.

In English *time* is a noun (a thing or object) and can be thought of like other nouns; we can refer to phases of a cycle, or the passing of time as if it occurred in discrete units or objects ("twenty minutes," "four hours," "six days"). In Hopi, terms signifying phases of cycles or the passing of time comprise a grammatical category that is distinct from nouns. Nothing is suggested about time other than the perpetual process of "getting later."

Whorf suggests that certain cultural characteristics may be linked to the grammar of a language. The Hopi, for example, place great emphasis on preparation; much time and effort go into the preparation of ceremonies, meals,

Metaphors of war are used by Americans to give meaning to various experiences, as in this poster designed to encourage eating habits that can reduce the risk of cancer.

and so on. This characteristic may be linked to the way the Hopi speak about time. Days are not totaled, as they are in English, but rather are referred to by their order. It is as if different days are thought of as successive reappearances of the same entity, and this year is a reappearance in a later form of last year. For this reason, the Hopi expect activities of one time to influence activities to be done at a later time; in other words, there is in Hopi a great sense of continuity of events through time. English speakers, on the other hand, do not expect their actions on one Monday to be specifically linked to the events of next Monday. That is, since time in English is spoken of as if it could be divided up, in the same way an object is divided up, activities are likewise divided up. We fail to appreciate the sense of continuity in our actions, in the way Hopi speakers do.

Another implication of our way of speaking of time has to do with our sense of controlling it. Since in English *time* may take the role of an object, we are able to quantify it and to speak of "saving" or "wasting" it. This would make little sense to a Hopi, for whom time is an attribute of events rather than a concrete object.

EXERCISE 3.1

One of Benjamin Whorf's points is that the structure of English grammar encourages a view of the world as filled with objects, whereas Hopi grammar emphasizes a world of events. Take the following sentence and translate it into an English sentence that a Hopi speaker would understand:

"I grasp the thread of the argument, but if it is over my head my attention may wander and I lose touch with the drift of it, so that when he comes to his point, our views differ widely and what he says appears arbitrary or even nonsensical."

___

The ideas of Edward Sapir and Benjamin Lee Whorf, generally referred to as the **Sapir-Whorf hypothesis,** are suggestive, and both were very careful to avoid claiming that there is a causal link between language and thought. Not all anthropologists are convinced of the hypothesis that there is an explicit link between the grammar of a language and the culture of the people who speak that language. But there is another sense in which language serves to give meaning to different events, and it has to do with the idea of metaphor.

Borrowing Meaning with Metaphor

One major characteristic of human language is its economy. That is, the same words we use to describe one area of experience can also be used to describe another area. If this weren't so, we would need a distinct vocabulary for every experience we wished to describe; instead of a working vocabulary of hundreds of words, we would need a vocabulary of millions! Fortunately, we can escape that problem through the use of **metaphor,** taking linguistic expressions from one area of experience and applying them to another. Expressions such as "the *shoulder* of the road" or "the *foot* of the mountain" illustrate the metaphoric extension of parts of the human body to refer to features of the landscape. "Joe is a *snake*," "Sally is a *fox*," "Jeff is a *dog*," or "Charley is a *pig*" are expressions that represent metaphoric extensions from the animal world to the human world. Metaphors take language from one **domain of experience,** such as the domain of the body or the domain of animals, and apply it to another domain, such as persons or landscape features.

When language is extended from one domain to another, meaning is also extended. In other words, metaphor involves not only speaking of one experience in terms of another but also understanding one experience in terms of another. For example, when we speak about an argument, we might say that "His point was right on *target*," or "Your claims are *indefensible*," or "She *attacked* my argument, and I had to *defend* my position." Or we might say that "She *shot down* my argument," or "I think I *won* the argument." We speak of argument in terms of war, taking the language from the domain of war and applying it to the domain of conversation. But we have not only transferred words; we have also transferred meaning. We don't simply talk about argument in terms of war, we actually *win* and *lose* arguments.

What would happen if instead of metaphors of war, we borrowed metaphors from the domain of dance to comprehend argument? We might talk about the *rhythm* of the interaction or the *grace* of the performance. In fact, this wouldn't be argument at all; instead of two protagonists in a win-or-lose situation, we would have two partners trying to coordinate their movements to arrive at a mutual accommodation.

Or think about the way our conception of illness is embedded in the language we use to describe it. Again we take language from the domain of war. We build our *defenses* against illness; we get ill because our *resistance* was low. We *fight* a cold, *destroy* germs, wage *war* on cancer, and have heart *attacks*. Not all societies borrow from the domain of conflict to give meaning to health. The Navaho, for example, see illness as a displacement of the person from his or her proper place in the universe. Illness is a disruption of *harmony*.

War, of course, is not the only domain from which Americans borrow to assign meaning to other areas of experience. They also borrow from the domain of economic exchange. In English time is spoken of not only as if it were a distinct thing, but also as if it were a specific type of thing: "Time is *money*," "You're *wasting* my time," "This gadget will *save* you hours," "I don't have the time to *give* you," "That flat tire *cost* me an hour," "You need to *budget* your time," "He's living on *borrowed* time," "Is that *worth* your while?" Time in American culture is a valuable commodity, a scarce resource that we quantify, invest, and spend.

Sports represents another domain from which Americans borrow heavily for metaphors. For example, a male baseball enthusiast might describe a romantic encounter in this way: "I met a girl, I thought she'd *play ball,* and that I'd not only get to *first base,* but *score;* but I *struck out*." A follower of astrology might describe the same event this way: "I met a girl, I thought we'd be *Leo* and *Cancer,* that we'd be in *conjunction,* and she would be the *sun* to my *moon,* but our *stars* were *crossed*." The differences between the two descriptions of the same event involve more than a simple difference in language. Metaphors from different domains of experience assign different meanings to the same event. The baseball enthusiast, using a metaphor common to Ameri-

can youth, sees the experience as a contest to be won or lost, as a way of demonstrating proficiency. The follower of astrology, on the other hand, sees the meeting as a fated, predetermined event; it involves not winning or losing but rather the discovery of preexistent compatibilities.

EXERCISE 3.2

Carefully examine the photograph above. Describe what you think is happening in the photograph, and see if you can draw some conclusions about the nature of baboon society from your description.

Metaphors, then, are not simply verbal devices that we use to make our language colorful and economical. Rather, they are like theories, templates, lenses, or filters we can use to help us understand one domain of experience in terms of another. By using language from one domain of experience to describe another, whole domains of meaning are transferred; arguments become wars, time becomes a commodity, and romantic encounters become contests. Moreover, the metaphors we use to describe experiences may predispose us to certain solutions to problems associated with those things and people. A Navaho cure seeks to return the patient to a state of harmony with the social and natural universe. Does our speaking of illness in terms of war and battle encourage us to take for granted that it is some kind of war? And, if it does, how does that view determine the kinds of treatment for illness that we devise and seek? Doesn't the language that we use to describe illness predispose us to cures that destroy the agent of disease rather than return the patient to health?

The fact that Americans borrow so heavily from the domains of war, sports, and economic exchange for metaphors suggests another way to understand how language operates to influence people's view of the world. Most societies seem to have one or more domains from which they borrow extensively for metaphor. These domains become **key metaphors,** which give to each culture a style or cast that makes that culture distinctive. By thinking and speaking of many domains of experience in terms of a particular domain, a certain coherence is achieved in the meanings in any culture.

Kwakiutl Metaphors of Hunger

Perhaps one of the most spectacular expressions of the elaboration of both a key metaphor and the human imagination is found among the Kwakiutl of British Columbia. Much of our knowledge of the traditional life of the Kwakiutl we owe to Franz Boas, one of the founders of American anthropology, his Kwakiutl assistant, George Hunt, and filmmaker and photographer Edward Curtis. The work of Boas and Hunt served as the basis for Ruth Benedict's description of the Kwakiutl in her classic *Patterns of Culture,* and more recently for Stanley Walens's analysis of Kwakiutl belief.

Walens suggests that the act of eating is a key metaphor for the Kwakiutl; that is, the Kwakiutl speak of many different things using the vocabulary and language associated with hunger, eating, and food. A fundamental meaning the Kwakiutl find in their experience is that the universe is a place in which some beings are eaten by other beings, and some beings must die so that other beings may eat them and live. Eating gives life in at least two ways; it provides nutrition, but it also frees souls. The Kwakiutl believe that when a person dies his or her soul leaves the body and enters the body of a salmon. But the soul cannot be freed until the physical body is destroyed, so they place their dead on scaffolds where the body can be devoured by ravens and other birds. Once the soul enters the body of a salmon it remains there, living in a salmon world that socially resembles the human world. However, when the salmon is caught and eaten by human beings, the soul is once again freed and enters the body of a newborn child. Thus for the Kwakiutl the act of eating becomes a metaphor through which they understand and describe much of their life.

The importance of eating for the meanings the Kwakiutl ascribe to experience is manifested in the images of mouths that visually dominate Kwakiutl art, ritual, and myth. Their world, says Walens, is replete with mouths, the mouths of animals killing to satisfy their hunger, and their art represents the gaping jaws of killer whales, fangs of wolves and bears, tearing beaks of hawks, eagles, and ravens. Dancers wear masks of cannibal birds with nine-foot-long beaks that shatter human skulls to suck out the brains. The woods are inhabited by wild women with protruding lips who wait to rip apart and devour travelers and misbehaving children. It is a world where suckling infants turn into monsters and devour their mothers.

The Kwakiutl use the eating metaphor to give meaning to a wide range of their experiences. Hunger is associated with greed, for, like unrestrained hunger, greed causes people to accumulate wealth far beyond what they need, often taking from others who are left without. Moreover, people who hoard food would, in effect, be hoarding souls, preventing the return of a soul from the spirit world. Consequently, the Kwakiutl place great emphasis on gift-giving and generosity. Hunger is also equated with immorality. The Kwakiutl have few means of maintaining social control; there are no police or courts, and violence is often the only recourse available to people who believe they have been wronged. Since the Kwakiutl believe that human desires create conflict and destruction that can quickly get out of hand, people must work together to prevent and control conflict before it threatens to destroy the group. And hunger is metaphorically associated with children, because they constantly demand to be fed and will, if allowed, devour all a family's food. To fully appreciate the impact of a metaphor, it is necessary to understand that by ordering and describing a view of the world according to a particular domain of experience, people are drawn to try to control their lives by controlling the domains of experience they use to represent aspects of their lives. The Kwakiutl believe that the real solutions to the problems of greed, conflict, and child rearing are to actually control hunger. Eating is highly ritualized and controlled; food must be carefully handled. Food must also be generously given to others to avoid accusations of greed. In fact, wealthy persons are said to vomit forth goods, vomit having for the Kwakiutl a distinctly different meaning than it has for Americans. For the Kwakiutl, vomit is a life-giving substance. Animals that regurgitate their food—wolves that vomit food for their young, and owls that regurgitate the bones of small animals they have eaten—occupy a special place in the Kwakiutl world. And the socialization techniques of the Kwakiutl are geared to teaching children to control their hunger. In sum, a single domain of experience—eating—has been elaborated by the Kwakiutl to give to their world a style and meaning that are unique to them.

EXERCISE 3.3

There are some interesting parallels between the metaphors of eating and hunger among the Kwakiutl, and the metaphors of sexual intercourse and sexual desire in America. Kwakiutl art, myth, and stories are filled with mouths and images of eating and hunger. What are some of the images that fill American expressive culture (advertising, for example)? Vomit is a life-giving substance for the Kwakiutl; what symbolizes life-giving in America? Are there other ways Americans use sexual symbolism that are similar to the ways the Kwakiutl use hunger and food?

There is no necessary connection between the domains from which people draw metaphors and the domains to which they apply them. There is no natural connection between commodities and time, war and health, or eating and immorality. These borrowings are the products of the human imagination. Many different metaphors can be applied to a specific experience, and one domain can never be the exact replica of the other. No man is really a tiger, no woman really a fox. Metaphoric borrowings are intrinsically absurd. Yet we constantly seem to confuse one domain with another; we really do *fight* disease; we really *win* arguments. By what magical means are people convinced that by controlling one domain of experience (e.g., eating), they can really control another (e.g., greed)?

QUESTION 3.2 *How Does Symbolic Action Reinforce a Particular View of the World?*

Is language the underlying factor?

Language represents one way that our experience of the world is socially filtered. By sharing a language we also share a view of the world that is expressed in the vocabulary, grammar, and metaphors of the language. But language is not the only way our social life mediates between our senses and the meanings we assign to experience. We also participate in activities that express a particular view of the world, not the least of which are symbolic actions such as ritual, myth, literature, art, games, and music. Symbolic actions carry bundles of meanings that represent public displays of a culture. They are dramatic renderings and social portrayals of the meanings shared by a specific body of people. More important, symbolic actions render particular views of the world in a way that makes them seem correct and proper.

chess = war

This idea can be illustrated with the game of chess, which originated in India or China as a favorite pastime of the aristocracy. Its original meanings are unknown, but the game is often considered to be a representation of war. It is, however, a war in which each side has exactly the same number and kinds of pieces, and the two sides alternate their moves. If it is a symbolic representation of war, it is a highly stylized and carefully regulated war, unlike any that has ever been fought.

But chess is more than a game; it is a statement, a story about hierarchy and the social order. Pieces (pawns, rooks, knights, bishops, kings, and queens) are ranked in terms of importance and are given a freedom of movement corresponding to their ranking. Consequently, each game of chess is a story about social hierarchy that reinforces the validity of a social system based on rank order. Each time the game is played, the authenticity of this social system is proven true; the side with the highest ranking pieces remaining is almost always the winner. And, significantly, the game validates the importance of the generals (the two players), who are the commanders over their sides' pieces on the board. It is the strategist, the thinker who wins the war (the game), not the soldiers. Even the king is dependent upon the general. Since in every chess game each side starts out with the same number and kinds of pieces, it must be the strategist, the head of the hierarchy, who determines the outcome of the game and, by extension, the well-being of the society. Chess reinforces the axiom that rank is power, and power is achieved by outwitting an opponent; a pawn, in itself, can never defeat a queen, any more than a peasant can threaten a king. There are winners and losers, but regardless of which side wins, the match in a crude way represents the superiority of the aristocracy over the peasants.

As a game, chess assures the players of the rightness of hierarchical forms of social organization. However, participating in a single game of chess is not likely to convince anyone that the world portrayed in the game works as the game says it works. Instead, the meanings that characterize a culture are repeated again and again in other symbolic actions, the most important of which may be **ritual.** The Kwakiutl provide a good example of how ritual portrays and reinforces certain meanings. Their view of the world, as noted in Question 3.1, rests on metaphors of hunger that are graphically expressed in their language, myth, art, and ritual. One of the most important Kwakiutl rituals is the Cannibal Dance. The description of the dance that follows is necessarily simplified but gives the basic outline of the ceremony.

The Kwakiutl Cannibal Dance

The Cannibal Dance is a four-day spectacle that serves as the highlight of the Kwakiutl Winter Ceremonial, a period of celebration and ritual observance in which all worldly activities cease. It is a time set aside for the spiritual world of the Kwakiutl, filled with monstrous and powerful beings and animal spirits, to intersect with the real world. The dance varies in some detail from group to group, but in all it is the focal point of a youth's initiation into the Cannibal Society, a group responsible for performing certain rituals. The initiate plays the role in the ceremony of the cannibal dancer, or *hamatsa*. Members of the Cannibal Society and others gather in a ceremonial house to call back the cannibal to the human world from his sojourn in the realm of Man Eater, one of the most important of the supernatural beings in the Kwakiutl pantheon of spirits.

At the beginning of the ceremony, the *hamatsa* (the initiate) is believed to be in the woods frantically searching for human flesh to devour. Some accounts of the dance report that he would actually eat mummified human remains. Meanwhile, members of the Cannibal Society gather around a fire in the ceremonial house to sing and recite prayers to entice the *hamatsa* into the house, periodically sending men out to see if he is approaching the village. Finally, the prayers and calls of the Cannibal Society attract the *hamatsa*. Dressed in branches of the hemlock tree, he arrives by pushing aside roof boards and jumping down among the celebrants; this is supposed to symbolize descent from the spirit world above to the world of the living. In a seeming frenzy, the *hamatsa* runs around the fire and then into an adjacent room, leaving behind the sacred hemlock branches he had worn. During the four days of the ceremony the celebrants try by various means to entice him back into the house and, in effect, to tame and socialize him, convincing him to forsake his craving for human flesh and accept normal food. For example, in one part of the ceremony the *hamatsa* flees the house and a member of the Cannibal Society is sent as the bait to attract him. The *hamatsa* rushes upon him, seizes his arm, and bites it. Each time he bites someone, he dashes into a secret room and vomits, an act that is repeated various times during the ceremony.

During pauses, members of the audience exchange gifts; wealthy persons are expected to give away more wealth than others. Later the *hamatsa* appears naked and is given clothes, but he flees again. At another point a woman who serves as a co-initiate appears naked, carrying mummified remains; she dances backward trying to entice the *hamatsa* to enter the house, but she fails. Finally the group succeeds in subduing the *hamatsa* by bathing him in the smoke of cedar bark that has been soaked in menstrual blood. After the conclusion of the public part of the Cannibal Dance, the initiate and a few members of the Cannibal Society go to another house and eat a normal meal, the final symbol that the *hamatsa* has been tamed, that his craving for human flesh has been replaced with a desire for ordinary food.

Ritual can be viewed as a symbolic representation of reality that makes it seem as if the reality were absolutely true. In another sense, the ritual presents participants in the ritual with solutions to real problems, in the same way symbolic representations suggest real solutions. For the Kwakiutl the *hamatsa* is the ultimate projection of the power of hunger, and his desire for human flesh is a manifestation of the forces that can destroy society. The participants in the ritual, by symbolically taming the hunger of the *hamatsa,* are asserting their moral responsibility to control greed and conflict. The ritual is the acting out of the successful efforts of the group to overcome forces that threaten society. Here is how Walens puts it (I've added italics):

> The *hamatsa's* hunger is fearsome; but it is the same hunger felt by every human, and thus every human has the *power* to control it. Ultimately the *hamatsa,* and the bestial ferocity he embodies, can be conquered. Morally the force of controlled social action, the strength of ritual, can conquer even a Cannibal's hunger. In fact, ritual can totally alter the impetus of the Cannibal's hunger, changing it from a destructive act to an affirmation of self-control, an act of creative power. The winter ceremonials *prove* that no matter how terrible the power of hunger, no matter how many fearsome guises it assumes, no matter how many masks it wears, and no matter how many voices it speaks with, morality will be the ultimate victor. So long as humans have the knowledge to use food correctly, they need never fear hunger nor its awful accompaniment, death. (Walens 1981:162)

The Cannibal Dance also contains a powerful message about socialization. Children, like the *hamatsa,* come from the spirit world and enter the world naked. Like the *hamatsa,* children have a female assistant, their mother, who must feed and socialize them; they dance and kick in the womb, where they live off the flesh of their mothers. Children come into the world hungry, threatening to devour their parents' wealth. In other words, in the Kwakiutl view of things, all humans are cannibals who must be socialized and tamed. Through swaddling, ritual fasting, denial of food, and other actions, parents transform their children from cannibals into moral human beings. The Kwakiutl, through ritual enactment, have made their symbols real. Their world really is as the ritual depicts it, and their lives in part revolve around living the reality they have created.

Dorothy Meets Luke Skywalker

The Kwakiutl Cannibal Dance probably seems exotic, but consider the power of **myth** in American society. In the same way societies have key metaphors that give meaning to a wide range of experiences, they may also be said to have **key scenarios,** stories or myths that, like ritual, portray their values and beliefs. In the same sense that people act out and communicate their views of the world in ritual, they can be said to act out the scenarios contained in their myths. Like others, Americans act out the key scenarios of their myths.

Joseph Campbell spent most of his life studying the myths of people around the world. In one of his earlier books, *The Hero with a Thousand Faces,* Campbell concludes that myths from all over the world contain stories about a hero who embodies the most valued qualities of a society. These myths have consistent scenarios. A hero, separated from home, family, or society, embarks on a journey in search of something—knowledge, a magical object, a person, or even a vision. In the course of the journey the hero encounters a mentor, someone who conveys some kind of power to the hero. When the hero meets up with strange creatures or powerful forces that make it difficult to reach a goal, helpers appear to offer assistance and protection. Eventually the hero faces death but, with the help of the mentor's power, escapes and ultimately reaches the goal.

EXERCISE 3.4 ━━━

From what you remember about *The Wizard of Oz* and *Star Wars,* how does each represent the process of coming of age? Are there key differences in the stories that are significant? Consider the following questions: What do each of the heroes, Luke and Dorothy, seek? From whom do they obtain their power? What form does the power take, and why are the differences significant? What helpers join the heroes, and what is the hero's relationship to them? How do the heroes destroy evil, and what is the reaction to their heroic deeds? Finally, what lesson does each hero learn, and in what way have their adventures transformed them?

If the scenario sounds familiar, it probably is; it has been the source for many stories, books, and films. George Lucas, for example, wrote the script for his movie *Star Wars* using Campbell's writings on mythology as a guide. The quest scenario is deeply rooted in American literature and myth. There are variations, however. Another popular American story that utilizes the quest scenario is Frank Baum's *The Wonderful Wizard of Oz,* which differs from *Star Wars* in that instead of a male hero (Luke Skywalker), it has a female hero (Dorothy). Consequently the meanings the stories contain differ; one is a story of growing up a male, the other a story of growing up a female. Regardless, reading, watching, or listening to stories such as these, and identifying with the hero, helps people learn something about growing up. Both *Star Wars* and *The Wizard of Oz* are coming-of-age tales. Both emphasize the American value of finding one's self; both define the qualities that are required for success. While one story concerns a male and the other a female, both present stories to live by, scenarios for solving real problems.

QUESTION 3.3 Can Humor Be Used to Resolve the Contradictions Inherent in Language and Metaphor?

While language, ritual, myth, and other forms of symbolic action help us make sense of our experience, they are all, in a sense, absurd. Metaphors are highly inexact ways of understanding things—after all, courtship is not a sporting event, and children don't eat their parents—and lives and experiences rarely follow the neat formulas laid out in ritual and myth. Ritual and myth are fictions. Dorothy recovered Toto and got home, and Luke Skywalker found the force and destroyed the Deathstar, but in real life solutions aren't this neat. Moreover, the meanings incorporated in language, ritual, and myth are problematic, and people often express considerable skepticism, doubt, and uncertainty about their beliefs. One area of human behavior in which these doubts and uncertainties gain expression is humor.

The subject of humor may seem out of place in a discussion of such mediums as language, ritual, and myth. But social scientists, beginning with the psychologist Sigmund Freud, have long recognized jokes as expressions of anxieties, doubts, and uncertainties. Humor is built on contradiction, anxiety, and ambiguity. The joke depends on an abrupt switch or change of interpretation that allows a person, situation, or experience to take on a new, sometimes incongruous meaning. The switch in interpretation may also overcome some anxiety or fear.

To illustrate the serious side of humor and the ambiguities of language, take one of the basic forms of humor, the pun. The joke in a pun rests on a basic ambiguity found in all languages, the fact that a word or expression can mean two things at the same time. "Tell me, Mr. Fields," a reporter once asked W. C. Fields (an actor who claimed to despise working with child stars), "do you approve of clubs for children?" "Only," said Fields, "when kindness fails." Here the humor focuses on the ambiguity of the term *club*—an association, like the Boy Scouts, or a large stick. The pun raises to consciousness the ambiguity of language. As Edmund Leach put it:

> A pun occurs when we make a joke by confusing two apparently
> different meanings of the same phonemic pattern. The pun seems funny
> or shocking because it challenges a taboo which ordinarily forbids us to
> recognize that the sound pattern is ambiguous. (Leach 1979:207).

Ludwig Wittgenstein Meets Alice in Wonderland

The ambiguities and contradictions in belief that make humor possible are the same as those that philosophers struggle with in earnest. In fact, Ludwig Wittgenstein, perhaps the foremost philosopher of the twentieth century, once remarked that he could write a serious philosophical work that consisted entirely of jokes. An example of how ambiguities in language can be the source of both philosophical concern and humor is found in George Pitcher's comparison of the work of Wittgenstein with the humor of Lewis Carroll in *Alice in Wonderland* and its sequel, *Through the Looking Glass*. The ambiguities in language that served as a philosophical concern for Wittgenstein were a source of humor for Carroll.

The basic assumption behind the use of metaphor is that if we know what something means in one context, we know what it means in another context. That is, if we know how to "measure" length, then we also know how to "measure" time. Wittgenstein claims that this simply isn't so; a person who knows what *W* means in one context does not necessarily know what it means in another context.

Carroll illustrates exactly what Wittgenstein means. He describes how, during the trial of the Knave of Hearts in *Alice in Wonderland*,

> ...one of the guinea-pigs cheered, and was immediately *suppressed* by the officers of the court. (As that is rather a hard word, I will explain to you how it was done. They had a large canvas bag, which tied up at the mouth with strings: into this they slipped the guinea pig, head first, and then sat upon it.) "I'm glad I've seen that done," thought Alice. "I've so often read in the newspapers, at the end of trials, 'there was some attempt at applause, which was immediately *suppressed* by the officers of the court,' and I never understood what it meant till now." (quoted in Pitcher 1965:598; italics added)

Alice, in effect, wrongly assumed that since she understood what "suppressing a guinea pig" meant, she also knew what "suppressing applause" meant. Yet our entire mode of knowing is based on the assumption that if we know what something means in one context, we know what it means in another, just as Alice thought she did.

Wittgenstein points out the absurdity of the metaphors English speakers use to understand the conception of time, and our tendency to think of time as a thing:

> We say that "the present event passes by" (a log passes by), "the future event is to come" (a log is to come). We talk about the flow of events, but also about the flow of time—the river on which the logs travel. Here is one of the most fertile sources of philosophic puzzlement: we talk of the future event of something coming into my room, and also of the future coming of this event. (quoted in Pitcher 1965:609)

Carroll used this absurdity in our language as a rich source of humor. During the tea party with the Mad Hatter:

> ...Alice sighed wearily. "I think you might do something better with the time," she said, "than wasting it in asking riddles that have no answers." "If you knew Time as well as I do," said the Hatter, "you wouldn't talk about wasting *it*. It's *him*. "I don't know what you mean," said Alice. "Of course you don't!" the Hatter said, tossing his head contemptuously. "I dare say you never even spoke to Time!" "Perhaps not," Alice cautiously replied; "but I know I have to beat time when I learn music." "Ah! That accounts for it," said the Hatter. "He won't stand beating...." (quoted in Pitcher 1965:609)

A central doctrine in Wittgenstein's philosophy is that similarities in English grammar cause confusion in our use of language. For example, the sentence "Nobody is here" is grammatically similar to the sentence "John is here," suggesting that "Nobody" can be interpreted as a name. As Wittgenstein says, "Imagine a language in which, instead of 'I found nobody in the room,' one said, 'I found Mr. Nobody in the room.' Imagine the philosophical problems which would arise out of such a convention." Alice's conversation with the King of Hearts builds on Wittgenstein's philosophical dilemma:

"Just look along the road, and tell me if you can see either of them."

"I see *nobody* on the road," says Alice.

"I only wish I had such eyes," the King remarked in a fretful tone. "To be able to see *Nobody!* And at that distance too! Why it's as much as I can do to see real people, by this light! . . .

"Who did you pass on the road?" the King went on, holding out his hand to the messenger for some more hay.

"*Nobody*," said the messenger.

"Quite right," said the King: "this young lady saw him too. So of course *Nobody* walks slower than you."

"I do my best," the messenger said in a sullen tone. "I'm sure *nobody* walks much faster than I do!"

"He can't do that," said the King, "or else he'd have been here first." (quoted in Pitcher 1965:610, italics added)

Carroll's routine is, of course, an early version of the classic vaudeville routine made famous by Lou Abbott and Bud Costello in which baseball players are identified as "Who" on first, "What" on second, "I don't know" at shortstop, and so forth. In sum, both Wittgenstein and Carroll draw attention to the fact that languages are imperfect vehicles of meaning. They contain contradictions and ambiguities that are sources of confusion—and humor.

Apache Humor: Laughing at the Whiteman

The ambiguities and contradictions in language are not our only source for humor. Often people create humor out of everyday life problems or events. The humor created by the Western Apache is a good example. Like most indigenous peoples of North America, they suffered greatly at the hands of Euro-Americans. Their lands were taken from them and they were confined to reservations in 1872, when Cochise made peace after a protracted struggle with the U.S. Army. The Western Apache, like many Native Americans, are victims of poverty, and even now whites, often insensitive to Apache culture, impose themselves and their values on them. The Apache view of whites is aptly summarized by Harold Cardinal:

> The biggest of all Indian problems is the Whiteman. Who can understand the Whiteman? What makes him tick? How does he think and why does he think the way he does? Why does he say one thing and do the opposite? Most important of all, how do you deal with him? Obviously he is here to stay. Sometimes it seems like a hopeless task. (quoted in Basso 1979:3)

Paradoxically, one of the richest sources of humor for the Western Apache is the Whiteman. As anthropologist Keith Basso describes it, most Whiteman jokes take the form of little skits or performances in which an Apache imitates a white person talking to an Apache. Here is one example that involves J, a cowboy (age 40 +), his wife K (age 37), and L, a kinsman of J (age 35 +). J and K have just finished a meal, and K is doing dishes while J is repairing a bridle. There is a knock on the door. J answers it and greets L. Basso describes the interaction:

> J: Hello my friend! How are you doing? How are you feeling L? You feeling good?
> [J now turns to K and addresses her.]
> J: Look who's here everybody! Look who just came in. Sure, it's my Indian friend L. Pretty good all right!

[J slaps L on the shoulder and, looking him directly in the eyes, seizes his hand and pumps it wildly up and down.]

J: Come right in, my friend! Don't stay outside in the rain. Better you come in right now.

[J now drapes his arm around L's shoulder and moves him in the direction of a chair.]

J: Sit down! Sit right down! Take your loads off your ass. You hungry? You want some beer? Maybe you want some wine? You want crackers? Bread? You want some sandwich? How 'bout it? You hungry? I don't know. Maybe you get sick. Maybe you don't eat again long time.

[K has stopped washing dishes and is looking on with amusement. L has seated himself and has a look of bemused resignation on his face.]

J: You sure looking good to me, L. You looking pretty fat! Pretty good all right! You got new boots? Where you buy them? Sure pretty good boots! I glad. . . .

[At this point J breaks into laughter. K joins in. L shakes his head and smiles. The joke is over.]

K: Whitemen are stupid! (Basso 1979:62–64)

The humor in this performance originates in mocking the behavior of whites toward Indians. Every bit of white behavior, for an Apache, was totally wrong and inappropriate. For example, the greeting "Hello my friend" is an expression that Apaches find irresponsible and presumptuous. Apaches think whites use it even when they meet someone for the first time, or even if they hold a person in contempt. "How are you feeling" is an unsolicited and intrusive inquiry into a person's emotional or physical health that would never be asked of one Apache by another. It is an invasion of privacy. "Look who's here everybody"—Apaches enter or leave a group unobtrusively, never calling attention to themselves or others. J addresses L by his name; Apaches rarely do that. A name is a personal possession, and to use it is likened to borrowing it without asking. J slaps L on the back, stares him in the eye, and guides him to a seat; Apaches, especially adult males, rarely touch each other in public. And staring at someone is an aggressive act, as is forcibly moving somebody to another spot. "Come right in, my friend! Sit down!" is viewed by Apaches as "bossing someone around." "Maybe you get sick"—Apaches believe that talking about adversity and trouble may increase their chance of occurrence. "You hungry? You want some beer? Maybe you want some wine? You want crackers? Bread? You want some sandwich? How 'bout it? You hungry?"—except in an emergency, Apaches think it rude to ask a question more than once, and since it is polite to give people time to respond, demanding an answer is considered boorish behavior.

From an Apache perspective, the behavior was all wrong. The joke, as Basso puts it, is a dramatized denunciation "of the ways in which Euro-Americans conduct themselves in the presence of Indian people." These performances give visible expression to Apache views of whites and to the problems Apaches face when the two interact. Basso points out, also, that the content of the humor has changed to incorporate different groups of whites that, over time, have appeared on the reservations. In the 1960s the Whiteman was portrayed as a hippie, mumbling and effeminate; in the 1970s, when VISTA volunteers arrived on the reservation, whites were portrayed as "gushingly altruistic," hopelessly incompetent at the simplest task, and, for some reason, always out of breath. When doctors arrived to stamp out diarrhea in infants and to "teach women how to breast feed," they were labeled "those-who play-with-babies'-shit."

Apache humorists, like Western humorists such as Lewis Carroll, highlight areas of experience that are somehow problematic. But there is a paradox. How can forms of expression—humor in this case—that draw our attention to problems and absurdities help us find meaning in our experience? Shouldn't humor make us even more skeptical and doubtful of the meanings contained in our language and ritual performances?

Humor and Life's Incongruities

Anthropologists have long noted the association of humor and ritual performance. For the Hopi the clown was an important part of all ritual performance, and the masked clown was featured in Iroquois rituals. Rituals are said to have the power to heal, and some people, such as the writer Norman Cousins, claim that humor also has therapeutic qualities. However, whereas ritual seeks to mask the ambiguities and contradictions in our lives, humor does just the opposite; it highlights and draws attention to them. In a very real sense, humor is anti-ritual. But the key, I think, is that when we laugh at the meanings in jokes, we laugh at the problems and contradictions of life, as the Apache laughs at the Whiteman for behavior that is the source of many Apache problems.

Most societies have their clowns who, in one way or another, make fun of what otherwise are very serious things. The clown serves as a guide to the incongruities and absurdities in our beliefs. But clowns play a dangerous game. If they succeed in getting us to laugh at the incongruity or problem, they succeed in helping us negate our doubts. But if they fail to make us laugh, they have succeeded only in making us aware of our failings. The clown must make us laugh at the joke in the same way that the priest must prevent us from laughing at the ritual. In his analysis of Apache humor, Basso makes the same point about the Apache jokester. The Whiteman that the Apache imitates is an example of someone who looks down on others. Too often the Apache who is the butt of the joking performance has been treated by Anglo-Americans with insolence and disdain. Consequently, if the imitation of the Whiteman is performed poorly or with the wrong person as the foil, the humor could backfire; the butt of the joke may take it seriously, feel that he or she is being insulted by being treated condescendingly, or even retaliate by physically attacking the jokester.

The clown serves another important purpose. By definition, the clown is not someone we take seriously; when a clown points out incongruities or absurdities in our lives, they lose some of their credibility. That may be why the clown is inevitably an asocial, and often asexual, figure, existing on the fringes of society. Perhaps it is no accident that most American comedians are Jewish or African American, and most British comedians are Irish. Psychologists have claimed that the clown or the comedian becomes the butt of our aggressions, a cathartic figure who encapsulates all our fears and anxieties. The clown and the joke are, in effect, receptacles in which we store our fears and anxieties about threatened disorder, receptacles we conveniently trash by our laughter.

There is in humor, as John Allen Paulos points out, a sense of the mathematical proof that takes the form, "To prove A, show not–A is nonsense."

This is a form of proof popular with theologians who wish to prove the existence of God; if they cannot prove that God exists, they try to prove that existence without God is impossible. In the same way, humor, by making jokes about the very real ambiguities and contradictions in our lives, makes the problems they represent seem nonsensical and, consequently, less threatening.

But, no matter how much fun it might be, we cannot laugh away all the inconsistencies, ambiguities, and contradictions in our lives. We must also be able to confront doubt and uncertainty in other ways, some of which will be examined next.

QUESTION 3.4 How Do People Collectively Defend Beliefs That Are Threatened?

In addition to being filtered by language, symbolic action, and humor, our experience is also mediated by collective judgments. Our individual beliefs about how the world works lead us to expect or predict that certain things will or will not happen. But whether or not we think that our expectations or predictions have been fulfilled depends on the collective judgments of the groups to which we belong. The fact that individual expectations are sometimes filtered through group expectations has two implications. Obviously, if most people in a group say that something is true, that is often enough for everyone else to accept it as true. Less obviously, even if an event that our beliefs lead us to expect or predict doesn't happen as predicted, we can collectively act to dismiss the event or nonevent in such a way that the beliefs that created the expectation can be upheld. In other words, a group can always preserve beliefs that are challenged.

Explaining Why the Sun Moves Around the Earth

For almost 2,000 years, Europeans believed that the earth was the center of the universe. Supposedly, there was a two-sphere cosmos consisting of a vaulted heaven across which the sun, planets, and stars circled eastward, and an earthly sphere that was at the center of the universe. Then as now, people spoke of the sun rising and setting. This conception of the universe was incorporated into myth with the biblical story of Joshua stopping the sun in the heavens. The idea of an earth-centered universe fits well with a society in which humankind was afforded the central place in the universe.

In spite of the extent to which people took for granted an earth-centered universe, there were problems with understanding the system. It was difficult to explain the behavior of planets that revolved around the earth, because they sometimes seemed to reverse their course or increase or decrease in brightness. Moreover, some early scholars, such as Aristarchus, a Greek grammarian who proposed a sun-centered cosmology, were aware of alternative views. But people were generally able to explain away apparent contradictions.

The history of astronomy illustrates some of the ways people are able to sustain what they believe, in spite of evidence to the contrary. For example,

In the Middle Ages, people accepted the idea that the earth is at the center of the universe and the sun and stars revolve around it, though they found it hard to understand.

people can rationalize inconsistencies in what they believe; that is, they can find some way to explain away the inconsistency without changing their belief. The behavior of the planets was a problem for medieval astronomers; sometimes the planets could be observed reversing direction, a phenomenon now explained as a consequence of the differing speed of rotation of the planets around the sun. As the earth catches up to or is passed by a planet, the planet seems to reverse its motion. In the Ptolemaic system, however, the inconsistency was rationalized by proposing that planets moved in epicycles, figure-eight loops they supposedly made as they rotated around the earth. The epicycle concept also explained why a planet could vary in brightness, since during its loops its distance to the earth would vary.

A British anthropologist, E. E. Evans-Pritchard, used the term **secondary elaboration** to define this type of rationalizing process, illustrating it with his classic account of divination among the Azande of northern Zaire. A Zande who needs to make an important decision or discover the cause of an event consults a diviner. The diviner or oracle worker feeds a poison to chickens and addresses questions to the oracle that is thought to be manifest in the poison. The poison used by the Azande sometimes kills the chicken and sometimes does not, so the questions are put to the oracle in the form, "If such is the case, kill (or don't kill) the chicken." The procedure is done twice to check its accuracy.

Sometimes, however, the oracle is wrong. It may reply positively to a question, and subsequent events prove the oracle false. It is easy for us to say, "We told you so," but the Azande can, if they wish, continue to believe in the power of the oracle by secondary elaboration. Instead of doubting the power of the oracle to predict, they can excuse the error by saying the oracle failed because the wrong poison was used, or because witchcraft interfered with the oracle, or because the poison was old, or ghosts were angry, or the diviner was incompetent.

Beliefs can also be sustained by **selective perception,** seeing only what we want to see. The earth-centered universe, for example, was easily confirmed by the evidence of the senses. There was certainly nothing to indicate the earth moved. In fact, the senses indicated just the opposite; if you dropped an object, it fell straight down. If the earth moved, the object should fall to the right or left of the spot it was dropped. You could see that the sun rises and sets. The Azande, for example, believe witches are people who have inside them a substance responsible for making them witches. This substance can be discovered through autopsy and is believed to be inherited from one generation to another. Someone accused of witchcraft can be convicted or acquitted if an autopsy is done on a kinsman who dies. The corpse is cut open, and an expert in the procedure sifts through the intestines in search of the witchcraft substance. If it is found, as it sometimes is, it is held aloft for everyone to see.

Another way to sustain beliefs is by suppressing evidence—not allowing evidence that contradicts a cherished belief. In the Middle Ages, for example, the Catholic Church declared as heresy any attempt to suggest that the earth moved around the sun, and astronomers would simply ignore evidence that suggested that the earth was not at the center of the universe. For the Nuer, a herding people of the Sudan in northern Africa, the animal world is divided into things that are human and things that are not. Occasionally, however, a phenomenon threatens the distinction; if a monstrous birth (a severely deformed infant) occurs, it obscures the Nuer distinction between human and nonhuman. The Nuer solve the problem by saying the infant is a baby hippopotamus born to a human parent and putting it in a river. They have suppressed evidence that threatens their view of the world.

EXERCISE 3.5 ────────────────────────────────────

One of the most persistent contradictions in Judeo-Christian thought has to do with the nature of God. The Judeo-Christian God, unlike creator figures in some other belief systems, is believed to be omnipotent; He controls everything. But, in addition, He is thought to be all-good. The problem is, how can God be all-good and all-powerful when evil, suffering, and injustice exist in the world? If evil exists, He must allow it, in which case He is not all-good. Or if He is all-good, and evil, suffering, and injustice exist, He must not be omnipotent. How might this contradiction be resolved? How can it be explained away while maintaining the idea of an all-powerful, all-good deity?

Beliefs can also be sustained by an appeal to faith or mystery. The earth-centered universe was sustained by an appeal to faith. If there were questions about it, people could be told that it was wrong to ask too many questions about the universe, that God sometimes worked in mysterious ways. The Catholic Church recognizes the concept of mystery in the anomalous features of such doctrines as the Trinity, the idea that God is one in essence but three in "person," Father, Son, and Holy Ghost; the Eucharist, the idea that the bread and wine of ritual are the body and blood of Christ; and the Incarnation, the idea that the human and divine natures of Christ are united. The church embraces these ideas even though they are problematic in some way by declaring each is a mystery, a doctrine whose truth cannot be demonstrated but must be taken on faith.

And beliefs can be sustained by appeals to authority; the authority of Scripture supported the truth of an earth-centered universe. If all else fails, it is possible to use violence or deceit to protect a belief that is threatened. In the seventeenth century, when Galileo proposed to support the idea that the earth revolves around the sun, he was imprisoned and tortured by Church officials until he recanted. He spent the rest of his life under house arrest.

One lesson of the history of astronomy is that beliefs are among the most enduring features of human societies, and they are changed only with difficulty. People tend to accept their beliefs as givens and find ways to defend and maintain their views of the world, even if they are confronted with experiences that cast doubt on their beliefs. But, as the history of astronomy also indicates, beliefs do change. The next question is, why do beliefs change?

QUESTION 3.5 *How Can People Reorder Their View of the World if It Becomes Unsatisfactory?*

The meanings that people assign to their experience do not change easily. We take it for granted that the view of the world created by the interaction of our own experiences with the mediums of language, symbolic actions, humor, and collective judgments is the right view. But beliefs do change. Often changes in the meanings that people assign to their experiences are triggered by periods of social upheavals in which the old way of looking at the world, for whatever reason, is no longer satisfactory. If sufficient numbers of people share this unease, they may together try to change both their view of the world and the organization of society. Anthony F. C. Wallace suggests the term **revitalization movements** for these attempts by people to construct a more satisfying culture.

Generally, a period of social or economic upheaval or oppression leads to the development of a new or revised belief system. This system may promise to return the society to a real or mythical previous state or offer a new vision of the world that promises to relieve the oppression or frustration. During such social upheavals, the usual explanations for events are unsatisfactory, traditional solutions to problems no longer work, and rituals may be abandoned. Doubt engendered by social upheaval is replaced with a new certainty born of religious fervor or conversion. Two examples of revitalization movements are expressed in the Ghost Dance of Native Americans and the colonies of the Shakers, a religious group who came to this country from England and settled in upstate New York.

Wovoka *(Jack Wilson)* and the Ghost Dance — *appealed to religions faith that would affect all ways of life*

American settlers migrating west in the nineteenth century came into contact with hundreds of Native American groups, and eventually conflict over land resulted in wars between these groups and American military forces. During the Indian wars, which covered a period from about 1850 to 1880, the U.S. government negotiated and signed treaties with Native American groups guaranteeing their rights to areas of land, financial compensation, and food and other provisions. But as more white settlers moved into the Indian territories, the government insisted on renegotiating the treaties if the settlers wanted land that had been given to native groups. For example, the Sioux were given rights to the Black Hills of South Dakota, but after gold was discovered there the government unilaterally renegotiated the treaties and reduced their land by more than half (in this case, however, courts later ruled that the government's act was illegal, and the Sioux never ceded their rights). Moreover, the buffalo on which the Plains Indians subsisted were virtually exterminated, sometimes in a conscious effort by the American military to destroy the economic basis of native society.

As a result of the Indian wars, treaty negotiations, government deceit, and the influx of new settlers, native groups were restricted to reservations, made dependent on government rations, and denied traditional pursuits such as hunting and horse raiding. Government deliveries of food and provisions were often late or did not arrive at all, and the indigenous population had little resistance to illness and disease brought to the New World by European settlers. Children were taken to boarding schools away from the reserves and prohibited from speaking their native languages. Government agents, often at the insistence of Christian missionaries, banned traditional ceremonies and rituals. In brief, the social fabric of indigenous society was destroyed. Those traditional things that help filter experience—language, ritual, and the ability of groups to collectively sustain particular views of the world—virtually vanished.

Revitalization movements usually receive their impetus from a prophet who claims to have received a vision or dream about a new way of viewing the world or a set of moral injunctions governing people's lives. The major prophet for the Ghost Dance was a Paiute named Wovoka. In 1889 Wovoka had a vision in which he was taken up to heaven where he saw God and all the native people who had died performing their traditional games and activities. God told him he must go back and tell his people to live in peace with whites and with each other. He was also given instructions for a ritual dance and told that if this dance were performed for five days and nights, friends and relatives would be reunited in the other world.

Converts to Wovoka's message spread the word from Nevada to Native American groups throughout the United States and Canada, but his message was often reinterpreted as it spread. In some versions the world would be destroyed and only the Native Americans brought back to life; in others, Euro-Americans and Native Americans would live together in harmony. In other versions, the buffalo would return, or a specific date was set for the millennium, or Wovoka was said to be the son of God. Whatever the interpretation, the Ghost Dance, as it became called, was adopted by numerous groups who were seeking a revival of a way of life disrupted by Euro-American expansion.

revesting buck

multi- culturalim

compromise

Black n. Revit.

create conflict → change instead of

conflict → create change

Religions were formerly the big revitalization movers—now science?

Among the groups that enthusiastically adopted the Ghost Dance was the Sioux. They had sent emissaries in 1889 to visit Wovoka and returned with descriptions of his vision and power. One account of the delegates' report is contained in James Mooney's work on the Ghost Dance. An anthropologist working for the Bureau of American Ethnology, Mooney traveled around the country interviewing key figures, including Wovoka, and collecting first-hand accounts of the dance. Here is his description of the report of the Sioux delegates:

> They were gone all winter, and their return in the spring of 1890 aroused an intense excitement among the Sioux, who had been anxiously awaiting their report. All the delegates agreed that there was a man near the base of the Sierras who said that he was the son of God, who had once been killed by the whites, and who bore on his body the scars of the crucifixion. He had now returned to punish the whites for their wickedness, especially for their injustice toward the Indians. With the coming of the next spring (1891) he would wipe the whites from the face of the earth, and would then resurrect all the dead Indians, bring back the buffalo and other game, and restore the supremacy of the aboriginal race. (Mooney 1965:64)

Based on these messages, the Sioux began to dance in October of 1890. However, for the Sioux, the Ghost Dance turned into a tragic reminder of Euro-American oppression. Frightened that the ritual might turn into open rebellion, the Indian agent at one Sioux reservation called in the military. Some of the Sioux fled the reservation, chased by the Seventh Cavalry, General George Custer's group that had been decimated by a combined Native American army at Little Big Horn in 1876. After the promise of a safe return to the reservation, the Sioux surrendered their arms at a place called Wounded Knee and were surrounded by the cavalry, equipped with Gatling guns. As soldiers rummaged through the Sioux shelters searching for guns, someone fired a shot. The army opened fire, killing over 150 men, women, and children.

The Ghost Dance virtually ceased among the Sioux after the massacre at Wounded Knee but continued among other groups, each of which hoped for the return of a traditional culture. Today it represents one attempt of a people to build a new culture, a new system of meaning after the destruction of a previous one.

Mother Ann Lee and the Shakers

Another example of a revitalization movement comes from one of the most dramatic periods of religious change in American history, the first half of the nineteenth century, when hundreds of religious movements warning of the coming end of the world led to the establishment of religious communities. This was also a period of great social change, as Americans began the transition from a rural-agricultural to an urban-industrial society. It was marked by considerable population movement, the growth of poverty, and the breakdown of the family as the prime maintainer of societal norms. Revitalization movements represented an attempt to reformulate society in ways that remain relevant today. Virtually all of them reacted to poverty by eliminating private property and requiring communal ownership of all things; reacted to inequality by recognizing the equality of men and women; and reacted to what they perceived as the breakdown of the larger

Wovoka, the major prophet of the Ghost Dance, in a photograph taken by James Mooney in 1891; and (right) Bertha Lindsay, one of the last surviving members of the Shakers in the United States, who died in December 1990.

society by requiring withdrawal of their communities. While almost all these movements eventually failed, the goals of many remain viable.

The Shakers, or the United Society of Believers in Christ's Second Appearing, as they called themselves, were one of the most interesting and most successful. The Shakers are known largely for their vows of celibacy and rejection of sexual intimacy. But that is only a portion of their ideology.

The founder of the Shakers was Ann Lee. We know little of her life other than that obtained from early nineteenth-century accounts written by her followers. She was born in Manchester, England, in 1736 and at age eight was working 12 to 14 hours a day in the textile mills of Manchester, one of the worst urban slums in England. When she was 22, she attended a series of religious revival meetings held by a group led by Jane and James Wardley. The Wardleys had been Quakers but broke away to form the Wardley Society, developing an expressive kind of worship characterized by emotional chanting, shouting, and shaking from which they got their name, the "Shaking Quakers."

Lee is said to have exhibited an antipathy to sex early in her life. When she was 25, pressured by her family, she married a blacksmith, Abraham Standerin; in a rare decision for its time, she continued to call herself by her maiden name. Her first three children died in infancy, and the fourth was stillborn. The chronicle of her life states that she was paralyzed by grief and guilt and became convinced that sex and marriage were the root of all evil and the cause of her misery. She gained support (over the objections of her husband) from the Wardleys and declared her celibacy.

The Wardleys preached that the second coming of Christ was near, and, since God was both male and female, the manifestation of Christ's second coming would be a female. In a public confession of sin, Lee poured out all her transgressions and then joined the Wardleys to preach. She and her father, brother, and husband, all of whom had joined her, were arrested for causing a public nuisance. While in jail, she had a vision of Adam and Eve "committing the forbidden sexual act" and began publicly preaching against it. She also claimed to have had a vision in which Jesus appeared to her and revealed that she was his chosen successor, that she was to be the Word of God, the second coming of Christ as a woman.

The Wardleys accepted her vision, and stories began to circulate about the miraculous healing power of Mother Ann Lee, as she came to be called. One woman claimed that she had a cancer of the mouth, and when Lee touched it, it disappeared. Others related how Lee was beaten for her beliefs but showed no injury. She later had another vision that told her to take her religion to America. In 1774, along with her husband, brother, niece, and four others, she journeyed to America to establish a church. Escaping New York City just ahead of the British in 1776, they journeyed to upstate New York and established a settlement outside Albany. The turning point for the Shakers in America came in 1780. There was a religious revival of Baptists in the nearby community of New Lebanon, and Calvin Harlow and Joseph Meacham, a Baptist minister, heard about the Shakers and traveled to see Mother Ann Lee. They were so impressed with her and what she had to say that Meacham became her first important convert in America.

Mother Ann Lee died in 1784, perhaps as a result of a journey she and members of her group undertook in 1781 to bring her message to others in New England. The journey was marked by persecution and beatings. But the movement continued to spread, and at its height in the 1840s there were over 6,000 members spread over 25 communities, from Maine to Florida and into the Ohio Valley.

The social message of the Shakers was relatively simple. Sexual relations were banned, both men and women shared authority, there were separate living arrangements for men and women, members were required to publicly confess their sins, and property was held in common. There was also a prohibition on eating pork; most Shakers ate no meat at all, even avoiding milk, butter, and eggs. The Shakers professed pacifism and sought to maintain a separate government apart from the rest of society. Each community was organized into groups called families and had a ministry consisting of males and females, usually two of each. Their religious principles included the idea that God is a dual being, male and female, that Mother Ann Lee was the second coming of Christ as spirit, and that the millennium had commenced with the establishment of their church.

Much of what we know of the Shakers in the nineteenth century comes from a book by Charles Nordhoff, *The Communistic Societies of the United States: From Personal Observations.* Nordhoff was a widely respected journalist who traveled among the Shaker settlements in 1874, recording his observations and interviewing members. He interviewed Frederick Evans, probably the most prominent of the Shakers of his time, who had met with President Abraham Lincoln to plead that Shakers should be exempted from military service, a request Lincoln granted. Evans described the advantages of Shakerism, asserting that celibacy is healthful and that it prolongs life: "The joys of the celibate life are far greater than I can make you know. They are indescribable."

Nordhoff found that the Shakers comprised a cross section of professions—teachers, lawyers, farmers, students, and merchants—and a cross section of religious denominations—Jews, Baptists, Methodists, and Presbyterians, but no Catholics. Since celibacy was a requirement, the Shakers could not reproduce themselves and had to recruit new members. In the early years they obviously did this with considerable success. They built their communities to be representations of heaven on earth and gave them heavenly names—City of Peace, City of Love, City of Union, Holy Mount, and so on. They became master builders whose physical structures were the envy of all and whose authentic furniture still brings astronomical prices. Their organization of space, their posture, the way they cut their food—all were prescribed as symbols of simplicity and symmetry. Restrictions on posture and movement were suspended only during religious meetings; then the same people who ordinarily walked straight, tiptoed, and never raised their voices sang, shouted, and whirled dizzily in circles.

We can speculate about what led the people who joined the Shakers to accept their beliefs. Women, obviously, were attracted to the movement because of its promise of equality, and all may have been attracted to the strong group support offered in Shaker communities. In many ways the physical layout, the rituals and the rules of the Shakers seemed to be a denial of anything urban, anything suggesting economic or social exploitation. The communities thrived from 1800 to 1850, but they began to decline after the American Civil War as fewer people were attracted to the message. In 1990 four Shakers survived in the last of the communities in Sabbathday Lake, Maine.

CONCLUSIONS

Our interpretation of experience cannot be based solely on our direct perception of the world, and our view of the world must in some way be filtered through such mediums as language, symbolic action, humor, and collective judgment. The problem is understanding how these processes affect belief.

How does language affect the meanings we assign to our experience? The ideas of Edward Sapir and Benjamin Lee Whorf demonstrate that the vocabulary of a language may direct perception to certain features of an environment, and the grammar of a language may encourage certain ways of looking at the world. The selection of metaphors also has an impact on the meanings we assign to experience. By taking the language from one domain of experience and applying it to another, we carry the meaning of one domain to the other.

Symbolic action reinforces a particular view of the world. Ritual, for example, symbolically depicts a certain view of reality in such a way that it convinces us of the truth of that reality. An example is the Cannibal Dance of the Kwakiutl, which portrays the values of Kwakiutl society and provides members with a way to control their lives.

One way the ambiguities and contradictions of our lives can be resolved is through humor. The philosophy of Ludwig Wittgenstein can be compared with the humor of Lewis Carroll, for example. The ways Western Apaches joke about the Whiteman also demonstrate how humor helps us deal with life's problems by making them objects of laughter.

When a particular view of the world or belief is threatened, people can collectively sustain what they believe by rationalization, selective perception, suppression of evidence, appeals to faith or mystery or to authority, or violence or deceit. But under certain conditions, people might be led to change what they believe or to accept alternative ways of interpreting experience. The experience of social upheaval may lead, as it did among the Plains Indians, to a new system of belief that promises to reorder society and, in the case of the Ghost Dance, promises to resurrect the past. In the case of the Shakers, the social change that marked the transition from an agricultural base to industrialization inspired an attempt to formulate a religious community that might bring the millennium and reshape the social order.

REFERENCES AND SUGGESTED READINGS

INTRODUCTION: THE PROBLEM OF BELIEF The epigraph comes from Barry Barnes, *Scientific Knowledge and Sociological Theory* (Routledge & Kegan Paul, 1974). An excellent review of how anthropologists have addressed the human way of knowing can be found in an article by Malcolm R. Crick, "Anthropology of Knowledge," in *Annual Review of Anthropology*, vol. 11 (1982), pp. 287–313.

HOW DOES LANGUAGE AFFECT THE MEANINGS PEOPLE ASSIGN TO EXPERIENCE? Edward Sapir's works span the period from 1910 to 1939, and many appear in a volume edited by David G. Mandelbaum, *Selected Writings of Edward Sapir in Language, Culture, and Personality* (University of California Press, 1949). Benjamin Lee Whorf's works are collected in *Language, Thought, and Reality: Selected Writings of Benjamin Lee Whorf*, edited by John B. Carroll (John Wiley & Sons, 1956). A good summary of the work of Sapir and Whorf can be found in *Language, Thought and Experience*, edited by Paul Henle (The University of Michigan Press, 1958). The treatment of metaphor was taken from George Lakoff and Mark Johnson, *Metaphors We Live By* (University of Chicago Press, 1980). Some of Franz Boas's work on the Kwakiutl is contained in *Kwakiutl Ethnography*, edited by Helen Codere (University of Chicago Press, 1966). The description of Kwakiutl metaphors comes from Stanley Walens, *Feasting with Cannibals: An Essay on Kwakiutl Cosmology* (Princeton University Press, 1981). A review of the role of language in socialization is Bambi B. Schieffelin and Elinor Ochs, "Language Socialization," in *Annual Review of Anthropology*, vol. 15 (1986), pp. 163–191.

HOW DOES SYMBOLIC ACTION REINFORCE A PARTICULAR VIEW OF THE WORLD? Information on the Kwakiutl Cannibal Dance, along with other aspects of their ritual and mythology, can be found in Franz Boas, *Kwakiutl Ethnography*, cited above, and Franz Boas and George Hunt, *Kwakiutl Texts*, Memoir of the American Museum of Natural History, vol. 5 (1905). A classic work is Ruth Benedict's *Patterns of Culture* (Houghton Mifflin, 1934). Interpretations of the Cannibal Dance are found also in Stanley Walens, *Feasting with Cannibals*, cited above. A social analysis of the *Wizard of Oz* can be found in David Payne, "The Wizard of Oz: Therapeutic Rhetoric in a Contemporary Media Ritual," *Quarterly Journal of Speech*, vol. 75 (1989). Joseph Campbell's *The Hero with a Thousand Faces* (Princeton University Press, 1949) is one of the classic works on mythology. The anthropological literature on ritual and symbolic action is extensive. Roy Wagner's "Ritual as Communication: Order, Meaning, and Secrecy in Melanesian Initiation Rites," in *Annual Review of Anthropology*, vol. 13 (1984), pp. 143–155, provides an excellent review of works on ritual, as does an article by John D. Kelly and Martha Kaplan, "History, Structure, and Ritual," in *Annual Review of Anthropology*, vol. 19 (1990), pp. 119–150.

CAN HUMOR BE USED TO RESOLVE THE CONTRADICTIONS IN LANGUAGE AND METAPHOR? Edmund Leach provides some fascinating insights into puns and profanity in "Anthropological Aspects of Language: Animal Categories and Verbal Abuse," in *Reader in Comparative Religion*, 4th edition, edited by William Lessa and Evon Z. Vogt (Harper & Row, 1979). The comparison of the philosophy of Ludwig Wittgenstein and the humor of Lewis Carroll comes from George Pitcher, "Wittgenstein, Nonsense and Lewis Carroll," *Massachusetts Review*, vol. 6 (1965), pp. 591–611. Keith Basso's analysis of Apache joking is in *Portraits of "The Whiteman": Linguistic Play and Cultural Symbols among the Western Apache* (University of Cambridge Press, 1979). John Allen Paulos, in a marvelous book entitled *Mathematics and Humor* (University of Chicago Press, 1980), provides a very accessible summary of the psychological and philosophical writing on humor.

HOW DO PEOPLE COLLECTIVELY DEFEND BELIEFS THAT ARE THREATENED? The analysis of medieval astronomy comes from Thomas Kuhn's *The Copernican Revolution: Planetary Astronomy in the Development of Western Thought* (Harvard University Press, 1957). The description of Azande witchcraft and divination is from E. E. Evans-Pritchard's classic *Witchcraft, Oracles and Magic among the Azande* (Oxford University Press, 1937). The example of the Nuer monstrous birth comes from Mary Douglas, *Purity and Danger* (Frederick A. Praeger, 1966).

HOW CAN PEOPLE REORDER THEIR VIEW OF THE WORLD IF IT BECOMES UNSATISFACTORY? Anthony F. C. Wallace provides a discussion of revitalization movements, as well as the ritual process, in *Religion: An Anthropological View* (Random House, 1966). The material on the Ghost Dance comes from James Mooney's *The Ghost Dance Religion and the Sioux Outbreak of 1890* (University of Chicago Press, 1965), and from Alice Kehoe's *The Ghost Dance: Ethnohistory and Revitalization* (Holt, Rinehart and Winston, 1989). The earliest work on the Shakers is contained in *Testimonies of the Life, Character, Revelations and Doctrines of Our Ever Blessed Mother Ann Lee*, published in 1816 by J. Tallcott & J. Deming, and much of what is known about Ann Lee is described by Nardi Reeder Campion in *Mother Ann Lee: Morning Star of the Shakers* (University Press of New England, 1990). Charles Nordhoff's *The Communistic Societies of the United States* was first published by Harper and Brothers in 1875 and reissued by Dover Publications in 1966. An excellent summary of Shaker life and the relationship of their beliefs to their architecture and living arrangements can be found in *Seven American Utopias: The Architecture of Communitarian Socialism, 1790–1975*, by Dolores Hayden (MIT Press, 1981). For a general review of other religious movements, see James W. Fernandez's article on religious change in Africa, "African Religious Movements," in *Annual Review of Anthropology*, vol. 7 (1978), pp. 195–234.

C H A P T E R   4

Patterns of Family Relations

PROBLEM 4: WHAT DOES A PERSON HAVE TO KNOW TO UNDERSTAND
THE DYNAMICS OF FAMILY LIFE IN A SOCIETY?

If ever thou purpose to be a good wife, and to live comfortably, set down this with thyself: mine husband is my superior, my better; he hath authority and rule over me; nature hath given it to him . . . God hath given it to him.

W. Whately, *The Bride Bush,* London, 1617

A WOMAN NEEDS A MAN LIKE A FISH NEEDS A BICYCLE
Automobile bumper sticker, 1988

INTRODUCTION: *Soap Operas and Family Relations*

Could a foreign visitor to the United States learn anything about American family life from watching our soap operas? Consider this recent plot from a popular soap: Holden is having an affair with Lilly while his wife Angel is undergoing psychiatric treatment because she had been sexually molested by her father, who was shot and killed by Kalib, Holden's brother. In the meantime Darryl is having an affair with Francine while he and his wife, Carol, are arranging to have a child through a surrogate mother. Francine's sister Sabrina has run off with Antonio, an apparent drug dealer who has shot Bob, the sisters' father.

A visitor certainly might conclude from the popularity of this one soap opera that Americans like to watch stories of illicit love, incest, infidelity, greed, and marital and family conflict. And while the behaviors of these soap opera characters may not really represent the daily lives of American husbands and wives, fathers and mothers, or sons and daughters, they must represent enough of reality to allow viewers to identify with the characters and their situations. In some way, the plots and the relationships between the characters must seem plausible and must reveal something about the dynamics of American lives. The assumption is that a person who understands and enjoys soap operas in America would have a good understanding of the dynamics of American family life. But what relevance does that have for understanding family life in other societies?

Americans are not alone in their fascination with soap operas. Most societies have fictional dramas and real-life tales about family life that reveal the concerns of the people. Brazilians, like Americans, are fanatical soap opera watchers, but the characters, situations, and plots are different from those on American television, and these differences reveal differences in family structure and dynamics. The focus in Brazilian soap operas tends to be on the **family of orientation**—father, mother, self, and siblings—rather than on the **family of procreation**—husband, wife, and their children. The theme of class mobility dominates Brazilian soaps with plots about women from poor, rural families marrying wealthy men from the city. Love is depicted as dangerous and often unrequited, as when a woman is hopelessly in love with a man destined to marry someone else. In Brazilian soaps, characters almost always interact with family and friends; in American soaps, they interact much more frequently with strangers. In addition, the setting for Brazilian soaps is usually the home—the sphere of private life. In American soaps, the setting is often the workplace or other locations in the sphere of public life.

Soap operas, like traditional dramas and real-life tales, reveal the reasons for domestic strife; they depict individuals with choices to make, choices that have an impact on others. They reveal character motivation and development. In whatever form they take, such stories are an interesting way to learn about family life in different societies. Moreover, if you were to learn enough about family life in another society that you could write a plausible soap opera about it, the chances are that you would also understand a good deal about family dynamics in that society.

What would you need to know in order to write a soap opera about families in other societies? First, you would need to know the composition of a typical family and how the family is formed or develops and is maintained. You would need to examine how the themes of sexuality, love, and wealth (all prominent in American soap operas and familiar themes in the stories of other societies) are dealt with, and what kinds of situations or conflicts can disrupt family life in the society.

QUESTIONS

4.1 What is the composition of the typical family group?
4.2 How is the family formed and the ideal family type maintained?
4.3 What are the roles of sexuality, love, and wealth?
4.4 What threatens to disrupt the family unit?

To make this task more manageable, I will focus on family life in three societies, the !Kung, the Trobriand Islanders of the South Pacific, and the traditional Chinese farm family. I've chosen these societies for three reasons. First, they represent very different levels of social, cultural, and technological complexity. The !Kung were gatherers and hunters, living in small, mobile groups; the Trobriand Islanders were horticulturists living in villages of up to 400 people. The traditional Chinese are representative of a large, agricultural society. Second, family structure and roles vary significantly among the three, but together they depict family types and relations that are representative of many, if not most, societies around the world. Finally, the three societies have been well studied in the anthropological literature. I will discuss these societies in what anthropologists refer to as the **ethnographic present;** that is, *although the actual descriptions may refer to situations that existed in the past, they will be described as if they still existed.* In reality, the !Kung, the Trobriand Islanders, and the rural Chinese are, to varying degrees, very different today than they were when the anthropologists whose work I will refer to studied them.

QUESTION 4.1 *What Is the Composition of the Typical Family Group?*

To understand family composition in different societies, you need certain concepts and tools. One place to begin is by examining how most Americans would respond if asked about the composition of their families. If unmarried, they would likely list their mother, father, brothers, and sisters. If asked, "Who else?" they would likely add grandparents, aunts, uncles, and cousins. If they were married, they would include their husbands or wives and perhaps children.

Certain features of the typical (although by no means the only) type of American family stand out. Americans consider themselves equally tied by kinship to both their mothers and fathers and both their maternal and paternal kin. In other words, Americans use a **bilateral kinship** system and reckon kinship through both parents. Second, Americans make no linguistic distinction between their mothers' siblings and their fathers' siblings—both are referred to by the terms *aunt* and *uncle.* Nor do they distinguish linguistically the children of aunts and uncles; they are all referred to as *cousins.* For most Americans, the ideal family grouping traditionally has been the **nuclear family**—the group consisting of father, mother, and their own or adopted children. Figure 4.1 illustrates the composition of the American nuclear family at various stages of development. The influence on family life of the extended family of grandparents and grandchildren, as well as uncles and aunts and cousins, nieces, and nephews, varies.

Families in other societies may be composed very differently. While Americans give equal recognition to peoples' ties to their mothers or their fathers, in other societies there is greater emphasis on ties to one parent or the other. In some cases, only people related through either the mother or the father may be considered family. Societies that emphasize persons' ties to their mothers are said to have **matrilineal kinship** systems; those that emphasize ties to fathers are said to have **patrilineal kinship** systems. However, an individual's relationship to one side of the family or the other is rarely totally ignored; rather, in most societies, relationships with mothers' families and fathers' families are viewed differently. For example, Americans traditionally inherit their surnames from their fathers, thus embracing the patrilineal principle, but in case of divorce, the American legal system usually gives priority to the matrilineal principle by awarding custody of a child to the mother.

The three examples of societies used in this chapter—the !Kung, Trobriand Islanders, and traditional Chinese—each define the composition of the family and relations between members differently.

Family Composition of the !Kung

For most of the year, the !Kung live in groups numbering 10 to 30 or 40 people, bilaterally related (through both parents), who hunt and gather in a territory associated with a particular water hole. Camp groups are often organized around a brother and sister pair who claim ownership of the water hole. They bring in their spouses and children to the group; in turn, the spouses might bring in their brothers, sisters, and even mothers and fathers (see Figure 4.2).

1. The traditional American household generally begins with a husband and wife pair moving from the households of their parents.

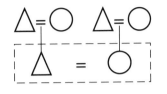

2. The arrangement is formalized with the birth of children, which produces a new nuclear family.

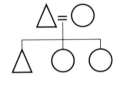

3. At some point the household might be composed of three generations, as married children join the household with their children.

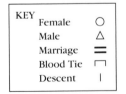

4. At a later stage, the household might consist of the original couple or a single person.

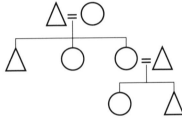

KEY		
Female	○	
Male	△	
Marriage	=	
Blood Tie	⌐	
Descent	│	

FIGURE 4.1   COMPOSITION AND DEVELOPMENT OF THE AMERICAN NUCLEAR FAMILY

1. Most !Kung camps are organized around brother/sister pairs who claim ownership of a water-hole.

2. Brother and sister are joined at the camp by their spouses and relatives of their spouses. The nuclear family is the main economic unit.

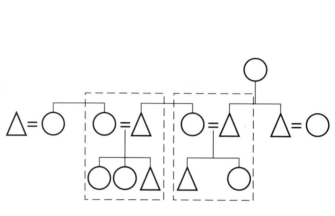

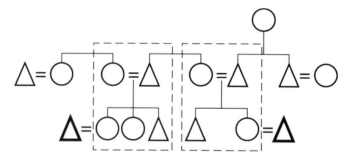

3. Bridegrooms join the camp of brides' parents for brideservice.

4. Camp composition changes as a result of changing social relations.

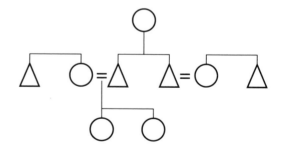

KEY
Female   ○
Male   △
Bridegroom   ▲
Marriage   =
Blood Tie   ⊓
Descent |

FIGURE 4.2   COMPOSITION AND DEVELOPMENT OF THE !KUNG CAMP

Membership in a camp is very fluid. People move freely from camp to camp based on hunting alliances or because conflict develops in the group. Within the camp, however, the basic family group is the nuclear family of husband, wife, and children. Children spend most of their time with their mothers. The !Kung acknowledge the fact that pregnancy results from sexual intercourse (not the case in all societies). They also believe that conception takes place at the end of the woman's menses, when the man's semen joins with the last of the menstrual blood.

One feature of !Kung society that figures prominently in the dynamics of family life is the custom of **brideservice** at marriage. When a couple marries, the groom is expected to come and live in his bride's parents' camp and work for her parents for as long as ten years. Tales of family life among the !Kung are often built around the effects of this arrangement on family dynamics.

Family Composition of the Trobriand Islanders

The people of the Trobriand Islands live in some 80 villages with from 40 to 400 people. Each village is surrounded by cultivated fields of yams, taro, and other crops and by water holes, fruit trees, and palm groves. A village is further divided into hamlets, each ideally consisting of a **matrilineage,** or *dala,* as the Trobrianders call it, a group of men related to each other through the female line, along with their wives and unmarried children (see Figure 4.3). The matrilineages are ranked relative to one another, and each village has a chief who is the eldest male of the highest ranking matrilineage. Since each person is a member of the lineage of his or her mother, neither a man's wife nor his children can be members of his *dala.*

Trobriand mythology and beliefs about procreation are a dramatic reflection of their matrilineal descent system. Their mythology tells how a long time ago, pairs of brothers and sisters emerged from the ground to begin each *dala. Dala* members trace their descent back to their mythological ancestors, and their claims to specific plots of land are based on the emergence of their ancestors there. Obviously, there is an incestuous theme in Trobriand myth, since the originators of each lineage were brothers and sisters. However, Trobriand ideas of procreation ostensibly deny a role to men in conception. They reinforce the matrilineal principle as well as the ties between brothers and sisters.

The Trobrianders say that when a person dies, the soul or spirit becomes young and goes to live on an island called Tuma. There the soul ages, but it regenerates itself by bathing in the sea. As the skin is sloughed off, a spirit child, or *baloma,* is created which returns to the world of the living and enters the womb of a woman of the same matrilineage as itself. In effect, a Trobriand matrilineage exists in perpetuity, as souls and spirits travel back and forth between the land of the living and the island of the dead.

The *baloma* may enter the woman through her head, or it may be carried by water into her womb. In some areas of the Trobriand Islands, if a woman wishes to become pregnant, a pail of water is brought to her dwelling by her brother. In fact, a woman cannot conceive without the "permission"

1. Each *dala* or matrilineage has its origin in a brother/sister pair who claim a plot of land.

2. *Dala* membership is traced in the female line, and individuals must marry someone from outside their own *dala*.

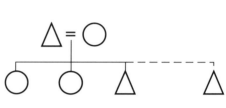

Dala   *Dala*

3. Trobriand Island households are composed of wives, husbands, and children. Males 12—15 years of age go to live in a bachelor's hut. If a male will inherit land from the *dala* of his mother's brother, he lives near his uncle.

Household   Bachelor's Hut

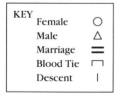

KEY
Female   ○
Male   △
Marriage   =
Blood Tie   ⌐
Descent |

FIGURE 4.3   COMPOSITION OF THE TROBRIAND ISLAND *DALA* AND HOUSEHOLD

of her brother. Consequently, the act of conception among the Trobrianders is a matter of three agencies—a woman, the spirit or *baloma* of a deceased ancestor, and the woman's brother. While sexual intercourse is said to play no role in conception, it does play a role in the development and growth of the fetus. Trobrianders believe that the man's semen provides food and nourishment for the fetus, and that is why children physically resemble their fathers. Sexual intercourse is also said to open the womb for the child to emerge.

While Trobriand procreation beliefs may seem strange to us, in the context of their ideas about descent they make perfect sense. When a person is believed to be descended exclusively from the mother, possible relations and ties to the father are excluded not only socially but physically as well. And the Trobrianders can rationalize and "prove" their beliefs about procreation very easily. Bronislaw Malinowski, who spent four years studying the people of the Trobriand Islands, tells of their response when he suggested to them that sexual intercourse plays a role in procreation:

> I sometimes made myself definitely and aggressively an advocate of the truer physiological doctrine of procreation. In such arguments the natives would quote, not only positive instances of women who have children without having intercourse, but would also refer to the many cases in which an unmarried woman has plenty of intercourse and no children. This argument would be repeated over and over again, with specially telling concrete examples of childless persons renowned for profligacy, or of women who lived with one white trader after another without having any baby. (Malinowski 1929:185–186)

EXERCISE 4.1

The procreation beliefs of the Trobriand Islanders prompted debate among anthropologists about whether the Trobrianders really do believe that men play little or no role in reproduction, or whether, to emphasize the matrilineal principle, they pretend not to acknowledge the male's role. In either case, we would expect to find in societies that emphasize the patrilineal principle that a woman's role in reproduction is deemphasized. What kind of belief about reproduction can you think of that would deny the importance of the female? How does this compare with the biological roles of men and women in American society?

To what extent the Trobrianders really deny a role to men in procreation is a matter of some debate. Annette Weiner, who worked with them in the early 1970s, some 50 years after the pioneering work of Malinowski, reports that they no longer denied the direct role of men in conception. However, she also reports a case where a grandmother claimed that she had used magic to make her granddaughter pregnant when the woman conceived while her husband was away.

Regardless of the extent to which the Trobrianders recognize the role of coitus, their ideas about descent and procreation reflect important features of the composition of their families. First, the key family relationship for them is not between husband and wife; it is between brother and sister. Second, the father of the family is an outsider to his children, a member of another family group. His interest, ideally, is in his sister's children, since it is they who are members of his matrilineage. Third, since the matrilineal extended family group, the *dala,* is more important than the nuclear family, the Trobrianders merge certain people under the same kin term, the same way Americans refer to different kinds of kin as aunt, uncle, or cousin. Trobrianders refer to all women of their matrilineage of the same generation by the same term; for example, a man refers to his mother, as well as to his mother's sisters by the term *ina.* A woman refers to her brother and to all other men of her matrilineage and generation as *luta.* Thus a man has many "sisters," and a woman has many "brothers."

Another consequence of matrilineal kinship is that men inherit property not from their fathers but from their mothers' brothers, and it is ideally in his maternal uncle's village that a young man goes to live. The fact that these ideal conditions are not always met creates some of the drama in Trobriand family life.

Family Composition of the Chinese

Family life in traditional rural China centers around the patrilineal extended family household of a married couple, their married sons and daughters-in-law, and their grandchildren and unmarried daughters (see Figure 4.4). To understand the traditional Chinese family, you have to understand the idea of temporal depth, for in China the patrilineage exists as much in time as it does in space. When Americans speak of family they generally limit it to the living; in traditional China the family includes a long line of patrilineal ancestors. Francis L. K. Hsu notes that the identity of each male is defined by his relations to the dead as much as it is by his relations to the living. His social worth and destiny are but reflections of the actions of his ancestors. He thus exists, as Hsu says, "under the shadow of his ancestors." Likewise, the spirits of the dead are dependent on the contributions of the living. These contributions are ceremonially made at altars, prominently positioned in each home where people present gifts to their ancestors by burning paper money, paper clothes, or other paper articles.

Given the interdependence between living and dead men of the patrilineage, it is apparent why it is essential to a Chinese male to have male descendants to look after his well-being and provide for him in the afterworld. Male children and grandchildren are living proof to a man that his line will continue. For this reason, unlike the !Kung or Trobriand Islanders, the Chinese express a marked preference for male children. Males are needed to maintain the patrilineal descent group, for if the only children born are daughters whose children in turn will belong to the patrilineage of her husband, a family line would die out. A son, as the Chinese put it, is a major happiness; a daughter is but a small happiness. Here is how one woman summed up the Chinese attitude toward daughters to Margery Wolf, who did research in the Taiwanese village of Peihotien:

> Why should I want so many daughters? It is useless to raise your own daughters. I'd just have to give them away when they were grown, so when someone asked for them as infants I gave them away. Think of all the rice I saved. (Wolf 1968:40)

A more lethal implication of the relative importance of sons and daughters in China is the differential rates of infanticide and abortion of males and females. In the area in which Hsiao-Tung Fei did research, there was a ratio of 100 girls to 135 boys in the age group 0–5 years. The population data suggest that a larger proportion of females had been killed.

In addition to a long line of male ancestors, ideally a Chinese household should include several generations of fathers and sons sharing a common

1. The traditional Chinese family exists in time as well as in space. Descent is traced patrilineally for generations.

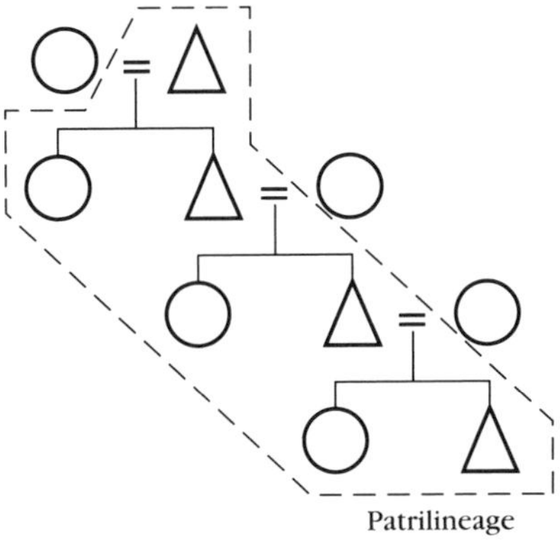

Patrilineage

2. An ideal family would be similar to that of the Lim household in Taiwan.

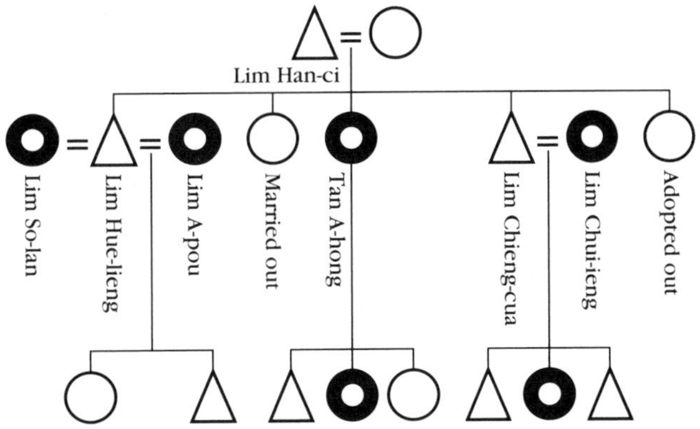

Lim Han-ci

Lim So-lan
Lim Hue-lieng
Lim A-pou
Married out
T'an A-hong
Lim Chieng-cua
Lim Chui-ieng
Adopted out

3. Most Chinese extended households eventually break up into separate nuclear family units, with wives of sons joining their husbands' households.

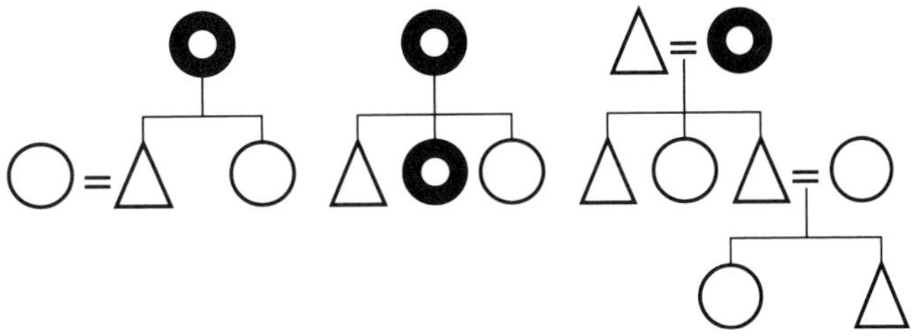

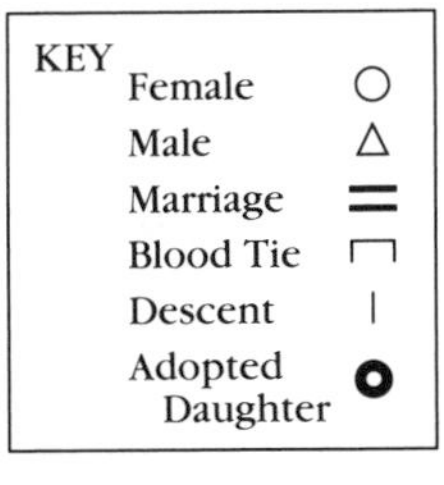

KEY
Female ○
Male △
Marriage ＝
Blood Tie ⊓
Descent |
Adopted Daughter ◉

FIGURE 4.4 COMPOSITION AND DEVELOPMENT OF THE TRADITIONAL CHINESE FAMILY

Source: Adapted from Margery Wolf, *The House of Lim: A Study of a Chinese Farm Family* (Englewood Cliffs, NJ: Prentice-Hall, 1968).

hearth or cooking stove and an ancestral altar, the symbols of the household. In the architecture of Peihotien, houses are constructed in such a way that they can easily be extended to accommodate additional sons and grandsons who bring their wives to live in the family home. In reality, it is very difficult to maintain this ideal; most households in villages such as Peihotien are small, consisting of a married couple and several dependent patrilineal relatives.

QUESTION 4.2 *How Is the Family Formed and the Ideal Family Type Maintained?*

Regardless of the size of family units or descent systems, in virtually all societies families require the socially recognized union of a male and female. Generally this takes the form of marriage, a publicly recognized joining of two people or two families. But while marriage makes or sustains families, the manner in which such an arrangement comes about varies significantly in different societies.

In American society, children begin learning about courtship and marriage at an early age; five- and six-year-olds are teased about their "boyfriends" or "girlfriends," and playing house together is a popular preschool pastime. Americans begin serious courting in their early teens and usually go through a series of relationships before choosing a partner for their first marriage, most often when they are between the ages of 18 and 30. While the choice of a marriage partner is supposedly based on feelings of love and sexual attraction, other factors also influence it. Americans, like people in virtually all societies, are prohibited by the **incest taboo** from marrying certain categories of kin, such as brothers or sisters, mothers or fathers, or, in some cases, cousins. Ideally, also, a spouse should be chosen from an appropriate income, ethnic, racial, or gender group. The conflict that may arise when an inappropriate marriage partner is chosen is often depicted in soap opera plots.

The marriage ceremony in American society is traditionally arranged and financed by the bride's family, and after the honeymoon, the couple ideally establishes an independent residence. Their relationship, based on love expressed in regular sexual intercourse, is later transformed by the arrival of one or more children—a wife transformed into a mother, a husband transformed into a father. That, of course, is the ideal for most Americans, and it is the disruption of that ideal that is the stuff of soap opera plots.

The cycles of events that create or sustain the family among the !Kung, Trobriand Islanders, and traditional Chinese illustrate the diversity of such arrangements. The soap opera themes of these groups would be quite different.

The !Kung Family Cycle

!Kung men and women, like Americans, begin to learn about courtship, sex, and marriage early. Since there is little privacy in a !Kung camp and children sleep with their parents, they soon are playing at marriage and imitating the bodily movements of parents making love. Most young men and women have

Trobriand Islanders are bound together by matrilineage kinship ties in extended family groups.

had sexual experiences by the time they are 15. !Kung men usually marry for the first time between the ages of 18 and 25, when they are able to hunt and work for their wives' parents. Marriage is important for a man for a number of reasons. It marks him as an adult worthy of taking part in !Kung public life, and he gains a sex partner and a mate to provide his food. While men are obligated to share and formally distribute the meat they obtain in the hunt with everyone in the camp, women are not obligated to share what they gather outside their nuclear family group, and women gather from 60 to 80 percent of the food in a camp.

Women often marry as early as 12 to 14 years of age, generally before their first menstruation, which occurs at about 17. Girls have fewer reasons to marry than men. Single or married men are always available as sex partners, and, since the product of male labor, meat, is widely shared, a woman needn't have a husband to ensure her share of the hunt. However, a girl's parents have good reasons for getting her married as soon as possible. The earlier she is married, the longer she and her husband will remain with her parents until she is of age, and the longer her husband will work for her parents. Moreover, the bride's family gains an alliance with another family and is less likely to get involved in open conflict between men over their daughter.

Marriages are almost always arranged by the couple's parents. Typically the mother or father of the male approaches the family of the female with a proposal for marriage. If her parents approve of the match, the families exchange gifts to indicate their agreement. An appropriate husband for a daughter is a man who is not too much older, is not yet married, is a good hunter, and is willing to accept responsibility. The prospective groom should also be cooperative, generous, and unaggressive.

The !Kung not only avoid choosing a spouse who is a close kinsperson, they are also restricted in the choice of a marriage partner by their naming system. There are only about 30 to 40 names that can be chosen for newborns, and people with the same first name consider themselves connected, regardless of their actual kinship connection to one another. Consequently, if a man's name is Toma, all the brothers and sisters of everyone else named Toma would be considered his brothers and sisters; all the sons and daughters of other Tomas would be considered his sons and daughters, and so on. Therefore, a marriage partner should occupy neither an actual prohibited kinship category nor one created by the naming system. A woman, for example, could not marry a man with the same name as her father or a man whose father had the same name as her father, since she and the man would refer to themselves as brother and sister. When Richard Lee was working with the kinship system of the !Kung he found that interpretations of the naming system varied, and disagreements about the kin connection between people would always be resolved by the interpretation of the older person in the relationship.

Once a suitable match is made, one more obstacle to the marriage remains. Perhaps because they have little to gain or much to lose, young women often object strenuously to the marriage or to their parents' choice of a husband. Kicking and screaming is one way women demonstrate their objections. If they protest long and hard enough, the marriage will be called off; if the protest is not sufficient to call off the arrangement, a marriage ceremony takes place. A hut set apart from the bride's village is built for the couple by members of both families. Friends bring the couple to the hut, and the bride, head covered, is placed in it. Coals from the fires of both families are brought to start the fire. Friends stay, joking, singing, and dancing, while bride and groom remain apart. Often, especially if the bride is young, a relative stays with the couple in the hut until she begins to adjust to her new status. However, "honeymoons" are fraught with danger and are often the source of continuing conflict.

Working among the !Kung, Marjorie Shostak forged a close relationship with a woman, Nisa, who described her wedding night. Nisa said that she cried so much and objected so strongly to spending the night with her new husband, Bo, that her parents asked a female relative, Nukha, to sleep between Nisa and Bo. She soon discovered that Nukha was having sex with Bo, and after a few nights she told her parents. They took her and moved to another water hole, leaving Nukha and Bo behind.

Typically, half of all first marriages fail among the !Kung, and they may enter several marriages over the course of their lives. Nisa's second marriage, to Tashay, followed the same lines as her first; on her wedding night she cried and cried and finally ran into the bush. Relatives tried to explain the benefits of marriage and to convince her to accept Tashay. When she finally agreed, Tashay took Nisa to his parents to live, and Nisa's parents followed. But not until Nisa and Tashay had been living together for a long time did they have sex. Nisa remembers the aftermath of their first lovemaking as being painful, and it was a long time before she allowed it again and began to enjoy it.

The Trobriand Family Cycle

Courtship and sexual play begin early in the Trobriand Islands. Children play erotic games at the ages of 7 and 8 and begin seeking sex partners at ages 11–13. Trobriand adolescents are permitted to openly display their affection for each other; girls scratch, beat, thrash, or even wound their lovers, and boys accept this treatment as a sign of love and display their wounds as proof of manliness and success in courtship. They sing about love, both successful and unrequited, and take great pains with their physical appearance. Here is what Malinowski says about adolescent male courtship:

> An adolescent gets definitely attached to a given person, wishes to possess her, works purposefully towards his goal, plans to reach fulfillment of his desires by magical and other means, and finally rejoices in achievement. I have seen young people of this age grow positively miserable through ill-success in love. (Malinowski 1929:63)

Since sexual activity before marriage is common and expected among the Trobrianders, the couple often has already been living together, and the marriage simply formalizes an existing relationship. While the couple may take the initiative in arranging a marriage, parents approve or disapprove of the choice of a spouse and sometimes arrange matches. There are certain categories of people a Trobriander may not marry. All Trobrianders belong to one of four clans, groups whose members consider themselves descended from a common ancestor. They must observe clan **exogamy**—that is, marry out of their own clan into another. In addition, the incest taboo applies to all close relatives, particularly brothers and sisters, who include all members of a matrilineage of the same generation. Trobriand myths tell of brother-sister incest that resulted in both parties committing suicide. Father-daughter incest is prohibited, but Trobrianders tell stories about it and joke about the idea of a father being overwhelmed by the beauty of his daughter. From their point of view, fathers are not related by kinship to their daughters. The best marriage for a man is to a woman from his father's clan, for then his children, who trace their descent from their mother, will be members of his father's clan. Consequently, the close relationship a man has with members of his father's clan will continue into the next generation.

There is no formal marriage ceremony; the girl simply stays overnight in her boyfriend's house. The next morning the bride's mother brings the couple cooked yams to share to indicate the bride's family's approval of the marriage. If they don't approve, they demand that the girl return home with them. Significantly, sharing food is considered by the Trobrianders to be more intimate than having sex. Later, the wife's mother and maternal uncle bring raw yams, and the groom's father and maternal uncle begin collecting **bridewealth**—valuables such as stone axe blades, shells, and money—to give to the wife's kin and her father. The requirement of bridewealth makes young men dependent on members of their matrilineage. This differs from the brideservice required of a !Kung man, which does not obligate a man to members of his family (see Question 4.1).

During the first year of marriage, the couple lives in the hut that served as the groom's adolescent retreat, and the groom's mother brings meals for them to share. At the end of the year the groom's mother builds a stone hearth for the couple, and the wife becomes responsible for the cooking. The end of the first year of marriage also marks a dramatic change in the husband-wife relationship. They no longer eat together, and the sexuality that bound them together as adolescents must be submerged. It is shameful for anyone to refer to the couple's sex life together; people may tease each other with such sexual taunts as "fuck your mother" or "fuck your father," but the epithet "fuck your wife" could get a person killed. In public, a husband and wife never hold hands or display affection. Their lives become segmented into a private domain in which affection and emotion can be displayed, and a public domain, in which the meaning of their relationship is dictated by their obligation to help ensure the continuity and honor of their respective matrilineages.

The matrilineal principle in the life of a Trobriand husband and wife requires each to have a continued involvement with others outside the nuclear family. In addition to his ties to and concerns for his wife and children, the husband is also involved in the family life of his matrilineage, his sisters and their children. The wife is continually involved with her own and her children's matrilineage—especially her brothers. This involvement is economic and centers around wealth such as yams, banana-leaf bundles, and skirts, all of which are controlled ultimately by women.

One reason men marry is to obtain yams. Yams are more than food in the Trobriand Islands; they are valuable symbols or objects of wealth and are used as gifts to create and sustain relationships among people. They are particularly important in marriage transactions and in the continued tie of a woman to her matrilineage. Trobriand family yam gardens belong to the wife, but they are tended first by her father and later by a "brother." Each year at harvest time the yams grown in her garden by her father or brother are ceremoniously taken to her. The amount and quality of the yams grown by a woman's brother are usually proportional to the bridewealth that was given to the wife's family by the groom's family when the couple was married. Early in the marriage these yams are stored in the rafters of the couple's hut, and the husband redistributes them as valuables to his kin who contributed the bridewealth. Later—often 10 to 15 years later—if a man is recognized as important by his wife's kin, they construct a yam house for him to store the yams they bring each year. The amount and quality of the yams stored and displayed by a man are indications of the regard in which he is held by his wife's kin, and of his status in the community. The yam house, according to Weiner, is like a public bank account.

As a man seeks a wife to obtain the yams grown for him by his wife's brother, brothers seek husbands for their sisters, not only for the children nurtured by the husbands for their wives' matrilineage but for the brother-in-laws' help in obtaining banana-leaf bundles. Sisters are obligated, with the help of their husbands, to have ready bundles of banana leaves to be used to finance the funerals of members of their matrilineage. Some are made by the woman, but her husband may have to purchase additional bundles. They are given away at funerals by members of the deceased's matrilineage to people who were important in the life of the deceased. The more important the person was to the deceased, the greater the number of banana-leaf bundles he or she receives. In this way, members of a matrilineage uphold their honor and status; to fail to fulfill these obligations would bring dishonor to the matrilineage.

The development of Trobriand family life, then, must be understood in the context of the movement of such goods as yams and banana-leaf bundles between husband and wife and members of the wife's matrilineage. It is the successful completion of the cycle of exchanges of yams and banana-leaf bundles that ensures the stability of a marriage and a matrilineage. The Trobriand nuclear family thus promotes stable bonds between husband and wife. Divorce is both frequent and easy to obtain, however; the initiative is usually taken by the wife. But most divorces occur in the first year of marriage, and they are rare after the couple has been together for a few years.

While fathers are not technically members of their children's family, they are very important to the lives of the children. Once children are weaned they sleep with their fathers, and later the father is responsible for enhancing their beauty with presents of shells, necklaces, and tiny tortoise-shell earrings. These objects are evidence of a father's presence in the life of his child; in fact, Weiner says, the term for a child with unpierced ears is translated as "fatherless." So important is the tie that develops between a man and his son that when the son marries, the father may try to convince him to remain in his village rather than moving to the village of his maternal kin, as expected.

The Chinese Family Cycle

The key relationship in the !Kung family is between husband and wife, and among the Trobriand Islanders it is between brother and sister. In China, the family centers on the relationship between father and son. Marriage in traditional China is less a matter of a man getting a wife than it is one of bringing a child-bearer into the household. As Hsu describes it, "A marriage is made in the name of the parents taking a daughter-in-law, not in the name of the son taking a wife."

Since marriage has far less to do with relations between the husband and wife than with those between the husband's family and a daughter-in-law, marriages in traditional China are almost always arranged, often far in advance, and there is little if any courtship. When a boy is six or seven years old, his parents might hire a matchmaker to find a girl who will eventually be an appropriate bride for their son. Since they believe that the time of a person's birth influences his or her personality and fate, the parents might also enlist the services of a diviner to make the appropriate match. The matchmaker takes a red paper with the time and date of a girl's birth to a prospective groom's family. The boy's mother brings this paper (or papers, if there is a choice of brides) to a fortune teller, who predicts the compatibility of the boy and girl. If a girl is deemed appropriate by the fortune teller, the matchmaker tries to convince the girl's parents to accept the match. If she is successful, the bridewealth, the marriage gifts of the husband's family to the wife's parents, is then negotiated.

Another way parents can obtain a wife for their son in traditional China is to adopt an infant girl who will be reared in the household and later will marry the son. While this kind of arrangement is not as prestigious as bride-wealth marriage, it has two advantages. Since the prospective bride was raised in the household of her future mother-in-law, she is more likely to be obedient, and it is not necessary to pay a brideprice for an adopted daughter-in-law. The major disadvantage is that the prospective bride and groom are

In the traditional rural Chinese family, the ability to produce male heirs assures the continuance of the entire patrilineage. The father's pride is evident in this nineteenth-century print titled "Five Sons Successful in Examination."

raised virtually as brother and sister and often find it difficult to make the transition to husband and wife.

The adoption of a boy to serve as a husband for a daughter is a third way marriages are arranged in traditional China. This is done only when a family has no sons. The adopted boy then assumes the family name so that his sons continue the line of his adopted father. Such marriages are not as respected as others, and a man who is adopted into his wife's family bears the stigma of having abandoned his parents and ancestors. For poor or orphaned boys, however, the prospect of heading a thriving household might outweigh such a stigma.

Compared to the !Kung or Trobriand marriage ceremony, the Chinese wedding is very formal and, for the groom's family, very expensive. The date and hour of the wedding are determined by a diviner, who even decides the exact time the bride will arrive in her sedan chair. The day before the wedding, the girl's **dowry** is sent to the groom's home in a procession accompanied by a band, drummers, and ushers. The dowry consists of such goods as leather chests, tables, stools, cosmetics, housewares, clothing, and cloth, but never land or a house. On the day of the wedding, the groom is carried in a sedan chair to the house of the bride; when he arrives, she shows token resistance, and she and her mother weep. Then she is carried to the groom's house in a red sedan chair decorated to suggest the early birth of sons. Offerings are made at the ancestor's altar to ensure success of the marriage. The couple is taken to pay respect to the boy's parents—the formal introduction of the bride to the groom's household. Feasting and dancing accompany the wedding, sometimes for three or four days.

After the wedding, there is little time or place for romantic relations between husband and wife. Hsu reports that husband and wife sleep in the same bed for only seven days, and there is no public expression of affection between them. Once the wife enters into her husband's family, she finds herself among strangers, virtually cut off from her parents and siblings. She must treat her mother-in-law with respect and acquiesce to the demands of sisters-in-law or other members of her husband's family. She occupies the lowest place at the table. She occasionally can go back to her mother and sob at her change of status, but, as the Chinese proverb puts it, "Spilled water cannot be gathered up." She does not acquire full status in her husband's family until she produces a male child. Until then, the husband must show indifference to his wife, addressing her through a third party; after the birth of a son, he can refer to her as the mother of his child. It is as if a man's wife is related to him through his children. For the groom, marriage is simply a continued expression of his duty to his father and his ancestors. In no way is his new relationship with a wife to interfere with that duty; rather, the marriage is an expression of his filial devotion and obligation to produce male heirs.

Whereas divorce is fairly common among the Trobrianders and the !Kung, it is virtually unheard of in traditional China. A husband can take a mistress with impunity, but, in theory, he can murder an adulterous wife. Wives have no rights of divorce. A wife may flee her husband's household, she may commit suicide, or she may become a prostitute, but a woman who wishes to leave her husband and in-laws has few other alternatives.

QUESTION 4.3 *What Are the Roles of Sexuality, Love, and Wealth?*

The themes of sex, love, and wealth are pervasive in American life. Young men and women use their sexuality and appearance to influence one another and to gain potential partners and spouses. Later, as husbands and wives, they attempt to manage their wealth (if they have any) to fulfill social obligations and to maintain or rise in status. Often they seek to cement their status both as individuals and as a family by having children. As mothers and fathers they face the task of guiding their children and trying to ensure their success and happiness.

The manipulation and negotiation of sexuality, love, and wealth dominate many of the plots of American soap operas. The ideas about romantic love expressed in these plots, however, often are not shared in other societies. Examining these ideas among the !Kung, Trobriand Islanders, and Chinese, and imagining how they might be expressed in soap operas, can help you understand our own beliefs about these things.

Sex, Love, and Wealth among the !Kung

Wealth plays virtually no part in the lives of the !Kung, but for women, especially, sex, love, and beauty are very important. A !Kung woman's sexuality is her major means of negotiating the conditions of her relationships with others. Sexuality is important first for her own well-being. As Nisa told Marjorie Shostak, if a girl grows up not learning to enjoy sex, her mind doesn't develop normally; if a grown woman doesn't have sex, her thoughts are ruined and she is always angry. Moreover, a woman's sexuality maximizes her independence. Sex attracts lovers, and a love relationship, being voluntary, recognizes the equality of the participants. By taking lovers a !Kung woman proclaims her control over her social life, because she can offer her sexuality to men as a means of vitalizing them. Talking candidly about sex, male impotence, and the contributions women make to men, Nisa said:

> A woman can bring a man life, even if he is almost dead. She can give him sex and make him alive again. If she were to refuse, he would die! If there were no women around, their semen would kill men. Did you know that? Women make it possible for them to live. Women have something so good that if a man takes it and moves about inside it, he climaxes and is sustained. (Shostak 1983:288)

There is one tradeoff for !Kung women who use their sexuality. Men see them as sources of male conflict and consequently as potentially dangerous.

Motherhood, on the other hand, is not easily bartered by !Kung women. In other societies, including our own, parents are apt to stress how much they have sacrificed or suffered for their children, thus using motherhood or fatherhood as a way of creating obligations and ties. It makes little sense for a !Kung woman (or man, for that matter) to make such a claim. Children owe their parents little; there is no need for bridewealth or dowries for marriage, and food and kin to care for them are plentiful. The dynamics of !Kung families are built on the need of individuals to avoid permanent ties and obligations and to maintain their independence.

Sex, Love, and Wealth among the Trobriand Islanders

Where the enhancement of sexuality is important throughout life for !Kung women, among the Trobriand Islanders it is important for women only prior to their marriage. Armed with the magic and bodily adornments contributed by her father, but without the wealth—yams, banana-leaf bundles, and other valuables—she will later acquire, an unmarried woman uses her sexuality to negotiate her relationships with others. Once married, she ceases to emphasize her beauty and sexual attraction and instead emphasizes her fertility and motherhood. A woman's worth, once measured by her father's concern for her and her own sexuality and beauty, is determined after marriage by her ability to collect yams for her husband, produce children, and provide banana-leaf bundles for her matrilineage.

Men's sexuality is viewed very differently. Since the Trobrianders claim that men play no role in reproduction, their sexuality is never very important anyway. Their physical attractiveness, however, is important, for this is what attracts lovers and later a wife to collect the yams by which a man measures his status. Beauty is especially important for chiefs. They must maintain an aura of physical attractiveness in order to attract more wives, whose fathers and brothers will supply the wealth they need to maintain their position of influence.

Wealth also forms different kinds of links for Trobrianders. The links !Kung men create with their wives' families are based not on wealth but on their labor; among the Trobrianders, men must use the wealth of members of their matrilineage as bridewealth payments to their wives' families. They are required to return this wealth to their family by redistributing the yams they later receive from their wives' brothers. The yams they receive also are in some ways payment for the children of the marriage, who will add to the matrilineage of wife and brother-in-law.

Sex, Love, and Wealth among the Chinese

The themes of sexuality, love, and wealth are played out very differently in the traditional Chinese rural family. Whereas both !Kung and Trobriand adolescents have considerable freedom to utilize their sexuality to attract and influence others, quite the opposite is true in China. If a girl comes from a family that is influential and wealthy enough to make an attractive match for her, she will have little to do with other boys. Virginity is both valued and necessary for a Chinese bride; for a !Kung or Trobriander woman it is almost no consideration. In China, if a girl is known to have been mixed up in an affair, her only chance of marriage is to someone in a distant village.

Romantic love and sexuality are irrelevant also in the relations between traditional Chinese husbands and wives. A wife's function is to produce children. A man who can afford it takes concubines; a man who can't afford it but does so anyway is criticized not for his infidelity to his wife but for squandering the wealth of his ancestors and descendants.

In fact, sexuality figures very little for a Chinese woman, either before or after marriage. Her sexuality is simply not negotiable; instead it is as a mother that most Chinese women establish significant relations. Her value consists in her potential to become a mother of a boy. Becoming a mother cements her relations with her husband, her father-in-law, and her mother-in-law, and it is her motherhood that secures her later life. While a son is obligated to care for his aged mother, the obligation is not so great as it is to care for a father. To compensate, a woman must establish bonds of emotion and affection with her sons, and she may do this with the assistance of her husband. After a boy is six or seven, fathers become aloof and withdrawn in order to assert and reinforce their authority and control over a son. A mother can use her husband's aloofness from his son to strengthen the son's ties to her. Even if she enjoys good relations with her husband, she will try to reserve the son's affections for herself, while preserving the son's respect for his father.

The only exception to the motherhood-over-sexuality rule is the woman who is unable to obtain a husband or who loses one. Such a woman may become a concubine or a prostitute. Margery Wolf tells the story of Tan A-Hong in the Taiwanese village of Peihotien, who was adopted by Lim Han-ci to be the wife of a son who later died. In such cases adopted daughters may be sold—to dealers who buy attractive women to train as prostitutes, to wealthy families as slaves, or to prostitutes who initiate them in their livelihood for support in their old age. Lim Han-ci arranged to have Tan A-Hong adopted into another family, but when the adoption didn't work out she went to southern Taiwan and became a prostitute. She ultimately moved back to Peihotien, bringing an adopted daughter she reared in her way of life to care for her.

The attitude toward prostitutes in traditional China is not the same as it is in the United States. The Chinese do not condemn women who choose prostitution. According to Wolf, prostitutes are said to be "more interesting" than other women, but people rarely make judgments about them because too many village girls "go out to work" in order to support family members.

EXERCISE 4.2

The American family is different from the !Kung, Trobriand Islander, or traditional Chinese families, as you might expect. While our families are embedded in an urban-industrial society, the !Kung are hunters and gatherers, the Trobriand Islanders horticulturists and fishermen, and the Chinese peasant farmers. Yet there seem to be features of family life in all three that are similar to life in the American family. Your problem is simply to list those features of family life among the !Kung, Trobriand Islanders, and Chinese that resemble American families. Put another way, what features of American family life would be familiar to a !Kung, a Trobriand Islander, or someone from rural China?

QUESTION 4.4 *What Threatens to Disrupt the Family Unit?*

If soap operas are in any way accurate reflections of American life, infidelity, sickness, authority struggles, and economic hardship are the principal threats to family formation and maintenance. As our soap operas constantly remind us, any threat to an established marriage endangers the continued existence of the family unit. Ideally, the American marriage is sustained by love; if either partner says "I don't love you anymore," it is generally grounds for divorce. Diminished sexual attraction or sexual activities and sexual infidelity are other grounds. Economic problems also threaten the stability of the American family; if a couple does not have the resources to sustain or to fulfill their obligations, strains inevitably develop.

There are also threats to the stability and maintenance of traditional Chinese, Trobriand, and !Kung families, but they of course differ from those that endanger the American family.

Threats to the !Kung Family

The major threat to family stability among the !Kung is conflict between husband and wife over infidelity or the efforts of a husband to secure a second wife. Like many societies around the world, the !Kung permit **polygamy.**

Men are allowed to have more than one wife (**polygyny**), and apparently women are permitted to have more than one husband (**polyandry**), though this is rare. In practice, however, polygamy is the exception rather than the rule. A survey conducted by Lee in 1968 of 131 married !Kung men found that 93 percent were living monogamously, 5 percent were living in polygynous unions, and 2 percent were living in polyandrous relationships.

One reason why polygamy is rare, even though having more than one wife is a sign of prestige, is the family difficulties it creates. According to Marjorie Shostak, a popular saying is, "There is never any peace in a household with two women in it." Stories of the complications resulting from polygamous unions are an endless source of humor for those who are single or monogamous. Here is how Nisa described polygyny in her society to Shostak:

> When a man married one woman, then marries another and sets her down besides the first so there are three of them together at night, the husband changes from one wife to another. First he has sex with the older wife, then with the younger. But when he goes to the younger wife, the older one is jealous and grabs and bites him. The two women start to fight and bite each other. The older woman goes to the fire and throws burning wood at them yelling "What told you that when I, your first wife, am lying here that you should go and sleep with another woman? Don't I have a vagina? So why do you just leave it and go without having sex with me? Instead you go and have sex with that young girl!" Sometimes they fight like that all night, until dawn breaks. A co-wife is truly a terrible thing. (Shostak 1983:172)

While polygamy is rare, marital infidelity is not. At one water hole with 50 married couples, Lee recorded 16 couples in which one or another of the partners was having an affair. The !Kung recognize certain benefits in taking lovers. For a woman, extramarital affairs add variety, as well as economic insurance. Here is Nisa again:

> When you are a woman, you just don't sit still and do nothing—you have lovers. You don't just sit with the man of your hut, with just one man. One man can give you very little. One man gives you only one kind of food to eat. But when you have lovers, one brings you something and another brings you something else. One comes at night with meat, another with money, another with beads. Your husband also does things and gives them to you. (Shostak 1983:271)

Men say that the emotion and passion of extramarital affairs are wonderful; "hearts are on fire and passions great," as the !Kung say. When Shostak asked a young married man about his lover, he said they fantasized about running away. She asked what it would be like, and he smiled and replied, "The first few months would be wonderful!" However, extramarital affairs are likely to be threatening to a husband, and they are the most common cause of conflict and violence among the !Kung. Wives are important to !Kung men because as long as they have wives they are dependent on no one. Male adulthood requires acquiring and demonstrating a willingness to fight for a secure marital status.

Nisa's marital history provides an example of !Kung family conflict. After her second husband, Tashay, died (see Question 4.2), Nisa married Besa. Nisa says that even though they began fighting soon after the marriage, she became pregnant. Besa then abandoned her at a settlement where they had been working, and she miscarried. Shortly after, she met some people from Besa's village and told them to tell Besa that their marriage was over. She began a relationship with Twi, an older man, who asked her to live with him, and together they went to live in the camp of Nisa's brother. Besa came to take her back with him, but Nisa refused to go. Besa and Twi fought, and Besa pushed Twi down. Later Nisa and Twi separated because Nisa's brother Dau liked Besa and sent Twi away.

Nisa still refused to return to Besa and resumed an affair with a past lover that lasted for a time, until he died. Then she began to see another man named Bo, but Besa returned to renew his claim on her. Violence again erupted; Besa and Bo pushed each other and called each other insulting names, such as "Big-Testicles" or "Long Penis." In an almost final confrontation with Besa, Nisa publicly stripped off her apron and cried, "There! There's my vagina! Look Besa, look at me! This is what you want!" Besa, consoled by a man who accompanied him, left. Soon after, Nisa and Bo married. Besa also remarried, but later began again to approach Nisa about renewing their relationship.

The story of Nisa's relationship with Besa reveals how much a !Kung man may have invested in a marriage, and how he is obligated to resort to violence against his wife's lover, even if she has rejected him.

Threats to the Trobriand Island Family

Among the Trobriand Islanders, it is not threats to the husband-wife relationship that are critical but threats to the matrilineage. Because the matrilineage is the major social unit, the honor of that family group relative to other groups is a central concern to all members. Lineages among the Trobriand Islanders are ranked according to the closeness of their genealogical connection to the founders of the lineage. Each lineage must be able to maintain its position vis-à-vis others through the ceremonial presentation of valuables, particularly yams and banana-leaf bundles. So important are yams in the relative ranking of matrilineages that groups compete with the vegetable and try to demonstrate their wealth by giving more yams to others than they receive. Since giving may be taken as a claim of superiority, however, it can be dangerous; as the Trobrianders put it, "When you give too much, people worry."

While it may seem implausible, yams could become the center of a Trobriand soap opera plot. For example, a man's political power, measured in yams, is a direct result of the support he receives from his wife's kin—it is her yams, grown for her by her father and brother, that create status for her husband. However, the annual yam gifts received by a husband can also be a source of conflict. If the amount or size of yams harvested does not live up to a husband's expectations, he may be insulted. On the other hand, if a woman's brother is unhappy over the bridewealth he received from the husband's family or the support given by the husband to his sister in collecting banana-leaf bundles, he may purposely communicate his unhappiness by not working hard in his sister's yam gardens. Other plots could be devised about unrequited love, attempts of fathers to convince their sons to remain in the fathers' villages, and even incest themes. But a theme that would be sure to attract a Trobriand audience would be sorcery.

The Trobrianders claim to know of spells and magic that are capable of killing. Generally only chiefs have this power, but others can seek out a chief and, for a price, convince him to use his power against their enemies. Someone who is believed to have this power is both feared and respected; Trobrianders tell of instances when they were challenged and retaliated with sorcery. Vanoi, an important Trobriand chief, told Weiner about being challenged by a Christian convert who openly mocked Vanoi's knowledge of sorcery. Vanoi offered the man a cigarette, saying that he should smoke it if he doubted the chief's knowledge of sorcery. The man smoked the cigarette, became ill that night, and died a week later.

A person who uses sorcery against another is dominating that person, and since each person's fate is tied to that of the matrilineage, a threat to one is considered a threat to all. That is why any death among the Trobrianders is a serious matter. Since all deaths are attributed to sorcery, every death is a sign that the power of a matrilineage is being challenged by someone from another lineage. Each funeral marks an attempt by the members of a matrilineage to reassert its power, while, at the same time, the mourners publicly assert their innocence of sorcery. The matrilineal kin of the deceased do this by distributing banana-leaf bundles and other valuables to those who have come to mourn and to assist with the funeral arrangements by decorating and carrying the corpse. In recognition of their contribution to the life of the deceased, they receive gifts. The deceased's matrilineage empties its treasury to announce its strength in the face of the threat to its integrity that is signaled by a death.

Maintaining one's identity and that of the matrilineage is a never-ending process among the Trobrianders, because death threatens the network by removing someone from it. Here is how Weiner sums up the meaning of death for them:

> Because of the expanding possibilities in a person's life, each
> Trobriander represents her or his matrilineal identity—originally
> conceived through a woman and an ancestral *baloma* spirit—as well as
> the accumulation of all the other relationships that parenthood and
> marriage made possible. Therefore, a death demands attention to this
> full totality, as the members of a matrilineage seek both to repay all
> "others" for their past care and to hold on to them now that this death
> has occurred. (Weiner 1988:161)

Threats to the Chinese Family

The biggest threat to the traditional rural Chinese family is the absence of a son. The lack of a male heir endangers not only the continuance of a household but the entire patrilineage through time. A man without sons, a spirit without descendants, has no one to offer incense for him and no altar on which his spirit can find refuge and honor. However, the existence of a son is no guarantee of smooth family relations. Fathers have enormous authority and power over sons, and sons are obligated to worship, respect, obey, and care for their fathers. But often fathers become overbearing or use force to assert their authority. Margery Wolf says that Lim Han-ci in the village of Peihotien (see Question 4.3) administered physical punishment to his sons with unusual frequency; once he beat them with a hoe handle and left bruises that lasted for weeks. However, regardless of how harshly a son may be treated (and most Chinese boys are, if anything, spoiled), breaking away from one's father is considered a violent act.

Wolf reports the case of the conflict between Lim Han-ci and his eldest son, Lim Hue-lieng, to illustrate both the dilemma of a father-son split and the difficulties that can arise in adopted marriages (see Figure 4.4). When Lim Hue-lieng was a child, Lim Han-ci adopted Lim A-pou, then nine months old, to be reared as the eventual wife of his son. Growing up in the Lim household, Lim A-pou was a model daughter-in-law. She accepted reprimands and punishment without becoming sullen, she did not complain, and she was a hard worker. However, her relationship with her prospective husband was not a happy one. When Lim Hue-lieng was 19, he committed what in traditional China is an act of moral violence; he left home and severed his relations with his father. So extreme is the act of a son deserting his father that if a son dies before his father and so is unable to care for the father in his old age, the father ritually beats the son's coffin to punish him. Lim Hue-lieng was able to leave home only because he had become a leader in the *lo mue,* a secret society which is involved in crime and extortion but which also protects the downtrodden and contributes heavily to religious festivals.

Years after leaving home, much to the excitement of the villagers, Lim Hue-lieng returned to Peihotien, reconciled with his father, and went through a simple ceremony that transformed him and his foster sibling, Lim A-pou, into husband and wife. While it must have been obvious to her that Lim Hue-lieng would be less than an ideal husband, Lim A-pou did not protest, for what alternatives did she have? She could not return to the family she had left as an infant, and to remain in the Lim household if she refused to marry Lim Hue-lieng was impossible. Moreover, there were advantages to marrying the eldest son; it would give her status and influence in the household. Thus when Lim Hue-lieng took a succession of mistresses after the marriage, and even took one to live in the family house, Lim A-pou complained very little. Since she had a son by Lim Hue-lieng, her status as the mother of the son of the eldest son in the family was secure.

Dramatic splits between fathers and sons are rare in traditional China. More frequent is conflict between brothers over the division and sharing of the family wealth at the death of the male head of the household. In most other rural, peasant societies around the world, the male head of the household designates his heirs before his death. He may in some fashion divide his property among his offspring—**partible inheritance**—or he may leave all his property to one or another descendant—**impartible inheritance.** In China the ideal is for brothers to continue to live together and share the inheritance, usually under the direction of the eldest son, thus avoiding the division of property. In fact, however, brothers rarely continue to share, and ultimately conflict between them leads to a division of household property.

Wolf documents the ultimate disintegration of the Lim household after the death of Lim Han-ci and the resulting arguments over property by the sons and their wives. When Wolf went to live in the Lim household, Lim Han-ci and his oldest son, Lim Hue-lieng, had already died. The two remaining family units consisted of the family of the second-oldest son, Lim Chieng-cua, and the family of Lim Hue-lieng's widow, Lim A-Pou. While Lim Han-ci was alive, his power and influence and his control over the family's wealth was enough to maintain the extended family. Once he died, conflict between Lim A-pou and her son on the one hand and Lim Chieng-cua on the other led to the division of family property. The wealth that had held the extended family together served, finally, to drive it apart. After dividing the property, brothers or their families often continue to live in the same house, but they partition it into separate family units with separate stoves, as did the son and grandson of Lim Han-ci. The once extended household becomes, in effect, a family compound.

EXERCISE 4.3

An international television production company has hired your company, Creativity Enterprises, to write a pilot episode of a soap opera to be marketed in rural China. The plot of the soap you will create will revolve around the Wang family. The Wangs are a relatively well-off farming family who live in rural China. The characters in the soap opera are to include:

Wang Zhou: the fifty-five-year-old male head of the family
Wang Lim: the wife of Wang Zhou
Wang Xiao: the eldest son of Wang Zhou
Wang Lao: the wife of Wang Xiao
Wang Jiang: the second son of Wang Zhou
Wang Jane: the wife of Wang Jiang
Wang Sally: the 20-year-old unmarried daughter of Wang Zhou
Wang Nai-Nai: the mother of Wang Zhou

Xiao and Lao have four children, two boys and two girls
Jiang and Jane have two children, both girls

You may, if you wish, add other characters to the story. The story line should be simple but clear, and you are free to embellish the characters in any way you want, but keep in mind that the soap must appeal to a rural Chinese audience.

CONCLUSIONS

This chapter has examined the structure and dynamics of family life of three peoples—the !Kung, the Trobriand Islanders, and the traditional, rural Chinese—by asking four questions. The first question has to do with the composition of the typical family group. Each society has different rules about who a person regards as a family member. In some societies such as that of the Trobrianders, family membership and descent are reckoned through females (matrilineal descent), while in other societies such as that of the traditional Chinese, descent is reckoned through males (patrilineal descent). In still other societies, such as that of the !Kung, family membership is reckoned through both parents (bilateral descent). In China, the family is extended in time to include many generations of living and dead ancestors. For the !Kung the nuclear family is the major social unit; for the Trobrianders it is the matrilineal extended family; and for the Chinese it is the patrilineal extended family.

The next question concerns how the family is formed and the ideal family type is maintained in these societies. Among the !Kung, marriages are arranged by the parents of boys and girls, often at a very young age, but if the girl protests strongly, the marriage does not take place. Among the Trobrianders, young men and women court freely and often choose their own marriage partners, but their choice must be approved by their parents. In traditional China, a marriage is almost always arranged by parents, often with the assistance of a matchmaker. Sometimes female infants or young girls are adopted into families to later marry a son. The economic responsibilities for making a marriage also vary. Among the !Kung, a man is obligated to perform brideservice for his wife's family; among the Trobrianders, as well as in traditional China, a man's family is obligated to pay bridewealth to the bride's family. Key relationships also vary in the different family types. For the !Kung the key relationship is between husband and wife; for the Trobrianders it is between brother and sister; for the Chinese it is between father and son.

Another question is what roles are played by sexuality, love, and wealth in family life. Love and sexuality figure prominently in the life of the !Kung. Women especially emphasize the power of their sexuality and men's dependence on it. Wealth plays little role among the !Kung. Among the Trobrianders, females and males begin sexual activities early in their lives, and they place great emphasis on being sexually attractive and on romantic love. Once they are married, however, couples deemphasize the sexual aspects of their lives, at least publicly. Instead, they work to repay the bridewealth payment made to the wife's family and to grow yams for the husband to present each year to his sister's husband. Wealth is important to maintain the social rank of the matrilineage. In traditional China, sexuality and love have little part in family life. The main obligation of a woman is to produce a son; it is her fertility, not her sexuality, that men value. Wealth is required by a man's family to pay bridewealth to the wife's family at the time of marriage. Wealth is also required to sustain the patrilineal extended family of a man, his sons, and his sons' sons.

The forces that threaten the family unit were the topic of the final question. Marital infidelity is the greatest threat to the !Kung family, and divorce is frequent, especially early in a marriage. For the Trobrianders the more serious threats are to the matrilineal extended family. Since death of a family member is believed to be caused by an act of sorcery, it is a serious threat to the family unit, as is the consequent depletion of economic resources. Divorce is almost nonexistent in traditional China; it is failure to produce a male heir that threatens the continuity of the family, as does the death of the head of the patrilineal extended family. Disputes among brothers over the distribution of family wealth often result in the breakup of the extended family.

REFERENCES AND SUGGESTED READINGS

INTRODUCTION: SOAP OPERAS AND FAMILY RELATIONS The epigraphs come from Lawrence Stone's *The Family, Sex and Marriage in England 1500–1800* (Harper & Row, 1977) and from an automobile bumper sticker observed in 1988. Susan S. Bean provides an analysis of American soap operas in "Soap Operas: Sagas of American Kinship," in *The American Dimension: Cultural Myths and Social Realities,* edited by William Arens and Susan P. Montague (Alfred Publishing, 1976). The study of Brazilian soap opera is provided by Conrad Phillip Kottak in *Prime Time Society: An Anthropological Analysis of Television and Culture* (Wadsworth Publishing, 1990).

WHAT IS THE COMPOSITION OF THE TYPICAL FAMILY GROUP? The descriptions of the !Kung are drawn largely from Richard Lee's *The Dobe !Kung* (Holt, Rinehart, and Winston, 1984) and Marjorie Shostak's *Nisa: The Life and Words of a !Kung Woman* (Vintage Books, 1983), with additional information from Elizabeth Thomas's *The Harmless People* (Alfred A. Knopf, 1959). The description of the Trobriand Islander family is derived from Annette B. Weiner's *The Trobrianders of Papua New Guinea* (Holt, Rinehart, and Winston, 1988); Weiner's *Women of Value, Men of Renown* (University of Texas Press, 1976); and from Bronislaw Malinowski's *The Sexual Life of Savages in North-Western Melanesia* (Halcyon House, 1929). The material on China comes largely from Margery Wolf, *The House of Lim* (Prentice-Hall, 1968); Francis L. K. Hsu, *Under the Ancestor's Shadow* (Anchor Books, 1967); and Hsiao-Tung Fei, *Peasant Life in China: A Field Study of Country Life in the Yangtze Valley* (Routledge & Kegan Paul, 1939). Additional information on traditional Chinese families can be found in *Village Life in China* by Arthur H. Smith (Little, Brown, 1970).

HOW IS THE FAMILY FORMED AND THE IDEAL FAMILY TYPE MAINTAINED? The observations about the significance of brideservice and bridewealth come largely from Jane E. Collier and Michelle Rosaldo, "Politics and Gender in Simple Societies," in *Sexual Meanings: The Cultural Construction of Gender and Sexuality,* edited by Sherry B. Ortner and Harriet Whitehead (Cambridge University Press, 1981). A good survey of kinship and social organization is provided in Burton Pasternak's *Introduction to Kinship and Social Organization* (Prentice-Hall, 1976).

WHAT ARE THE ROLES OF SEXUALITY, LOVE, AND WEALTH? The extent to which women in different societies are valued for or emphasize their sexuality or their role in procreation is discussed by Collier and Rosaldo in their article cited above and by Michele Rosaldo and Jane Monnig Atkinson in "Man the Hunter and Woman: Metaphors for the Sexes in Ilongot Magical Spells," in *The Interpretation of Symbolism* (John Wiley & Sons, 1975). A good general review of works on the social construction of sexuality can be found in an article by D. L. Davis and R. G. Whitten, "The Cross-Cultural Study of Human Sexuality," in *Annual Review of Anthropology,* vol. 16 (1987), pp. 69–98.

WHAT THREATENS TO DISRUPT THE FAMILY UNIT? A good analysis and review of factors that influence family structure is "Family and Household: The Analysis of Domestic Groups," by Sylvia Junko Yanagisako, in *Annual Review of Anthropology,* vol. 8 (1979), pp. 161–205. An interesting collection of articles by anthropologists on divorce, largely in America, can be found in *Divorce and After,* edited by Paul Bohannan (Doubleday, 1970).

Picasso, Pablo. SEATED WOMAN, 1927.

THE SOCIAL CONSTRUCTION OF IDENTITY

PROBLEM 5: HOW DO PEOPLE DETERMINE WHO THEY ARE AND COMMUNICATE WHO THEY THINK THEY ARE TO OTHERS?

When an individual enters the presence of others, they commonly seek to acquire information about him or to bring into play information about him already possessed. They will be interested in his general socioeconomic status, his conception of self, his attitude toward them, his competence, his trustworthiness, etc. Although some of this information seems to be sought almost as an end in itself, there are usually quite practical reasons for acquiring it. Information about the individual helps to define the situation, enabling others to know in advance what he will expect of them and what they may expect of him. Informed in these ways, the others will know how best to act in order to call forth a desired response from him.

Erving Goffman

INTRODUCTION: *The Importance of Self*

Of all the products of our culture, the one we most take for granted is our self. We are not born knowing who we are or what our places are on the social landscape; we learn to be American or Japanese, male or female, husbands or wives, Amy, Richard, Michael, or Rebecca. As we become who we are, we learn how we stand in relation to others. We learn how we relate to others as sons, daughters, students, friends, or lovers. In this sense, society is a collection of **social identities** distributed over a landscape. Individuals strive to arrive at some identity/destination from which they can relate to other social identities, while they seek confirmation from others that they occupy the positions on the social landscape that they claim to occupy.

To appreciate the importance of the self, try to imagine a faceless society in which every person is identical to every other person. How would people in such a society know how to behave toward one another? Whenever we interact with another person, the interaction must be based on some idea of who *the other* is: Is it a friend? a stranger? a family member? a teacher? At the same time, the other must have some idea of who we are, a conception of the relationship that exists between us. The necessity of knowing the social identity of others is apparent when strangers meet and, directly or indirectly, seek to elicit information about one another. Each tries to place the other in some identity, at some spot on the social landscape.

The opposite of a faceless society, one in which every person is unique, is as implausible as one in which everyone is identical. In this case, every interaction would be unique, and there would be no way to learn from one situation how to behave in another similar situation. Each person would need to have an infinite variety of behaviors with which to interact with an infinite variety of types of people. We avoid this situation by categorizing people, placing them in groups so that not everyone in our social universe is unique. We group them into categories constructed from such criteria as gender (women and men), ethnicity (Irish, Italian, Chinese), personal characteristics (short, tall, husky, thin), and so on.

Try to imagine, also, a social landscape in which no person acknowledges any other person or communicates in any way who she or he thinks the other is. This too would be an impossible situation. People would have no way of acquiring from others confirmation that they occupy the social identities they think they occupy. Instead, our social identities are constructed in large part by others who, by their behavior toward us, confirm that we occupy the spot on the landscape we claim to occupy. Put another way, nobody is anybody except in relation to somebody.

Finally, try to imagine a social landscape on which everyone communicates to everyone else that they occupy the *wrong* spot on the landscape. Every person actively disagrees with every other person about who they are. This situation would be, if not impossible, at least chaotic.

To examine how people in a society determine who they are and communicate who they think they are to others, this chapter raises five questions about the ways that different societies define the person, the ways that individuals are differentiated from others, the manner in which individuals find out who they are and convey their identities to others, and the consequences of disagreements over identity.

QUESTIONS

5.1 How Does the concept of personhood vary
    from society to society?
5.2 How do societies distinguish individuals from one another?
5.3 How do individuals learn who they are?
5.4 How do individuals communicate their identities to one another?
5.5 How do individuals defend their identities that are threatened?

QUESTION 5.1 *How Does the Concept of Personhood Vary from Society to Society?*

In all societies, personal names are intimate markers of the person, differentiating individuals from others. Names also can reveal how people conceive of themselves and their relations to others. For Americans, names are perhaps the most enduring aspect of the self; assigned at birth, our names remain with us throughout our lives. Some people may choose to modify them—to shorten Kathleen to Kate, or Philip to Phil. But whatever form a name takes, it represents the self.

How much of the self is revealed by a name varies by culture and situation. College students meeting for the first time exchange personal names, rarely bothering with family names. Theirs is a self independent of any group or past. When American businesspeople meet they exchange first names, last names, and business titles. Businesspeople are linked to their organizations. When Moroccans from different towns meet, the names they offer to others include not only those of their families but the names of the towns they live in. The Moroccan self is embedded in family and place of origin. Among the Gitksan of British Columbia, the names people use depend on their social position, for when they enter adulthood, get married, or assume a higher rank in society, they change their names. The Gitksan self is inseparable from social position.

The differences in naming practices among different societies reveal the different ways societies conceptualize what a person is and how a person relates to the group. Most Americans believe that individuals are stable, autonomous entities who exist more or less independently of whatever situations or statuses they occupy. As Americans move from status to status or place to place—from student to husband or wife, to employee, to father or mother—they believe themselves to be the same persons nevertheless. Otherwise, each time we changed situations or statuses we would in effect become different people and would have to change our names. In this regard the American view of the self is highly **individualistic.**

This does not seem to be the case in other societies where individuals are not thought to be capable of having identities distinct from their social positions or groups. In societies such as the Gitksan, the relationship between the person and the group, or the person and her or his social position, is more **holistic**; the person cannot be conceived of as existing separately from society or apart from one's status or role. The holistic view of the self is expressed in Gandhi's metaphor of individuals as drops in the ocean; the drops cannot survive without the ocean, and the ocean loses its identity without the drops.

The Egocentric and the Sociocentric Self

These differences between the individualistic and holistic conceptions of the self led Richard A. Shweder and Edmund J. Bourne to distinguish two distinct ways in which the person is conceived in different societies: the egocentric and sociocentric views of the self. In the **egocentric** view, typified in many ways by the Western view adopted in American society, each person is defined as a replica of all humanity, the locus of motivations and drives, capable of acting independently from others. For Westerners, the individual is the center of awareness, a distinct whole set against other wholes. Social relations are regarded as contracts between autonomous, free-acting beings. Individuals are free to negotiate their own places in society, and the dominant idea is that everyone is responsible for what and who they are. Moreover, individuals possess intrinsic qualities such as generosity, integrity, or beauty. In the egocentric view of the person, a high value is placed on individualism and self-reliance.

Robert Bellah and his coauthors examine American ideas of the individual in *Habits of the Heart*. The American self, they say, seeks to work out its own life plot by individually pursuing happiness and satisfying its wants. Unlike individuals in some other societies, Americans seek to cut themselves off from the past, especially from their parents. Each wishes to become his or her own person, to find his or her self. Americans seem to want to give birth to themselves; young women and men need to demonstrate that they can stand on their own two feet and be self-supporting. This belief in a self-reliant, independent self underlies the American belief in success as the outcome of free and fair competition among individuals in an open market. Bellah notes that most successful Americans claim they achieved success through their own hard work. They seldom acknowledge the contributions made by their families, their schooling, or their position as members of the upwardly mobile middle class. The only way they can say they deserve what they have achieved is if they maintain that they have succeeded *through their own efforts.*

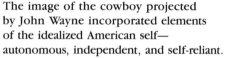

The image of the cowboy projected by John Wayne incorporated elements of the idealized American self—autonomous, independent, and self-reliant.

In contrast to the egocentric view of the person the **sociocentric** view of the self is context-dependent. Shweder and Bourne say it exists as an entity only within the concrete situations or roles occupied by a person, in much the same way the Gitksans' names are linked to their positions in society and not to some autonomous, separate self. From a sociocentric view, there is no intrinsic self that can possess enduring qualities such as generosity, integrity, or beauty. Such qualities can apply only to concrete social situations. Instead of saying that a man is generous, a sociocentric perspective would be, "He gives money to his friends." Instead of saying that a woman is principled, the perspective would be, "She does not give away secrets."

Personhood in Japan and America

Some anthropologists attribute a sociocentric view of the self to the Japanese. Christie Kiefer, for example, explains that the Japanese are apt to include within the boundaries of the self the social groups of which the person is a member, whereas the American self-concept does not extend beyond the physical body. Japanese children are not trained to be self-reliant, as American children are. They are taught that interdependence between the person and the family or group is more important than independence.

EXERCISE 5.1

People begin to learn from childhood the ways that their self relates to others and their groups. That is, by the behavior of others toward them, they come to see themselves as distinct entities or as beings intimately linked to others.

Schools in America are significant environments for learning about self. Try to list the ways that American school settings, and how children act in them, convey to children their degree of individuality and responsibility for their actions. Are there ways in which individualism is submerged? Might school settings differ in the extent to which the egocentric as opposed to the sociocentric self is developed?

Robert Smith notes that the Japanese view of the self is expressed in their language. For example, Japanese language lacks anything resembling our personal pronouns. In American society, children quickly learn to use the two personal referents, *I* and *you;* in Japan, boys must learn six and girls must learn five. The personal referent used in Japan depends on the relationship of the speaker to the listener. It expresses the contingency of self in Japan and how the self is defined relative to a specific social interaction.

In addition, Japanese language is lacking vocabulary that is status-neutral. Rather, it is characterized by what the Japanese call *keigo,* or "polite speech." *Keigo* has the effect of establishing at the outset of a conversation the relative social standing and degree of intimacy of speaker and listener. Japanese speakers use different forms of address, depending on their social position relative to the person to whom they are speaking. Since the Japanese language is status-based, people must be careful of the linguistic forms they use in conversations. When conversing with someone in a superior social position, the speaker must linguistically acknowledge his or her inferiority. Japanese advertisers have a problem with *keigo* because actors should not give imperative commands (e.g., "drink Coke"), for fear of offending people. They solve the problem by having low-status people who are nonthreatening (e.g., clowns, coquettish women, or children) issue the commands.

The sociocentric Japanese differ also from the egocentric Americans in their approach to social interaction. Americans believe it is desirable to assert themselves; some even undergo assertiveness training. They believe people should stand out, take charge. The Japanese believe that social interaction should be characterized by restraint or reserve, traits they identify as *enryo.* Americans may aggressively present themselves to others; the Japanese are more reticent. With *enryo,* giving opinions is avoided; it is best summed up in the proverb, "The nail that sticks up shall be hammered down."

Nevertheless, the Japanese do conceive of themselves as separate entities. They are as attached to their personal names as Americans are, if not more so. Moreover, they believe in self-development. But for the Japanese, the autonomy of the individual is established not through interaction with others, as it is for Americans, but away from society, where self-reflection and introspection are legitimate. It is through introspection that the Japanese find their true heart (*kokoro*) and are put in touch with their true nature—their *hara* (belly) and *jibub* (self).

The remaining questions in this chapter will look at the self less from our own egocentric perspective and more from the sociocentric perspective, as something contingent and relative to the situation. The focus is on that part of the self that is defined by social relations and social processes and that is subject to change and redefinition.

QUESTION 5.2 *How Do Societies Distinguish Individuals from One Another?*

Differences and similarities among persons are the materials from which we construct our social landscapes, which allow us to distinguish individuals from one another or assign them to one group or another. From these similarities and differences we construct our social identities. However, all societies do not use the same similarities and differences to construct a social code, nor do they all use these similarities and differences in the same way. Some characteristics of persons are almost universally used to differentiate and to group. Family relations, gender, and age, for example, are used in every society as categories of a social code. Other characteristics figure prominently only in some societies—ethnic group membership, skin color, and wealth, for example. Take the variety of personal characteristics used to construct a social landscape by students and teachers in a suburban New York high school. They include (not necessarily in this order): participation or nonparticipation in sports, performance in sports (as measured by the number of points an individual contributes to a team), participation in extracurricular activities, dress, scholastic achievement, will to achieve, disruptive or nondisruptive behavior, willingness to cooperate with teachers and administration, gender, ethnicity (Italian, "nothing" [American], Irish, Afro-American, Hispanic), family wealth, health, age, grade, and so on.

Perhaps the most important set of characteristics used to define the self is related to kinship and family membership. In traditional societies, kinship is the central organizing principle—the main determinant of a person's social identity. Anthropologists working with traditional societies are often "adopted" by a family. While this act is a signal of acceptance, it also serves the practical purpose of assigning to an outsider a social identity through which she or he can be approached by others. To have no kinship label or designation in such societies is to have no meaningful place on the social landscape.

Language spoken is another identity marker that is sometimes viewed as essential for the maintenance of a group identity. The way a language is spoken is often important; think of how Americans use dialect to identify people as being New Englanders, New Yorkers, Texans, and the like. Language is often tied strongly to a national identity, and many countries have established institutions to oversee the "purity" of the national language. The Academie Française is charged with keeping the French language free of foreign borrowings, such as "le hot dog" or "le hamburger." In some countries conflict between groups focuses on issues of language. In Quebec, for example, efforts of one group to preserve French as the official language of the province, and thus to protect what it sees as essential to group identity, have led to a movement for independence from the rest of English-speaking Canada.

The importance of group identity can also be observed in Northern Ireland, where the fundamental marker people use to locate others is religious affiliation. The Irish people acquire the skill of "telling," which involves determining whether another person is Catholic or Protestant. Adults in Northern Ireland claim that they can tell people's religious affiliation by such cues as their area of residence, the school they go to, their given names or surnames, speech, clothing, and even facial features. Some have suggested that group identity as Protestant or Catholic is the most important defining feature of social identity for the Irish. This is reflected in the joke about a man who is stopped on a Belfast street and asked his religion. "Jewish," he replies. "Yes," says the questioner, "but are you a Catholic Jew or a Protestant Jew?"

Northern Ireland also illustrates the importance of having either a positive identity or a negative identity. Members of each group attempt to build a **positive identity,** to attribute to themselves characteristics they believe are desirable, and to construct a **negative identity** for others by attributing undesirable characteristics to them. In Northern Ireland they often do this by comparing themselves with the other religious group, Catholics to Protestants, Protestants to Catholics. Catholics build a positive identity by emphasizing their Celtic heritage, their "decency," while Protestants emphasize their past military triumphs and their loyalty to Great Britain. Protestants believe themselves to be "neater" and "cleaner" than Catholics; Catholics think of themselves as the only true Irish.

Learning to Be Male or Female

While personal attributes of individuals are used to construct identities in almost all societies, they are not always used in the same way. Gender is a good example of an identity feature that Americans take for granted, on the assumption that it is a biological construct. But gender is at least as much a cultural creation as it is a biological construct; that is, different standards apply to being male and being female.

American parents, for example, teach male children that it is manly to endure pain, to be strong and tough. Male children are discouraged from expressing discomfort and encouraged when they can withstand it. Female children, on the other hand, are comforted when they hurt themselves. Traditionally, male American children are encouraged to be aggressive and competitive; they learn to compete in games and play with toys that require aggressive behavior. Females are taught to be caring and helpful; they are given toys such as dolls that encourage "feminine" behavior.

The idea that gender is more a matter of culture than biology was first investigated by Margaret Mead, who compared three New Guinea societies, the Arapesh, the Mundugumor, and the Tchambuli. She describes the gender differences among these societies in *Sex and Temperament in Three Primitive Societies,* first published in 1935. Among the Arapesh, both male and female children are discouraged from fighting or other acts of aggression, and they are never taught to accept discomfort. Children are fed when they are hungry and taught to share. The Arapesh do not believe that sex is a powerful driving force for either women or men. As a consequence, Mead says, both females and males are gentle, cooperative, and responsive to others, much like American females. Unlike the Arapesh, both Mundugumor men and women are expected to be ruthless and aggressive, much like American males. Among the Tchambuli gender definitions are the reverse of those in American society. Women are taught to be dominant and controlling, while men are expected to be emotionally dependent. On the basis of these findings, Mead concludes that culture defines and creates gender differences in personality, values, and behavior.

The number of gender categories recognized in a society also varies. For example, many Native American societies traditionally recognized a third gender, the *berdache* among the Cheyenne and Lakota and the *nadle* among the Navajo. The *berdache* or *nadle* is a biological male who does not fill a standard male role. Such individuals are not seen as men, nor are they defined as women. They occupy a third role, one that is culturally defined, accepted, and in some cases revered. Children in the Navajo, Lakota, Cheyenne, and other groups thus could choose from three gender categories, rather than learning that gender roles are defined by physiology. Among the Lakota male children learned that if they desired, they could adopt the dress and work roles of women and have sex with men, although the berdache role did not necessarily involve sexual behavior. The *berdache* or *nadle* did not play only women's roles, however; some were noted for their hunting skills and exploits in war. In American society, in contrast, persons who do not assume the gender roles associated with their anatomy are often defined as deviant, abnormal, or nonconformist.

According to Harriet Whitehead, one reason Americans have difficulty recognizing a third gender is that they make ethnocentric assumptions about what characteristics are most important in defining gender roles. Americans define gender largely by sexual preference, whether a person prefers to have sex with someone of the same or the opposite gender. They pay less attention to preferences in dress, behavior, and occupation. Native North Americans traditionally placed a different emphasis on these characteristics. Groups that included the socially legitimate identity of *berdache* or *nadle* defined gender primarily by choice of occupation; the gender of a sexual partner was least important.

In every society, therefore, the members have various identities. Not all, of course, are appropriate for everyone. Individuals must learn not only the characteristics of different identities but where on the social landscape they belong.

QUESTION 5.3 *How Do Individuals Learn Who They Are?*

We are not born with an identity; it is something we learn. Moreover, identities are not static phenomena. In all societies people are constantly changing their identities as they move through the life cycle. Consequently, there must be ways in which identity changes are announced.

In a classic work published in 1908, Arnold van Gennep introduced the concept of **rites of passage.** These rituals mark a person's passage from one identity to another, as a person's progress through a house might be marked by going through door after door. Van Gennep identifies three phases in rites of passage: first, the ritual separates the person from an existing identity; second, the person enters a transition phase; third, the changes are incorporated into a new identity. These phases are not always elaborated in specific ceremonies, however. The separation phase, for example, is a part of funeral ceremonies designed to help the living let go of the deceased; transition is a part of initiation ceremonies marking the passage of a person from, say, childhood to adulthood; and incorporation is emphasized in marriage ceremonies that, in most societies, mark the transfer of a person from one social group to another.

Anthropologists have studied how American corporations use ceremony and ritual to help employees define their identities within the work organization. Some corporations use ceremonies not only to change a person's identity but to remind others in the organization of unacceptable behavior. The W. T. Grant Corporation reportedly humiliated poor-performing store managers by throwing custard pies in their faces, cutting their ties in half, and inducing them to push peanuts across the floor with their noses. W. T. Grant was later dissolved through bankruptcy.

A more successful example of the use of ritual to define identity in business is the Mary Kay Cosmetic Corporation's ceremonies to enhance employees' identification with the company. Each year awards are presented to sales personnel, all of whom are women, in a setting that has been compared to the Miss America pageant. Honorees, dressed in evening clothes, are seated on the stage of a large auditorium in front of a cheering audience. The ceremony celebrates the personal saga of the founder, Mary Kay—how, through personal determination and optimism, she was able to overcome her separation from her husband, support her children as a salesperson, and ultimately found her own company. The ideology of the corporation is symbolized by a bee-shaped pin with the legend, "Everyone can find their wings and fly."

The Transition to Male Adulthood

In many societies around the world there are ceremonies that mark the transition of a male from boyhood to manhood, and most of them involve some kind of test of courage. According to David Gilmore, one reason societies incorporate tests of masculinity and tortuous initiation rituals only for males is that the male identity is more problematic than the female identity. For every individual there is in the beginning of life a subliminal identification with the mother, and it is more difficult for boys than for girls to differentiate themselves from their identification with their mothers. This is why societies incorporate rituals that symbolically separate the boy from his mother and at the same time incorporate him into manhood.

One example Gilmore gives is the initiation rite of the Maasai, a cattle-herding people of East Africa. For a Maasai male to attain the identity of "worthy man," he must own cattle, be generous to others, and be autonomous and independent, capable of defending his homestead and his honor. He must also demonstrate bravery on cattle raids against neighboring groups. The road to being a man (what the Maasai call a *moran*) begins with a boy's father looking for a sign that the boy is ready to assume the responsibilities of manhood. Tepilit Ole Saitoti tells in his autobiography how he begged his father to let him be initiated. One day Tepilit confronted and killed a huge lioness that threatened the family's cattle. Shortly after, his father gathered the family and said, "We are going to initiate Tepilit into manhood. He has proven before all of us that he can now save children and cattle."

The central feature of the Maasai initiation is circumcision. This rite is intensely painful, since the cutting, which may last up to four minutes, is done with no anesthetic. The boy, placed on view before male relatives and prospective in-laws, must remain absolutely still and silent. Tepilit describes how, shortly before his circumcision, he was told, "You must not budge; don't move a muscle or even blink. You can face only one direction until the operation is completed. The slightest movement on your part will mean you are a coward, incompetent, and unworthy to be a Maasai man."

Americans also have their rites of passage into adulthood, some of the most spectacular being those associated with high school and college fraternities. As with the Maasai, sexual identity and separation from the female identity often is a major theme in these ceremonies. To illustrate, I will describe a study whose initial focus was an instance of fraternity gang rape. The study began in 1983, when Peggy Reeves Sanday learned from one of her students of a gang rape at a college fraternity. Sanday's subsequent research produced a vivid portrait of how the male identity in American society is represented in college fraternity behavior.

Gang rape, or "pulling train," as it is called in fraternities, begins with the coercion of a vulnerable young woman who is seeking acceptance (or who may be high on alcohol or drugs) and who may or may not agree to have sex with a certain man. When she passes out or is too weak or intoxicated to protest, a "train" of men proceed to have sex with her. While the incident that triggered Sanday's study occurred in a fraternity on a large, prestigious college campus, gang rape is not unique to college fraternities. It is also associated with sports teams, street gangs, and other groups of men for whom the act often serves as a male-bonding ritual.

Pulling train occurs with some frequency. During one six-year period in the mid-1980s, there were 75 documented cases on college campuses, and in the investigation of the event that led to Sanday's study, witnesses reported that it occurred on that campus once or twice a month. It is likely that many cases go unreported. One reason is that both perpetrators and victims often do not recognize it as rape. Most men believe that if a woman has consented with one man, does not vigorously resist, and is not violently overpowered, the sex act does not constitute rape. Rather, they say, the woman is "asking for it." These men are unaware that any sex act in which the woman is *not able* to give consent constitutes a legal definition of rape. Victims may not recognize it as rape, either, and may take the responsibility, saying, "I went too far," or "I let things get out of hand." Other victims are reluctant to report it because of the publicity or negative treatment they receive from authorities. Where fraternities are concerned, colleges often cloak these events in secrecy to protect the offenders, the victims, and themselves.

As Sanday and her associates interviewed fraternity members, women who were associated with them, and victims of rape, they sought to explain what it is about the male identity, as represented by college fraternities, that encourages these actions. Three things stand out in her account. First, there is

One way men's groups help define the male identity in American society is through male-bonding rituals such as this fraternity food fight.

a heavy emphasis in fraternities on male bonding and male-bonding behavior, to the extent that a college man's self-esteem and social identity are dependent on first gaining entry to a fraternity and then being accepted by the brothers. Fraternities confer status; on most college campuses where they exist, they are recognized as places "where the action is." They also provide reassurance, security, and ready-made identities. Membership in a fraternity transforms outsiders into insiders.

Second, sex constitutes a major status and identity marker. Masculinity is defined and demonstrated by sexual conquest. For example, in the fraternity in which the gang rape occurred, a major activity was "hitting" or "riffing" on women, or "working a yes out." This involves persuading a woman to have sex by talking, dancing, or drinking with her. Men who are expert riffers gain status; those who are not successful are in danger of being labeled "nerds," "wimps," or, worse, "fags." Sex in this case is a public thing. Men in the fraternities that Sanday interviewed bragged publicly about their sexual conquests and arranged for brothers to witness them. Some fraternities posted weekly newsletters listing the brothers' sexual conquests.

A third element in the identity of fraternity men concerns their attitudes toward women. Many of the fraternity members interviewed by Sanday implied that women are sex objects to be abused or debased. A woman's identity among these fraternity men was determined largely by her sexual interactions with them. Women who are sexually unresponsive were labeled as "frigid" or "icicles"; women who allow advances only up to a point and refuse intimacy, as "cockteasers"; and women who have sex with many men, as "sluts" or "cunts." Such labels indicate that the role of girlfriend is virtually the only role with no negative connotations that a woman can play for fraternity men. In one fraternity, brothers marked women who attended their parties with "power dots," black, red, yellow, white, or blue stickers they attached to a girl's clothing to indicate how easy the girl was to pick up.

For the fraternity men, the debasement of women was interwoven with the themes of male bonding and sexual conquest. Part of the reason men bond in college, says Sanday, is to achieve domination and power they think is owed to males. One fraternity man explained how verbally harassing a girl increases male bonding: "I mean, people come back the day after a party and say 'you should have seen me abuse this girl.' They're real proud of it in front of everyone."

EXERCISE 5.2

In her book on gang rape, Sanday also discusses the role of pornography in the definition of male and female identities in America. She suggests that pornography depicts women as subservient to men and that it reinforces sexist attitudes and encourages behavior toward women that is characteristic of men in fraternities. Do you agree or disagree, and why?

Sanday calls the use of sex and the debasement of women to demonstrate masculinity **phallocentrism,** "the deployment of the penis as a concrete symbol of masculine social power and dominance." Phallocentrism, as well as the themes of male bonding, sexual prowess, and the debasement of women, all are manifested in the act of pulling train. It is a form of bonding, it publicly legitimizes a male's heterosexuality, and it makes women an object of scorn and abuse.

Sanday is quick to emphasize that not all college men subscribe to the ideology of phallocentrism, and not all fraternity men measure their masculinity by sexual conquest and the victimization of women. In the case that initiated her study, the six men charged with gang rape were all described by girls who knew them as "among the nicest guys in the fraternity." Individually, probably none of them would have committed the act they were charged with. However, in the context of the fraternity, gang rape is the credible outcome of a process of identity formation that is manifested in fraternity life in general and the fraternity initiation in particular.

The fraternity initiation ritual on most college campuses is the culmination of a period of pledging in which initiates are required to perform various demeaning acts. Particulars may vary from fraternity to fraternity and campus to campus, but in general the ritual stigmatizes the initiates as infants, children, or girls and then proceeds to cleanse them of this negative identity prior to incorporating them into the fraternity as full-fledged brothers. In one fraternity initiation described to Sanday, the initiates were blindfolded and stripped down to their jockstraps. Then they were told to drop their jockstraps and were ridiculed: "Look at the pin-dicks, pussies, fags. They're all a bunch of girls, it's amazing they don't have tits." As the brothers screamed at them, their testicles were rubbed with Ben-Gay. After about ten minutes, a brother said, "Sorry we had to do that, but we had to cleanse you of your nerd sin." Then the pledges were put to tests of trust. In one case, a pledge was thrown to the ground and swords were placed at his crotch by one brother and at his chest by another. The pledge was then asked if he trusted the brothers not to kill him. As the pledge nodded yes, the brother brought the sword down on his chest; since it was made of wood, it shattered. In another fraternity initiates were taken blindfolded to a bathroom and told to eat some feces out of a toilet bowl and trust they would not become sick. As they picked it out and ate it, they realized it was a banana.

The final stage of most fraternity initiations generally includes a secret ritual in which the pledges come before the brothers, who are dressed in robes and hoods or other ritual paraphernalia. In one ritual reported to Sanday, a brother addressed the initiates with the following words:

> You have shown trust in the fraternity and trust in the brothers. We know we can trust you now. A bond has been formed between us. No one has experienced the hell you have except us and the brothers before us. Bonded by strength, loyalty, and trust we are one. Cleansed of weakness and filth, we are men. As men we stand tall. As men we stand for the fraternity, and [name of fraternity] stands for us. (quoted in Sanday 1990:163)

In these ceremonies the abusers of the initiates then gain credence by accepting those they had just heaped with abuse. One initiate described to Sanday how he felt at this point:

> I felt exhilarated. I kept saying, "Oh wow!" and hugging my big brother and shaking hands with everybody. I was incredibly happy. I was made to feel worthless by the fraternity as an individual, and now that it was all over, I was made to feel wonderful by the fraternity as a brother. My worth was celebrated by the same process that had previously denied it, because of the change that it had effected within me. I now saw myself as a *brother,* and what may feel terrible to an individual confronted by brothers feels tremendous to an individual who *is* a brother. (quoted in Sanday 1990:149)

Sanday concludes that fraternity initiation rituals serve to solidify a fraternity man's identity by separating him from his previous identity as a member of a family, and perhaps separating him from his mother. The ritual incorporates the man into a group whose activities reinforce a male identity, defined largely by degradation of the negative identity of female and acted out in sexual conquest and abuse of females. Pulling train is both an expression of male sexuality and a display of the power of the brotherhood to control and dominate women. In other words, gang rape is but one instance of the abuse and domination that begin in the initiation and are continued later in relations with women and new pledges. Sanday says that once initiates have suffered abuse as a means of establishing their bond to the fraternity, they "resort to abusing others—new generations of pledges and party women—to uphold the original contract and renew their sense of the autonomous power of the brotherhood."

QUESTION 5.4 *How Do Individuals Communicate Their Identities to One Another?*

There is an episode in Jonathan Swift's *Gulliver's Travels* in which Gulliver learns of an experiment conducted by professors at the Academy of Lagado. They believe that since words are only names for things, they can abolish words by having people carry with them everything they need to engage in discourse with others. Gulliver describes such a "conversation": Two people meet, open their packs of things, "talk" by using them for an hour, pack up their things, and go off.

In many ways our interactions with others are similar to the interaction of the inhabitants of Laputa. We too communicate with things by using them to make statements of our identity—who we think we are, or who we want to be. The clothes we wear, the things we possess, the people we associate with are all used to convey an identity that we think we have or wish we had. For example, if sex or gender is used as a criterion to distinguish individuals, there must be ways that sexual differences are displayed so they can be read by others. In some groups in New Guinea, for example, men wear penis gourds, and in seventeenth-century Europe they wore codpieces to emphasize the male anatomy. In areas in Africa, people from different villages have different hairstyles; in America, teenagers encode their schools, or gangs, or teams by the jackets they wear. People signal their connectedness to others by holding hands, wearing rings, or feasting and drinking together.

EXERCISE 5.3 ━━━━━━━━━━━━━━━━━━━━━━━━━━━━━━━━━━━ COUNTRY
JOB
FAMILY
RELIGION
(?)

Suppose you were to travel to Gulliver's island of Laputa. If you could only communicate to people with objects that you carried with you, and you could take *only* five things with you to "tell" people about yourself, what would they be?

One of the most influential works in the history of anthropology is a book written by Marcel Mauss, modestly entitled *The Gift*. Mauss identifies what he calls **the principle of reciprocity,** or the giving and receiving of gifts. His major point is that gifts, which in theory are voluntary, disinterested, and spontaneous, are in fact obligatory. The giving of the gift creates a tie with the person who receives it and who, on some future occasion, is obliged to reciprocate. To Mauss, what is important is not what is given but the relationship that is maintained or established by the gift. The types of things given and received signal the identities of the participants in the exchange and the kind of relationship that exists between them. If the gifts are roughly of equal value, the relationship is one of equality. But if the gifts are unequal in value, the person who gives the more valuable gift is generally of higher status than the receiver.

The Kula Ring and the Potlatch Feast

A well-known example of gift-giving in the anthropological literature is the *kula* ring of the Trobriand Islands, the circulation of gifts among trading partners on different islands. The seagoing Trobrianders leave their homes on islands off the eastern coast of New Guinea and travel from island to island, visiting and trading. Trading partnerships are designated with gifts of red shell necklaces or white shell armbands. As a man travels and trades objects, he also gives and receives necklaces or armbands. A man who receives either object does not keep it but passes it along to another trading partner. There is a set pattern to the exchange; necklaces travel from island to island in a clockwise direction, while armbands move counterclockwise. The time between exchanges and the distances between the islands are so great that it may take two to ten years before the necklaces and armbands make a complete circle.

The *kula* ring serves as a concrete representation of ties between individuals. Any change in the pattern of gift-giving reflects a change in the nature of the social ties. In addition, special gifts that are individually owned are also circulated, and the owner's status and renown grow as the goods he owns circulate along predetermined paths. A successful *kula* operator participates in many such exchanges and can profit from them by keeping items for as long as he can before passing them along. Of course, if he keeps them too long, others will be reluctant to exchange, so a good deal of social skill is required to *kula* successfully.

Another famous example of gift-giving is the potlatch ceremony on the northwest coast of North America. Among the Gitksan the potlatch is a feast at a funeral; the person who dies vacates a spot on the social landscape or, more specifically, leaves empty a name. The Gitksan are organized into patrilineal clans or houses. Each house has associated with it a fixed number of personal names, and each name has associated with it specific spiritual powers, honors, and objects of wealth. As the Gitksan move through the life cycle they are given different names associated with their standing in the group. The names they hold when they die are vacated until they are claimed by or given to others. If the name vacated belonged to a chief or someone else of high rank, numerous people may claim it and the honors and privileges associated with it. The person who contributes the most wealth to the potlatch or funeral feast is the one who gets the name. The higher ranking the name, the greater the wealth that is given away. Around 15 years ago, the cost of a name ran anywhere from $100 to $500, and some chiefs have held eight to ten names at one time. However, the more names held by a Gitksan, the greater is the burden of upholding the power and honor of each name by being generous, loyal, and upstanding. Those who disgrace their names by doing something wrong (such as having an automobile accident or being put in jail) must give feasts to "clean the name."

The potlatch feast, however, does more than allow a Gitksan to obtain a new name and identity. It also serves to symbolically reorder and validate the names, and hence the social positions, of everyone at the feast through the distribution of gifts. Members of the house of the deceased generally serve as hosts to members of the deceased's father's house. The guests are feasted for the services they perform at the funeral—they prepare the corpse and dig the

Trobriand Island trading partners exchange wealth in the form of necklaces and bracelets as a way of defining, maintaining, and protecting their social identities.

grave—and as repayment for the gifts they had given to help the deceased acquire a name. Guests are seated by their hosts according to rank. Those who think they have been given a "wrong" seat, one that assigns them to a lower rank than they think they deserve, complain to the leader of the host group, who gives them a gift of money to "wipe away" the disgrace or insult. When the guests are seated, the hosts announce the gifts they are giving to the guests, along with the name of the person from the host group who contributed the gift. Higher-ranking guests receive more gifts at a potlatch than lower-ranking guests. Consequently, the seating arrangements and the value of the gifts given to guests at the feast serve to announce or publicly notarize the social position or identity of each guest.

Exchanges that convey recognition of identities needn't be limited to material goods. The exchanges also may consist of affect, emotion, and sentiment. Hawaiians, for example, define a desired identity in part by expressions of gregariousness and hospitality. The affective qualities of a person's relationships are one criterion by which others judge, interact with, and respond to that person. For example, if you accept an offer of hospitality in Hawaii, it is a signal that you recognize the generous nature of the offer and you wish to maintain the social link. If you reject the offer of hospitality, it would be seen as a hurtful sign that you do not recognize the generous nature of the person making the offer and do not wish to maintain the relationship. Hawaiians attempt to keep social pathways open with altruistic exchanges of love (*aloha*), sincerity of feeling (with heart, *na'au*), and warmth (*pumehana*).

QUESTION 5.5 *How Do Individuals Defend Their Identities That Are Threatened?*

In defining themselves and others, people sometimes disagree on their relative positions on the social landscape; that is, they disagree on their respective identities. Anthony F. C. Wallace and Raymond Fogelson refer to such a situation as an **identity struggle,** an interaction in which there is a discrepancy between the identity a person claims to possess and the identity attributed to that person by others.

Take the medicine fight among the Beaver Indians of British Columbia, as described by Robin Ridington. The Beaver believe that a man's identity relative to others is determined by the amount of supernatural power or medicine he possesses. This power determines a man's success in hunting and protects him and his family from illness and misfortune. Any personal misfortune a man experiences, such as illness or failure to kill game, is interpreted by others as a loss of supernatural power and hence a loss of prestige. However, the man experiencing the misfortune does not interpret it in that way; for him, the misfortune is the result not of a loss of his supernatural power but of someone using supernatural power against him. In other words, his view of his identity is different from the one that he believes is attributed to him by others. The person experiencing the misfortune will dream the identity of the attacker and publicly accuse him. The accused may deny the charge, responding that his accuser is experiencing misfortune because he has committed some wrongful act. This begins the medicine fight, a series of accusations and counteraccusations that sometimes leads to violence.

Making Moka in New Guinea

The Beaver claim or defend their social identities through spiritual means. More common is the manipulation of material goods. Andrew Strathern uses the example of the Melpa who live around the area of Mt. Hagen in the Central Highlands of Papua New Guinea. The people of Mt. Hagen live by growing crops such as sweet potatoes and raising pigs. Pigs serve not only as a source of protein but also as signs of wealth and objects of gift exchange. The most important identity on the Highlands social landscape is the Big Man. Because they are leaders and among the wealthiest in terms of pig ownership, Big Men are the most independent from others. A man who is poor and dependent on others for food and sustenance is called by a term that translates into English as "rubbish man."

Becoming a Big Man requires courage in warfare. War, in the form of highly ritualized battles with spears and arrows or raiding and murder, has long been a part of New Guinea Highland society. Big Men play a pivotal role in planning war as well as establishing peace, either with their oratorical skills or with their wealth. The greatest skill required of a Big Man, however, is making *moka,* a form of ceremonial gift exchange in which a man makes a gift to a trading partner and receives in return more than he gave. Ceremonial gift exchanges serve two purposes: They establish and maintain links between the individuals and their groups, and they establish a rank system that enables men to earn status and prestige and become Big Men. Big Men from the same clan can make *moka* with each other, but it is most common for a man to have partners outside his clan and among ex-enemies or groups tied to his through marriage. Items that are included in exchanges include pigs, shells, bird plumage, salt, decorating oil, and stone axe blades. Pigs and shells used to be the most important items, but today Australian money, bicycles, cattle, and even trucks are used.

The major idea in making *moka,* and consequently establishing the status of Big Man, is for a man to give his trading partner more than he received at the last exchange. Thus if A gives 100 pigs to B, and B returns a countergift of 150 pigs that A cannot repay, then B is the Big Man because he gave the last gift. A series of *moka* exchanges between two trading rivals might look something like this:

First exchange: A gives x amount of goods to B.
  Result: B owes x amount of goods to A.

Second exchange: B gives two times x goods to A.
  Result: A owes x amount of goods to B.

Third Exchange: A gives two times x goods to B.
  Result: B owes x amount of goods to A.

Since after each exchange a man has returned the debt he owes his partner and added an increment equal to the debt, the result of the interaction is that one person always owes the other. The two participants never reach the point where things are even; the pattern of gift exchange assures that one party is always indebted to the other. The basic rule is to give more than you receive. It is strictly the incremental change in the debt that allows a man to say he made *moka.*

The negotiation of identity between *moka* partners is never an isolated affair, because a man rarely is able to make *moka* solely on the basis of what he possesses at a given time. For example, if a man wants or is being pressured to make *moka* with a rival to whom he must give six pigs or ten shell bracelets, and he doesn't have that many pigs or bracelets at that time, he must either call in outstanding *moka* obligations others owe him or must get what he needs from friends or kin. Thus any given exchange may involve a host of people and groups. A map of the circulation of *moka* goods around Melpa society would provide a pretty good idea of how different people and groups are related to others and would indicate the social identities of each person in the exchange network. These exchanges serve the Melpa as public statements of social identities—the relations between people and groups—at any given time. It is as if everyone in an American town publicly announced the present state of their social relations with each other person and group in town.

At a fairly typical *moka* exchange, many Big Men from different groups may make *moka* at once. The ceremony takes place at a ceremonial ground associated with a particular clan or lineage and is usually built by the Big Man of that group. Preparations for the *moka* exchange begin months before the actual presentation, and Big Men of donor groups negotiate the timing of the exchange. Those who are ready can push the *moka* through, but those who do not have enough to give to their trading rivals in the other group risk defaulting. They can try to delay the timing of a *moka* ceremony but may be taunted as procrastinators or rubbish men.

Before making *moka,* each man reviews his partnerships and ties to others, perhaps dropping some and adding others. Men scheduled to receive gifts at the *moka* exchange make initiatory gifts of shells, pigs, and legs of pork to their *moka* partners. Discussions about the ceremony are held at the ceremonial ground of the main group, and the men scheduled to give gifts set up stakes to indicate how many pigs they will give away to their partners. They also clear the ceremonial ground, make speeches, and review the history of the relations between the two groups. At each meeting the Big Men try to contract for more gifts, egging their clanmates on to give more pigs to their trading partners and increasing the competitive spirit. They insist that they must surpass in wealth the gifts received from their partners the last time they received *moka*. The climax of these discussions is the showing of the gifts.

Then the final transfer takes place, with dancing and oratory. The Big Men among the donors step forward and make speeches. On the final day men and women of the recipient group converge on the ceremonial ground. The donors decorate themselves with pearl shell pendants, fine bark aprons and belts, pig grease or tree oil, and charcoal and red ochre; they run up and down the row, crying *"hoo-aah, hoo-aah,"* and performing a war dance. Their speeches are boasts, claiming that by the amount they have given, they have "won." Here is an excerpt of such a speech:

> My sisters' sons, my cross-cousins. I am your true cross-cousin, living close to you. My sisters' sons, my cross-cousins, you say you see big pigs, big shells, well, now I have given you large pigs on the two olka stakes, given you a bicycle too, given you all the food you like to eat. Further, I have given you two steers, and so I win. I have given you all the things which are your food; I give you two steers also and so I win. (Strathern 1971:241)

Recipients who do not get what they expect at the ceremony (and they never know exactly what they will get until the ceremony takes place) complain loudly and bitterly. Thus the ceremony is an anxious occasion in which the honor, and consequently the social identity, of both donor and recipient is on the line. Sometimes actual fighting breaks out. If a man does not meet his commitments to his partner and does not give gifts commensurate with what he received at the last ceremony, his partner can do little but shout insults or physically attack him.

At the end of the ceremony, an orator counts the gifts while the recipients offer stylized thank-yous. The recipients of *moka* then gather their shells and pigs and knock over the pig stakes, except for one that is left standing as proof that the donors have made *moka* at their ceremonial ground.

CONCLUSIONS

The concept of the self, or personhood, varies from society to society. In the egocentric view, the self is viewed as an autonomous, discrete individual; in the sociocentric view, the self is viewed as contingent on a situation or social setting. The sociocentric view is often taken by social scientists who are interested in the social processes by which social identities are formed and maintained.

Societies distinguish individuals from one another by using such criteria as age, gender, kinship, ethnicity, and language. Differences and similarities in characteristics among individuals are used to construct social landscapes, on which each person's place, or identity, is indicated. The characteristics that determine identity, such as gender, are treated differently in various societies.

One way individuals learn who they are is through rites of passage or initiation ceremonies such as those characteristic of college fraternities. Initiation rituals prepare individuals to accept new ways of looking at themselves and at others.

People must also be able to communicate their identities to one another. One way to do this is through the process of gift exchange and the principle of reciprocity. The *kula* ring, or the circulation of gifts among trading partners by the Trobriand Islanders, is an example. And individuals must be able to defend their identities if they are threatened. An example of how this is done is making *moka* by the Big Men among the Melpa, who thus both claim and defend their places on the social landscape.

REFERENCES AND SUGGESTED READINGS

INTRODUCTION: THE IMPORTANCE OF SELF The epigraph is taken from the opening passage of Erving Goffman's classic work *The Presentation of Self in Everyday Life* (Doubleday, 1959).

HOW DOES THE CONCEPT OF PERSONHOOD VARY? An excellent treatment of the relationship between names and identity can be found in Richard D. Alford's *Naming and Identity: A Cross-Cultural Study of Personal Naming Practices* (HRAF Press, 1988). Naming among the Gitksan is discussed by John W. Adams in *The Gitksan Potlatch: Population Flux, Resource Ownership and Reciprocity* (Holt, Rinehart and Winston of Canada, 1973). The Gandhi reference is from Ramashray Roy, *Self and Society: A Study in Gandhian Thought* (Sage, 1985). The discussion of the differences between the sociocentric and egocentric self is based on an article by Richard A. Shweder and Edmund J. Bourne, "Does the Concept of the Person Vary Cross-Culturally?" in *Cultural Conceptions of Mental Health and Therapy,* edited by A. J. Marsella and G. M. White (D. Reidel Publishing, 1984). The discussion of American individualism draws on Robert Bellah et al., *Habits of the Heart* (University of California Press, 1984). The nature of the self in Japan is discussed in Robert J. Smith, *Japanese Society: Tradition, Self and the Social Order* (Cambridge University Press, 1983); Christie W. Kiefer, "The Danchi Zoku and the Evolution of the Metropolitan Mind," in *Japan: The Paradox of Progress,* edited by Lewis Austin (Yale University Press, 1976); and Dolores and Robert Cathcart, "Japanese Social Experience and Concept of Groups," in *Intercultural Communication: A Reader,* 4th edition, edited by Larry A. Samovar and Richard E. Porter (Wadsworth Publishing, 1984).

HOW DO SOCIETIES DISTINGUISH INDIVIDUALS FROM ONE ANOTHER? The information on identity in Northern Ireland comes from Ed Cairns, "Intergroup Conflict in Northern Ireland," in *Social Identity and Intergroup Relations,* edited by Henri Tajfel (Cambridge University Press, 1982). Margaret Mead's comparison of gender roles in New Guinea comes from her classic *Sex and Temperament in Three Primitive Societies,* first published in 1935 (Dell, 1963). Excellent accounts of the *berdache* role can be found in Walter L. Williams, *The Spirit and the Flesh: Sexual Diversity in American Indian Culture* (Beacon Press, 1986), and in Harriet Whitehead, "The Bow and the Burden Strap: A New Look at Institutionalized Homosexuality in Native North America," in *Sexual Meanings: The Cultural Construction of Gender and Sexuality,* edited by Sherry B. Ortner and Harriet

Whitehead (Cambridge University Press, 1981). Susan U. Philips discusses the ways language is used to convey gender identity in "Sex Differences and Language," in *Annual Review of Anthropology,* vol. 9 (1980), pp. 523–544. For a review of anthropological studies of human sexuality, see "The Cross-Cultural Study of Human Sexuality," by D. L. Davis and R. G. Whitten, in *Annual Review of Anthropology,* vol. 16 (1987), pp. 69–98.

HOW DO INDIVIDUALS LEARN WHO THEY ARE? The classic work on rites of passage is Arnold van Gennep, *The Rites of Passage,* translated by Monica B. Vizedom and Gabrielle L. Chaffe, originally published in 1906 (University of Chicago Press, 1960). A description of how American businesses use rites of passage is in Harrison M. Trice and Janice M. Beyer, "Studying Organizational Cultures through Rites and Ceremonials," *Academy of Management Review,* vol. 9 (1984), pp. 653–669. David D. Gilmore's work is represented by *Manhood in the Making: Cultural Concepts of Masculinity* (Yale University Press, 1990). The account of the initiation of a Maasai man is from *The Worlds of a Maasai Warrior,* by Tepilit Ole Saitoti (Random House, 1986), an excerpt of which is reprinted in *Anthropology 90/91,* edited by Elvio Angeloni (Dushkin Publishing, 1990). Peggy Reeves Sanday's account of gang rape is in *Fraternity Gang Rape: Sex, Brotherhood, and Privilege on Campus* (New York University Press, 1990). Another account of American college life is Michael Moffat's study *Growing Up in New Jersey* (Rutgers University Press, 1990). An interesting account of sorority initiation rites is contained in the article by Gary Schwartz and Don Merten, "Social Identity and Expressive Symbols," *American Anthropologist,* vol. 70 (1968), pp. 1117–1131.

HOW DO INDIVIDUALS COMMUNICATE THEIR IDENTITIES TO ONE ANOTHER? The use of *Gulliver's Travels* to illustrate the importance of goods in identity work is taken from Annette Weiner, *The Trobrianders of Papua New Guinea* (Holt, Rinehart and Winston, 1988). The classic work on the importance of the gift is Marcel Mauss, *The Gift: Forms and Functions of Exchange in Archaic Societies,* translated by Ian Cunnison, published originally in 1925 (W. W. Norton, 1967). The material on the *Gitksan* is from John W. Adams, *The Gitksan Potlatch,* cited above. The original description of the *kula* ring was the foundation for Bronislaw Malinowski's classic *Argonauts of the Western Pacific,* originally published in 1922 (E. P. Dutton, 1961). A reinterpretation of the *kula* ring can be found in Annette Weiner, *The Trobrianders of Papua New Guinea,* cited above.

HOW DO INDIVIDUALS DEFEND THEIR IDENTITIES THAT ARE THREATENED? The article by Anthony F. C. Wallace and Raymond D. Fogelson, "The Identity Struggle," can be found in *Intensive Family Therapy,* edited by I. Boszormenyi-Nagy and J. L. Framo (Harper & Row, 1965). The description of the Beaver medicine fight is from Robin Ridington, "The Medicine Fight: An Instrument of Political Process among the Beaver Indians," *American Anthropologist,* vol. 70 (1968), pp. 1152–1160. The material on "making *moka*" comes from Andrew Strathern, *The Rope of Moka: Big Men and Ceremonial Exchange in Mount Hagen New Guinea* (Cambridge University Press, 1971).

"Hey . . . this could be the chief."

CHAPTER 6

THE SOCIAL CONSTRUCTION OF HIERARCHY

PROBLEM 6: WHY ARE MODERN SOCIETIES CHARACTERIZED BY SOCIAL, POLITICAL, AND ECONOMIC INEQUALITIES?

131

> Every social hierarchy claims to be founded on the nature of things. It thus accords itself eternity; it escapes change and the attacks of innovators. Aristotle justified slavery by the ethnic superiority of the Greeks over the barbarians; and today the man who is annoyed by feminist claims alleges that woman is *naturally* inferior.
>
> Robert Hertz, 1909

INTRODUCTION: *The Rationale for Social Inequality*

The uneven distribution of wealth, status, and privilege is a significant problem in societies throughout the modern world. To Americans it is visible in the starving faces that stare out from our television screens in documentaries and on the evening news, interspersed with advertisements for such luxuries as automobiles, cosmetics, and household conveniences. Some people can purchase the finest amenities, while others lack the basic necessities of life, such as food, shelter, and health care. There are few if any modern nations in which one portion of the population does not in some way enjoy privileges that other portions do not share. In most of these cases, inequality follows from the assumption that some people are somehow better than others. Individuals are judged by certain traits—gender, age, physical appearance, occupation, wealth, group membership, and so on—that seem to make them more or less worthy compared to others.

Some believe that the hierarchical ordering of people and groups is unavoidable. For them, scarce resources, occupational specialization, and the power of an elite group to control the behavior of others necessarily result in some form of social stratification. Others maintain that stratification is not only avoidable, it is counter to human nature. According to Thomas Belmonte:

> Since the emergence of stratification, man's history (his changing ways of relating to nature and other men) has stood opposed to his humanity. The emergence of power-wielding elites . . . laid the basis for a new kind of anticollective society whose vastly accelerated growth was founded, not on the reconciliation of antagonisms between men, but on their origination and amplification in slavery, caste, and class. (Belmonte 1989:137)

Those who support this view note that in societies such as the !Kung and Inuit, there are no "poor," no "rich," no "inferior" or "superior" people. This is not to say that these societies are totally egalitarian; even in small-scale societies, valued statuses are unavailable to some members. Rather, the question is why modern societies are characterized by such extremes of poverty and wealth.

This chapter examines how societies construct social hierarchies and why some groups erect social edifices that are partitioned according to social dominance or submission, high or low status, oppressors or oppressed. Other questions are why most people in stratified societies—both those at the top and those at the bottom—consider social ranks to be natural; how people at the bottom levels of the hierarchy (those in poverty, for example) adapt to their conditions; and whether a nonstratified community can exist within a large-scale society.

QUESTIONS

6.1 How do societies rank people in social hierarchies?
6.2 Why do societies construct social hierarchies?
6.3 How do people come to accept social hierarchies as natural?
6.4 How do people living in poverty adapt to their condition?
6.5 Can a nonstratified community exist within a larger society?

QUESTION 6.1 *How Do Societies Rank People in Social Hierarchies?*

Social hierarchies in different societies vary along several dimensions: the criteria used to differentiate people into one level of society or another, the number of levels that exist, the kinds of privileges and rights that attach to people at different levels, and the strength of the social boundaries that separate the different levels. In American society, for example, people are stratified by **social class,** according to their income or wealth and personal possessions (e.g., lower class, middle class, and upper class). They are classified by cultural or family background into ethnic groups (e.g., Italian, Jewish, Hispanic, WASP—white, Anglo-Saxon Protestant), or by physical appearance or skin color into racial categories (e.g., black or white). They are also classified by gender and by age, as well as by such standards as education. People in the United States may move from class to class, and they may choose to emphasize or deemphasize their ethnic group membership, but generally their racial category and gender are fixed.

EXERCISE 6.1

Below is a list of personal attributes. Your task is to rank them by number from *most* to *least* important to you in judging a person's social or personal worth. No ties allowed. If there is an attribute not included in the list that you wish to add, do so.

RANK #

_____ PERSONAL APPEARANCE
_____ MONETARY INCOME
_____ GENDER
_____ AGE
_____ RELIGION
_____ ETHNIC OR COMMUNITY ORIGIN
_____ FAMILY BACKGROUND
_2_ INTELLIGENCE (as indicated in school performance)
_____ ATHLETIC ABILITY
_____ PERSONAL POSSESSIONS (clothes, car, etc.)
_3_ PERSONALITY (fill in your description of type of personality) _____

_1_ CONTRIBUTION TO COMMUNITY

In India, the population is stratified by **caste** into hundreds of different groups into which a person is born, must remain in, and may not marry outside of. In a caste system, individuals are assigned at birth to the ranked social and occupational groups of one or both of their parents. A person's place in the social order is fixed; there is no mobility from one caste to another. Castes are separated by strict rules that forbid intermarriage and regulate other forms of interaction, such as eating together, speaking to one another, or working together.

In any stratified society, people's access to jobs, wealth, and privilege is determined largely by their position in the hierarchy. The caste system in India was based on traditional roles, for example. The *Brahmins,* priests whose lives were devoted to worship and teaching, occupied the top of the caste hierarchy. Directly under them were the *Kshattriya* castes, whose members comprised the soldiers, politicians, and administrators. Next were the *Vaisya* castes, made up of farmers and merchants. At the bottom of the hierarchy were the *Sudra* castes, which were devoted to the service of other castes. The *Sudra* castes included "untouchable" or "unclean" persons whose occupations were believed to be polluting to others. Untouchables included washermen, tanners, shoemakers, and sweepers, people whose occupations required them to come into contact with animal or human wastes. While the Indian government has outlawed discrimination against untouchables, it nevertheless persists, based on caste membership.

The Feminization of Poverty

In the United States, gender and age are significant determinants of the likelihood of living in poverty. In *Women and Children Last,* Ruth Sidel draws an analogy between the doomed ship *Titanic* and American society at the end of the 1980s. Both, she says, were gleaming symbols of wealth that placed women and children at a disadvantage. When the *Titanic* went down, women and children were indeed saved first, but it was those in first-class and second-class accommodations, not the women and children in third class and steerage, who were saved. While only 8 percent of the women and 3 percent of the children traveling first and second class drowned, 45 percent of the women and 70 percent of the children in steerage died. As with the *Titanic,* Sidel says, certain women and children in the United States are not the first to be saved, they are the first to fall into poverty.

There have been dramatic changes in the role of women in the United States over the past half century. One measure is their steadily increasing participation in the work force. In 1960, only 32 percent of married women worked outside the home; in 1989, 58 percent were wage earners. Yet women in American society make up a disproportionate share of the poor. Americans are witnessing what sociologists call the feminization of poverty. According to the U.S. Bureau of the Census, in 1990 over 15 percent of all Americans had incomes at or below the amount established by the federal government as the official poverty level, and this level is set well below what is required for basic subsistence. That year the poverty level was $12,195 for a family of four, the pretax annual income for a person working full time for $6.10 an hour. Two out of every three poor adults were women, including

At the bottom of the social hierarchy in American society are those who live in poverty, including one out of every five children under the age of 12 in 1990. This homeless family now has a home of their own.

more than a quarter of all women over 65 who were not living in families. The 16 percent of all American families that were headed by females represented 53 percent of the families officially classified as living below the poverty level.

Children pay an even greater price. Living in poverty in the United States in 1990 were one out of every four preschoolers and one out of every five children under the age of 12. Nearly 40 percent of the American poor were children under 12, and over half of these were in families headed by females. In other words, it can be said that women and children make up the majority of America's poor. If, in addition, a person is Afro-American, Hispanic American, or Native American, the chances of being among America's poor are even greater. For Afro-American children, the poverty rate was almost 50 percent in 1990, and for Afro-American and Hispanic-American children in female-headed households it was over 70 percent. The greatest disadvantage in American society is to be a child or a female, and Afro-American, Hispanic American, or Native American.

There are various explanations for the unequal distribution of resources in the United States and other countries. Americans, who generally are highly individualistic, tend to believe that if people live in poverty it's their own fault, a rationale often referred to as "blaming the victim." In the case of children, most say poverty is their parents' fault. But since the surest predictor of adults' income has been found to be the income of their parents, more than individual work effort and motivation must be responsible for a person's position in the social hierarchy.

QUESTION 6.2 *Why Do Societies Construct Social Hierarchies?*

Does differentiation necessary'y equal stratification?

The construction of a social hierarchy is not a necessary feature of all human societies. Moreover, there seems to be no universal inclination to rank people by one criterion or another; in some societies skin color makes a difference, in others it doesn't. In most societies men are accorded far greater status than women, but in some there is little if any difference in gender rank. Even the use of age as a criterion of rank varies from society to society. The only general rule that seems to hold is that as societies become more complex and populous, their propensity for social stratification increases.

Integrative and Exploitative Theories of Social Hierarchy

integrative: structural functional

exploitative: conflict theory

Also: Lenski's Evolutionary theory)

There are various explanations for the existence of social hierarchies. Some claim that social stratification emerged with the origin of private property; others claim that it was created to satisfy the organizational needs of war. I will examine two explanations, the **integrative theory of social stratification,** based on the assumption that social hierarchy is necessary for the smooth functioning of modern society, and the **exploitative theory of social stratification,** in which the assumption is that hierarchy exists because one group of individuals seeks to take advantage of another group for economic purposes.

Proponents of the integrative theory of social stratification assume that as societies become more populous and there are more people to feed, house, and clothe, more labor-efficient or technologically sophisticated means are required to produce more food and other necessities, as well as to erect the necessary infrastructure. Unlike the smaller societies of hunters and gatherers and horticulturists, larger-scale societies require individuals to specialize in certain tasks or occupations, as noted in Chapter 2. This results in a **division of labor** that requires greater coordination of tasks, more efficient management, and more complex leadership systems, all of which inevitably lead to some form of social stratification. In addition, as societies become more complex, they need to organize systems of defense against other groups who may attack them, and the development of a military organization requires the centralization of power, which again leads to the emergence of an elite group. As resources become scarce, an internal policing system may also be required to keep order and prevent crime. In any case, the integrative theory of social stratification is based on the assumption that a society's need for greater integration, along with the need to assert greater controls on individual behavior, requires some form of centralized authority that offers citizens security, protection, means of settling disputes, defense against other groups, and sustenance. All these are offered in exchange for the people's acceptance of and loyalty to state authorities and officials.

In the integrative theory, society is viewed as resembling a living organism whose parts must be regulated by a controlling device if they are to function efficiently for the survival of the whole. The nineteenth-century social philosopher Herbert Spencer suggested that complex societies, like complex living organisms, exhibit greater differentiation as they evolve. With greater differentiation there follows a greater degree of interrelation among parts, which in turn requires greater control by government, management, and the military. Without control, society, like a living organism, would cease to exist.

In American society, the military is cited by integrationists as an example of the necessity for stratification. They say that without generals or commissioned officers, privates, corporals, and sergeants could not function efficiently to do their jobs, and the military would disintegrate. Industry is another example; in this view, if there were no executives to control those who do the work, corporations would collapse. The reason the !Kung require no hierarchy, integrationists might say, is because each person or family is self-sufficient, and there is no need for the coordination or control of activities. As societies become more complex and the division of labor increases, greater control is necessary. The fact that those who assume the responsibility of control are given greater rewards is simply a way of assuring that the society as a whole survives. The Indian caste system, for example, is sometimes said to perform an integrative function by providing benefits to both higher-caste landowners and lower-caste workers. Landowners get the workers they need to work their land and do not have to perform ritually polluting work, and workers are assured of economic support.

While others might agree that in complex societies it is necessary for integration to occur, they disagree that social hierarchy is required for integration. Proponents of the exploitative theory of social stratification claim that it arises when one group seeks to exploit the resources or labor of others. The exploitation might take the form of military conquest, as in the case of the Spanish conquest of South America, where thousands of indigenous people were forced to labor on farms or in mines to increase the wealth of Spanish conquerors, or it might take other forms of manipulation and control.

Karl Marx and the Origin of Class

The most influential and controversial of the exploitative theories of social stratification is that of Karl Marx and Friedrich Engels. As witnesses to the squalor of British cities during the industrial revolution of the nineteenth century, Marx and Engels concluded that landlords and factory owners (*capitalists,* in their terms) were able to use their control of resources to exploit the unlanded laborers in the newly emerging factories and mines of England. To understand how landlords and factory owners were able to exploit the masses, you have to understand the meaning of some key concepts in Marxist theory. The most important of these concepts is social class.

Social classes are an outgrowth of capitalism, not a necessary feature of modern society. According to Marx, classes arise when a group—a ruling class, landlords, bosses, and so on—gains control of the means of production. The **means of production** consist of the materials, such as land, machines, or tools, that people need to produce things. A group that controls the means of production can maintain or increase its wealth by taking advantage of the surplus value of labor.

The idea of the **surplus value of labor** works something like this: Take a product or commodity, such as bricks. Say that the labor value of bricks on the open market is $300 per 1,000 bricks; that is, people are willing to pay $300 above the cost of materials for each 1,000 bricks they purchase. If the same people both make the bricks and sell 1,000 of them for $300 plus the cost of materials, they are getting a 100 percent return on their labor. But what if the person who owns or controls the means of production for bricks hires people to make the bricks and only pays them $30 for every 1,000 bricks they make? The value of the labor to produce the bricks is still $300 per 1,000, but the laborers are getting only one-tenth ($30) of what their labor is worth, while the person who controls the means of production is getting the surplus value of labor, or the other nine-tenths of the labor value of the bricks ($270). In other words, the capitalist, the person who controls the means of production (the brickworks, in this case) is expropriating $270 worth of labor from the worker who produced the bricks.

Why would a worker labor under such conditions? The reason is political or social repression, which occurs because the ruling class, the group that controls the means of production, also makes the rules of the society. Members of this class elect or choose representatives who pass laws that serve their interests. Such laws may require people to work for the ruling class, prohibit workers from organizing into labor unions, require them to accept whatever wages they are offered, and forbid them from protesting these laws or the working conditions they produce. Because the ruling class can enforce these rules with the threat of joblessness, jail, or even death, most people allow it to exploit their labor. Moreover, the workers readily accept their situation if the ruling class also controls the distribution of information so it can create, for its own benefit, an ideology of class.

The **ideology of class** is a belief that the division of society into classes is both natural and right. According to Mark and Engels, if the ruling class controls the institutions that are responsible for determining how people view the world (institutions such as the churches, schools, and newspapers), it can promote the view that its dominance of society is in the best interests of all. The church, for example, can encourage the lower class to accept its fate because it is "God's will," or it can teach poor people that their poverty is not the fault of the ruling class but is due to their own "fall from grace." The ruling class may allow only children of its own class to go to school and at the same time make education a criterion for membership in the ruling class. Or, through its control of educational institutions and mass communications media, it can convince people who do not have an education that they are unworthy of being members of the ruling class, while it makes education so expensive that only the rich can afford it. The ruling class can use the media to popularize the view that the society would perish without it, or to promote an ideology based on the belief that if you are poor, it's your own fault. As a result of an ideology of class, the lower class comes to believe that its position in society is as it should be, and nothing can or should be done about it.

The ideology of class thus produces a society in which a few people control the means of production through the expropriation of the surplus value of labor. These people maintain their position of control through repression and the manipulation of ideology through religion, education, and the me-

TABLE 6.1   INCOME DISTRIBUTION IN THE UNITED STATES BY POPULATION
QUINTILES, 1980-1989

	Percentage of Total Income Received by Families				
Year	Lowest 20%	2nd 20%	3rd 20%	4th 20%	Highest 20%
1980	5.1	11.6	17.5	24.3	41.6
1981	5.0	11.3	17.4	24.4	41.9
1982	4.7	11.2	17.1	24.3	42.7
1983	4.7	11.1	17.1	24.3	42.8
1984	4.7	11.0	17.0	24.4	42.9
1985	4.6	10.9	16.9	24.2	43.5
1986	4.6	10.8	16.8	24.0	43.7
1987	4.6	10.8	16.9	24.1	43.7
1988	4.6	10.7	16.7	24.0	44.0
1989	4.6	10.6	16.5	23.7	44.6

1989 Income Ranges for Each Quintile:
Lowest: Under $16,003   2nd: $16,003–28,000   3rd: $28,000–40,800
4th: $40,800–59,550   Highest: Over $59,550

Source: Data from U.S. Department of Commerce, Bureau of the Census.

dia. The only way the lower class can rectify this situation, according to Marx and Engels, is **violent revolution;** because the ruling class controls the means of repression (e.g., police, militia, and the military), it won't relinquish its positions of privilege and control unless it is violently overthrown. Thus repression and poverty brought about by the existence of social classes ultimately push the lower class (the workers), in desperation, to revolt in order to regain control of the means of production and receive the surplus value of their labor.

While the application of Marxist solutions to political and economic governance in eastern Europe seems to have failed, there are two areas of Marx and Engel's theories that remain relevant today. First, the position that class structure is very resistant to change is supported by income distribution figures in the United States over the past decade. Table 6.1 shows how total income in the United States has been distributed among the total population from 1980 through 1989. For example, in 1980, the 20 percent of the population with the highest income accounted for 41.6 percent of the total income received, while the 20 percent of the population with the lowest income accounted for 5.1 percent. In 1989, the highest 20 percent took in 44.6 percent of the total income, while the lowest 20 percent took in 4.6 percent. In other words, the rich are getting richer, and the poor are getting poorer. This phenomenon did not just emerge in the 1980s; it is a trend that goes back at least to the 1950s.

A second lasting theoretical contribution of Marx and Engels lies in their ideas about the ideology of class, the notion that people in class societies come to believe that social stratification is "natural." That idea will be examined next.

American ideology holds that with hard work, dedication, and self-sacrifice, anyone can achieve the American dream—a home, a car, a good job, and a happy family life. This upper-middle-class black family has overcome some of the barriers of racial stratification.

QUESTION 6.3 *How Do People Come to Accept Social Hierarchies as Natural?*

Many people living in stratified societies accept the idea that the relative rankings in the social hierarchy have been dictated by nature or somehow are the work of the gods. Even those occupying the bottom levels of a social hierarchy may accept their positions. They have been educated and trained by experience to accept an ideology that justifies the principles of social stratification.

In the United States, for example, the ideology of class is based on the assumption that a person's position in the class hierarchy is determined largely by achievement or individual effort; that is, individuals who work hard and dedicate themselves to their work will succeed. Some Americans also assume that a person's place in the hierarchy is biologically determined. The hierarchical ordering of society thus is simply an expression of a natural law that some people are born more fit to lead and succeed. The clearest expressions of biological determinism have been in the stratification by race and gender.

Constructing the Ideology of Racism

For centuries, European and American societies have been characterized by racial stratification. The original position was that membership in certain racial or ethnic categories was enough to place people in particular positions in the status hierarchy that defined their social, political, and economic worth. In the United States, for example, position in the racial hierarchy often determined whether a person could vote, hold political office, follow one occupation or another, live in a certain area, use certain public facilities, attend certain schools, or marry a particular person. Until the second half of the twentieth century, racial stratification was written into the laws of many states.

Stratification by race and ethnicity has existed for a number of reasons. It was certainly economically profitable to people who could buy black slaves or obtain workers from among groups who were legally or socially barred from anything but low-paying jobs. It was advantageous, also, to those who did not have to compete for jobs with people who were socially or legally barred from them. But stratified societies frequently claim that the ranking of people by race and ethnicity is natural, and a social hierarchy is not socially constructed. In the case of racial stratification, some proponents claimed that it was God's will that some persons were inferior to others; others claimed that God created different races as He created different species of animals, and the Bible says the species are to be kept apart. Others claimed that members of one race or another were intellectually or morally superior to members of other races. Generally, of course, it was the race of the person making reference to God or the Bible that was somehow superior.

Most people had little trouble constructing an ideology to justify racial stratification, especially since it was reinforced by state and religious authorities. Even the supposedly objective findings of scientists assisted in building a racist ideology. In the nineteenth century, reputable scientists devoted much time and energy to proving that the racial stratification of society was "in the nature of things." Their research findings supposedly proved that members of one race (usually whites or Europeans) were intellectually superior to members of another (usually blacks or Asians).

Samuel George Morton was a respected scientist and physician who began in the 1820s to collect and measure skulls from all over the world. When he died in 1851, he left a collection of some 6,000 skulls. Like many in the nineteenth century, Morton believed that a person's intelligence is related to the size of his or her brain; the larger the brain, the more intelligent the person. Since the size of the brain could be determined by the size of the skull, he believed that a ranking of the races could be objectively achieved by a ranking of skull size.

Morton first measured the size or, more specifically, the cranial capacity, of skulls by filling them with mustard seed and then pouring the seed into a container to measure each skull's volume in cubic inches. Dissatisfied with the inconsistency of measurements obtained with mustard seed, he later used one-eighth-inch diameter lead shot. Morton concluded from his measurements that "white" skulls had a mean value of 92 cubic inches, "American Indian" skulls 79 cubic inches, and "black" skulls from America, Africa, and Australia 83 cubic inches. Among "white" skulls, the largest were those of Germans and English people, in the middle were those of Jews, and the smallest were those of Hindus. In other words, the social hierarchy of whites at the top, with the English and Germans at the top of the top, and blacks on the bottom was said to be supported by the evidence of brain size and intelligence.

Thus whites (more specifically, northern European whites) were considered to be not merely socially superior but biologically superior. Morton believed he had provided objective evidence that the distribution of status and power in nineteenth-century America accurately reflected not merely social but biological merit.

When Stephen Jay Gould, a Harvard biologist, reexamined Morton's published data in 1977, he concluded that Morton's summaries were a "patchwork of fudging and finagling" to reach conclusions that supported a socially constructed hierarchy. Gould found no evidence of conscious fraud. He concluded that Morton had simply selected or rejected certain data to ensure that the results confirmed what he and most other Americans knew: that whites were naturally more intelligent than the people they called Indian or black.

Working with the same skulls Morton had used over 150 years earlier, Gould discovered that the sample of 144 Native American skulls included proportionally more small-brained Inca skulls from Peru and fewer large-brained Iroquois skulls. This naturally produced a lower mean cranial capacity for indigenous Americans than would have occurred had Morton correctly adjusted for this discrepancy. Moreover, Gould discovered that Morton's failure to include the small-brained Hindu skulls with his "white" skulls had produced a higher average cranial capacity for whites. When Gould corrected for Morton's sample biases, he discovered that there was no difference between Euro-American and indigenous American cranial capacity. As for comparisons between "white" and "black" skulls, Gould discovered that Morton had ignored the facts that skull size is related to body size and that male skulls are larger than female skulls. Examination of Morton's black skulls indicated that the group included proportionally more female skulls and fewer male skulls. When Gould remeasured the "black" and "white" skulls, he discovered that the mean cranial capacity of black males was slightly higher than the mean for white males, while the mean for white females was just slightly higher than that of black females.

Gould does not believe that Morton consciously manipulated his skull measurements to prove that whites were intellectually superior to Native Americans or blacks. Rather, he thinks Morton simply assumed that this is what his measurements would prove and set about achieving the results he expected. For example, Gould observed that when Morton used mustard seed to measure cranial capacity, he obtained even greater differences between his "white" and "black" skulls than he obtained using lead shot. Gould concludes that because mustard seeds are smaller and lighter than lead shot, Morton, probably unconsciously, packed more mustard seed into "white" skulls. Morton's measurements were obviously in error, as was his assumption that cranial capacity reveals intelligence, and his conclusions were dictated by the socially constructed hierarchy of his day. Nevertheless, they served well into the twentieth century to support an ideology that the racial ranking of persons in a society could be justified on natural rather than social grounds.

Scientists have long rejected the idea that brain size and intelligence are related. At the beginning of the twentieth century, anthropologists, led by

Franz Boas, began to discredit the idea of any link between race and intelligence. But it took much longer to discredit attempts to justify racism with biology. After IQ tests were introduced as a standard measure of intelligence, some scientists who claimed to find consistent differences between the IQs of blacks and whites concluded that these tests provided objective evidence of the intellectual superiority of whites. In the late 1970s, for example, Arthur Jensen reported finding a mean difference of 15 points in IQ scores favoring whites over blacks. Jensen later qualified his findings as generalizations only and reported a study in which he found that on certain dimensions of intelligence, blacks generally do better than whites. A British psychologist, Cyril Burt, working about the same time was found to have invented data and falsified results to support his findings of whites' superior intelligence.

Constructing Stratification by Gender

Looking back at Morton's mismeasurements, it is easy to condemn the biases that seemed to create a scientifically supported system of stratification by race. Yet the biases that falsely linked race to biology also led to the linkage of gender stratification and biology—the belief that the superiority of men over women is not socially constructed but is "natural." Many people believed that women's bodies defined both their social position and their function, which was to reproduce, in the same way men's bodies dictated that they manage, control, and defend. At the beginning of the twentieth century, the Supreme Court of the United States ruled that women should be prohibited from jobs that might endanger their reproductive function. The Court concluded that a "woman's physical structure and the performance of maternal functions place her at a disadvantage in the struggle for subsistence. Since healthy mothers are essential to vigorous offspring, the physical well-being of women becomes an object of public interest and care in order to preserve the strength and vigor of the race."

The view that their biology makes females lesser persons than males remains embedded in American culture, sometimes in very subtle ways. One example is the language used by professionals to describe women's bodily processes of menstruation and menopause. In the nineteenth century, Americans regarded the female body as if it were a factory whose job was to "labor" to produce children. Menopause was viewed negatively because it marked the end of productive usefulness, and menstruation was described as a sign of the failure of the implantation of a fertilized egg. Medical writers of the time such as Walter Heape, a Cambridge zoologist and militant antisuffragist, described how in menstruation the entire epithelium (cellular tissue) is torn away, "leaving behind a ragged wreck of tissue, torn glands, ruptured vessels, jagged edges of stroma, and masses of blood corpuscles, which it would seem hardly possible to heal satisfactorily without the aid of surgical instruments."

An anthropologist who has studied attitudes toward females' reproductive functions, Emily Martin, says that the same attitudes persist today, encoded in contemporary medical and biology textbooks. For example, menopause is described as a breakdown of communication between the brain and the reproductive parts of the female body. One college textbook says that the ovaries become *unresponsive* to hormonal stimulation, and, as a result *re-*

gress. The hypothalamus, which controls hormone production, has gotten estrogen *addiction* from years of menstruation. Because of the *withdrawal* of estrogen at menopause, the hypothalamus gives *inappropriate* orders. Menopause is described as a breakdown of authority: functions *fail* and *falter;* organs *wither* and become *senile.* This language, as it did in the nineteenth century, depicts the female body as a machine or a control device that in menopause is no longer able to fulfill its proper goal; it can no longer produce babies. In this view, at menopause the female body becomes a broken-down factory.

Menstruation is likewise described even today as a breakdown in the reproductive process. When an egg is not implanted, the process is described in negative terms as a disintegration or shedding. Here is how Martin describes it:

> The fall in blood progesterone and estrogen "deprives" the "highly developed endometrical lining of its hormonal support," constriction of blood vessels leads to a "diminished" supply of oxygen and nutrients, and finally "disintegration starts, the entire lining begins to slough, and the menstrual flow begins." Blood vessels in the endometrium "hemorrhage" and the menstrual flow begins. . . . "the menstrual flow consists of this blood mixed with endometrial debris." The "loss" of hormonal stimulation causes "necrosis" (death of tissue). (Martin 1987:45)

Another otherwise objective text says, "When fertilization fails to occur, the endometrium is shed, and a new cycle starts. This is why it used to be taught that 'menstruation is the uterus crying for lack of a baby.' "

Menstruation is depicted as a sign of an idle factory, a failed production system, a system producing "scrap" or "waste." Note the language used in the following passage from another textbook:

> If fertilization and pregnancy do not occur, the corpus luteum *degenerates* and the levels of estrogens and progesterone *decline.* As the levels of these hormones decrease and their stimulatory effects are *withdrawn,* blood vessels of the endometrium undergo *prolonged spasms* (contractions) that reduce the blood flow to the area of the endometrium supplied by the vessels. The resulting *lack* of blood causes the tissue of the affected region to *degenerate.* After some time, the vessels relax, and allow blood to flow through them again. However, capillaries in the area have become so *weakened* that blood leaks through them. This blood and the *deteriorating* endometrial tissue are discharged from the uterus as the menstrual flow. As a new ovarian cycle begins and the level of estrogen rises, the functional layer of the endometrium undergoes repair and once again begins to proliferate. (Martin 1987:47, italics added)

Martin notes that very different language is used in the same textbooks to describe male reproductive functions. For example, the textbook from which the above description of menstruation is taken describes the production of sperm as follows:

> The mechanisms which guide the *remarkable* cellular transformation from spermatid to mature sperm remain uncertain. . . . Perhaps the most *amazing* characteristic of spermatogenesis is its *sheer magnitude:* the normal human male may manufacture several hundred million sperm per day. (Martin 1987:48, italics added)

This text, which speaks of menstruation as "failed production," does not mention that only about one of every 100 billion sperm ever makes it far enough to fertilize an egg. Moreover, other bodily processes that are similar to menstruation are not spoken of in terms of breakdown and deterioration. Seminal fluid picks up shredded cellular material as it passes through the male ducts, and the stomach lining is shed periodically. Why are these processes not described in the same negative terms as menstruation? Martin says the reason is that both men and women have stomachs, but only women have uteruses. The stomach falls on the positive side, the uterus on the negative.

Rather than describing menstruation as failed production, Martin suggests that it might be more accurate to describe it today as the successful avoidance of an egg implant. If a couple has done anything to avoid the implantation of an egg, is it still appropriate to talk of the reproductive cycle in terms of production? The following description of menstruation represents it not as a failure to reproduce but as the successful avoidance of a pregnancy:

> A drop in the formerly high levels of progesterone and estrogen creates an appropriate environment for reducing the excess layers of endometrial tissue. Constriction of capillary blood vessels causes a lower level of oxygen and nutrients and paves the way for a vigorous production of menstrual fluids. As a part of the renewal of the remaining endometrium, the capillaries begin to reopen, contributing some blood and serous fluid to the volume of endometrial material already beginning to flow. (Martin 1987:52)

Emily Martin's analysis reveals that in contemporary American society, the ideology of gender stratification remains embedded in our language and in our ideas about the bodily functions of males and females. Describing the bodily processes of women in negative terms makes women seem to be lesser human beings. Moreover, negative descriptions of menstruation and menopause may lead some women themselves to believe that their bodily functions are less clean and less worthy than those of men.

QUESTION 6.4 *How Do People Living in Poverty Adapt to Their Condition?*

The position in a social hierarchy occupied by each person is like a window through which she or he sees the world; different windows, different worlds. The term **culture of poverty** was coined by Oscar Lewis to describe the lifestyle and worldview of people who inhabit urban and rural slums. Other anthropologists object to that term, since it implies that poverty is somehow rooted in the subcultural values that the poor pass on from one generation to another, rather than in the social and cultural values of the larger society. The implication is that if it weren't for the culture of poverty, the poor would have no culture at all. Challenging that view, these anthropologists maintain that the behavior of people in poverty represents their adaptations to their socioeconomic condition—no money and no jobs. These conditions are the result of inequality, usually reinforced by racism and buttressed by an economic system that requires a source of cheap labor. Moreover, descriptions of poor families as broken, fatherless, or female-centered are misleading. Many of the behaviors of the poor that are viewed negatively by the dominant society are actually resilient responses to the socioeconomic conditions of those living in poverty.

Kinship as an Adaptation to Poverty

One of the classic studies of how families cope with poverty was conducted by Carol B. Stack in the late 1960s. She worked closely with a predominantly black community she called The Flats, a section of a small, midwestern city of some 55,000 people. Unemployment in The Flats was over 20 percent, and 63 percent of the jobs held were in low-paying service occupations such as maids, cooks, and janitors. While only 10 percent of whites in the city lived in housing classed as deteriorating, 26 percent of blacks did. Moreover, blacks had inadequate access to health care, and their infant mortality rate was twice that of whites.

Stack's interest was in how the residents responded to their impoverished conditions. She discovered that they fostered kinship ties and created fictive kinship links to form close, interlocking, cooperative groups in order to ensure economic and social support in times of need. Few people earned enough to provide them or their families with enough to eat or a place to stay on a regular basis; even welfare payments could not always guarantee food and shelter for a family. Accordingly, people in The Flats regularly "swapped" food, shelter, child care, and personal possessions. In this respect the community resembled societies like the !Kung, in which a person shares with others but expects them to reciprocate at some later time. Anthropologists call this type of sharing **generalized reciprocity,** as distinguished from **balanced reciprocity,** in which items are exchanged on the spot; direct trade would be an example. **Negative reciprocity** is an attempt to get something for nothing or to make a profit. The advantage of generalized reciprocity is that widespread sharing ensures that nobody lacks the basic needs for survival. People in The Flats cultivated diffuse kinship and friendship relations by giving when they could, so that others would give to them when they were in need. These networks were often framed in a kinship idiom, even though no biological kin tie existed.

Another adaptation to poverty in The Flats involved child care. Given the unpredictability of employment, the sometimes young age at which women had children, and the need to respond to unpredictable living conditions and substandard housing, a child might reside with three or four different adults. Often different people performed the roles of provider, discipliner, trainer, curer, and groomer. Stack points out that those who provided child care did so because they considered it a privilege as well as a responsibility. Children were valued, but they were considered the responsibility of a wide network of kin and friends.

Male and female relations were most affected by the difficulty men had in finding steady employment. Generally a couple would not marry unless the man had a steady job. Men in The Flats had accepted the mainstream American model of the male provider, and their inability to find regular employment prevented their assumption of that role. Moreover, marriage removed people from the widespread sharing network, since on marriage their major obligations belonged to their husbands or wives. Because women were cut off the welfare rolls if they married, kinship networks and welfare benefits offered them more security than a husband could. Nevertheless, men and

A poor urban neighborhood in New York City is the setting for a busy social life which may also provide some residents with a way to supplement their incomes. Anthropologists have studied the strategies used by people living in poverty to adapt to their condition.

women in The Flats did form intimate relationships, out of which children were born. The fathers took considerable pride in their children, as did the paternal grandparents, to whom the children often went for help. Many of the mothers regarded the fathers as friends to be called on as needed, rather then as fathers who had failed to fulfill their parental obligations. Thus the conditions of poverty drew people into kinship and friendship networks, rather than the nuclear family patterns valued by the larger society.

Making Ends Meet on the Lower East Side

Another way poor people adapt to their situations is by developing their own economic strategies. An example is provided by Jagna Wojcicka Sharff's study of how Hispanic Americans on the Lower East Side of Manhattan compensated for their inadequate income in the late 1970s. Her first impression of the neighborhood in which she conducted her study was dominated by the numerous children playing on the sidewalks, riding skateboards or broken bicycles, or hitching rides on the bumpers of passing cars and buses. The area seemed rich in social life, with clusters of young men on street corners and women talking together and watching their children from stoops and windows. However, Sharff soon realized that the street-corner gatherings of young men were more than social gatherings; the little corner cigarette store was not only selling tobacco; the nearby storefront was not just the home of a popular bachelor with lots of friends; and the mechanic was doing more than simply repairing cars. And the children were not simply playing. After months of working in the community she discovered that almost every man, woman, and older child in it was working to earn income for a household through legal or illegal means.

These activities served as the basis for an underground economy built around self-employment, manipulation—sometimes illegal—of public assistance, or enterprises defined as illegal by the larger society. To understand how this underground economy worked, Sharff and her colleagues closely studied 36 neighborhood households that included 133 people. Sixty-one of the individuals (18 of whom were under the age of 17) reported receiving incomes of from $5 to $300 weekly from "regular" jobs such as police guard, hospital aide, and community worker. Others were self-employed; three people, for example, said they were "dog breeders," selling stud services or puppies from purebred dogs they purchased or stole. One person was a paid advocate who accompanied recent immigrants to institutional settings such as courts, police agencies, or welfare agencies to translate and offer support. Another man earned money as an "extra" in police lineups, and one woman worked as a street vendor, buying clothes at wholesale and selling them door to door.

However, the underground economy provided neither enough regular jobs nor sufficient opportunities for people to earn money on their own. Two-thirds of the households, consisting almost entirely of women and children, required some form of public assistance, but what was provided was inadequate to satisfy their basic needs. In the late 1970s in New York City, a family of four received an average of $346 each month in public assistance and food stamps to cover food, gas, electricity, telephone, clothing, transportation, furnishings, cleaning materials, personal care, school supplies, and miscellaneous items. According to the Consumer Price Index for New York City during the same period, however, a family of four required $352 for food alone. Rent was paid by public assistance, but because of a shortage of low-cost housing, people often had to move in with others or to pay more than the maximum allowed by public assistance and make up the difference from their food budgets. Sharff's study found that 51 percent of the help provided through public assistance, rent allotment, and food stamps went for food and 36 percent for rent, leaving 13 percent for all other necessities. The question for the people of the Lower East Side was how to acquire the money needed to provide for their basic subsistence.

The residents used a number of strategies to close the gap between the income they needed and what they could receive through regular means. Sometimes they pooled resources and shared living space, but they also relied on "irregular" sources of income that would be defined by the larger society as criminal or fraudulent. Generally, however, these sources were not so defined by the residents of the Lower East Side. Too many people engaged in irregular practices for the residents to see them as criminal, and were it not for these methods, many families would have been destitute. The most common means of closing the income gap with irregular sources included lying to public assistance authorities about living arrangements, stealing, gambling, and selling drugs.

Since any reported income of household members was deducted from social service payments, most households reported that there were no male household heads, although 62 percent of the "female-headed" households included males who performed the husband/father role in relationships recognized by members of the community as common-law marriages. They justified the failure to report resident males or their income as being "for the children." Another strategy was for women to find part-time work using stolen Social Security cards purchased for $25, so their income would not be reported and deducted from their public assistance payments. Women also found work in service industries in which employers allowed them to work "off the books." For the women, this meant their wages would not be reported, and for the employers it meant that they did not need to pay social security taxes or other benefits, and they could pay lower than the minimum wage.

Another irregular means of generating income was through petty theft, or "geesing," mostly by young adolescents. This generally took the form of group shoplifting, usually for clothes. Geesing activities began to increase around August just before the beginning of the school year, when youngsters began to worry about getting the clothing they believed was required for high school. Sharff says it was not uncommon to see parties of three to five boys setting out on a raid and returning a few hours later with trousers, socks, and shirts. As winter approached, the boys would take bigger risks to get jackets and other winter clothes and often could end up in jail.

Some people earned money by working *bolita,* the illegal numbers lottery controlled by racketeers outside the neighborhood, who skim off most of the profits. Neighborhood residents worked as collectors, managers, and cashiers. The lottery is simple; the bettor chooses a three-digit number, and the winning number is based on some random combination derived from the finish of horses in a specific race. The bets are small, 25 cents to $1, and payoffs are significant, $150 for a 25-cent bet and $600 for $1. In some ways, *bolita* serves as a banking system for the poor; players invest a small amount each week, and if they hit a number, as most do eventually, they receive a lump sum in return. Since public assistance recipients are not allowed to have bank accounts, numbers betting represents for many their best chance of acquiring a significant sum of money at one time.

Drug sales were another way of supplementing household income for the East Side residents Sharff studied. The drug trade is also controlled by people outside the community; residents worked in low-level, high-risk retail distribution jobs. For example, there was what the researchers called the "drug-o-matic," a hole in an apartment house door through which buyers would pass money and receive drugs. Anywhere from 150 to 300 people each day, many of them well-dressed outsiders, used the device. Street vendors and small stores sold marijuana cigarettes, and other irregular activities included buying and selling stolen goods, mugging, and robbery.

In the 36 households studied by Sharff and her colleagues, most of the irregular income was generated by young men. Sixty-seven irregular jobs were performed by the residents, more than half by males under the age of 21. The high-risk nature of these jobs is revealed in the high rates of violent death among young men. During the period 1976–1979, there were 11 violent deaths of young people aged 19–30 among members of the 36 households studied.

Sharff also discovered that children played a critical role in the economic life of the residents of the Lower East Side in the 1970s. They were not only sources of income from public assistance for the families studied, they generated income through their own irregular activities. The Hispanic-American families were large; for example, the average number of children for women over 35 in the households studied was 4.38, as compared to an overall average for New York City of 2.4 children. Child-rearing patterns generally reflected the economic and social roles of the children; most male children were trained to be macho men, while girls were trained to be gentle and competent mothers. However, the researchers found that about a quarter of the children were encouraged to develop nontraditional skills and attributes. Some girls were trained to be strong and militant, and some boys to be gentle and passive.

The children were directed to specific household roles, which Sharff labeled street representative, young child reproducer, scholar/advocate, and wage earner. The street representative was a macho man whose job was to protect his mother, brothers, and sisters. The young child reproducer, a girl, brought in additional assistance money and assisted with the housework. Because of the high death rate of young men, the young reproducer could also provide replacements for lost members of the household. One 14-year-old who gave birth to a son within a year of her older brother's death named the child after her brother. Gentle boys and strong girls were also productive. Freed from traditional roles, the boys did not have to prove their manliness by taking risks, and the girls were not trapped into premature reproduction. Both girls and boys might be subsidized by the household to complete their educations and eventually help support it. However, this was only possible at the expense of the street representatives, who usually dropped out of school at 16 or 17, and the child reproducers, who dropped out even earlier, at 14 or 15. It was from the ranks of the wage earners or scholars/advocates that occasional upward mobility was possible through good jobs or marriage into middle-class families. Children therefore were essential for the present functioning of the household as well as for its future benefit. Moreover, since Hispanics have a strong family ethic, they generally do not resort to homes for the elderly, so children represent insurance for aging parents.

The studies by Carol Stack in The Flats of a midwestern city and by Jagna Sharff of the Lower East Side of Manhattan provide convincing evidence that people do not passively accept their position at the bottom of a stratified society; rather, like people in other environments and economic conditions, they adapt to their poverty as best they can. Moreover, they have the same social and economic aspirations as people higher up in the social hierarchy who have greater income and opportunity. While Stack, like others, emphasizes this, she concludes that

...those living in poverty have little or no chance to escape from the economic situation into which they were born. Nor do they have the power to control the expansion or contraction of welfare benefits or of employment opportunities, both of which have enormous effect on their daily lives. In times of need, the only predictable resources that can be drawn upon are their own children and parents, and the fund of kin and friends obligated to them. (Stack 1974:107)

QUESTION 6.5 *Can a Nonstratified Community Exist within a Larger Society?*

Many people who are convinced of the harmful effects of social stratification believe nevertheless that in a modern, industrial society, the system is inevitable. It may be possible for the Inuit or !Kung to have a relatively egalitarian society, for example, but it is not possible in a modern industrial state. Yet for thousands of years there have been attempts by some groups in stratified societies to create classless, egalitarian, utopian social settings. Christianity began as a utopian dream of universal equality, and the ideal of a real-life utopia emerged with the idea that man, under God, has the power to create an earthly paradise. Among the earliest expressions of this idea was Christian communalism, which led to the founding of Catholic monastic orders—isolated, virtually self-sufficient communities in which the work was collective and egalitarian. In the nineteenth century, industrialists such as Robert Owen attempted to build utopian factory communities, and Karl Marx's goal also was to build a national utopian society. In the middle of the twentieth century, psychologist B. F. Skinner outlined a utopian society based on scientific technology in *Walden Two,* a controversial novel that inspired an attempt to translate his fiction into a real-life utopia at Twin Oaks in Virginia. All of these attempts to construct utopian societies are evidence of the long history of the search for an egalitarian social order.

EXERCISE 6.2

Imagine for a moment that you have just been hired by NASA to plan the development of the first human extraterrestrial settlement. They want you to use your knowledge of other societies to build an ideal community, avoiding the problems of modern society. How would you go about the task? For example, what communities or societies that you know about might you choose as models for extraterrestrial settlements? What would be the main values that you would build into your community? How would people be rewarded for the work they performed? How would you maintain order and settle conflicts? What kind of educational system would you propose? Finally, what are the most serious problems in modern society that you would want to avoid?

Charles Erasmus examined hundreds of utopian communities in an effort to discover why most failed but some succeeded. He concluded that the main problem for these communities is trying to motivate community members to work and contribute to the common good without the promise of individual material rewards, status, or prestige. Of the successful utopian communities in this country, the most notable are those of the Hutterites, a Protestant sect that originated in Moravia in the sixteenth century. Why did the Hutterites succeed while so many others fail? Is it possible to use communities such as theirs as models for modern communities?

The Hutterites and the Colony of Heaven

"If there will ever be a perfect culture it may not be exactly like the Hutterites—but it will be similar." These words of a member of a Hutterite colony express the feeling that the group has succeeded in building utopian communities. In fact, the Hutterite colonies are among the most successful products of the Christian communal movement, which includes the Mennonites and the more familiar Amish.

The Hutterites originated during the Protestant Reformation. In 1528 they began to establish colonies throughout what are now Germany, Austria, and Russia. Their pacifism and refusal to perform military service brought them into conflict with European governments, and in 1872, to avoid conscription, they fled to South Dakota and established colonies. During World War I, a confrontation over military conscription with U.S. state and federal authorities resulted in a Hutterite move to Canada. But their successful agricultural techniques were valued in the United States during the Great Depression of the 1930s, and they were convinced to return and establish new colonies here. In the early 1970s there were over 37,000 Hutterites distributed among 360 colonies in the United States and over 9,000 in 246 congregations in Canada.

The goal of the Hutterites is to create a "colony of heaven." Drawing their inspiration from the Old and New Testaments, the Hutterites believe in the need for communal living and the proper observance of religious practice. They reject competition, violence, and war and believe that property is to be used and not possessed. They respect the need for government but do not believe they should involve themselves in it or hold public office. A Hutterite colony is governed by an elected board that includes the religious leaders and the community teacher, so authority is group-centered. It is a family-based, agricultural community in which everyone is expected to contribute to the work and to share equally in the bounty. Unlike the Amish, whose beliefs they in essence share, the Hutterites accept and use modern technology; they are acknowledged to be among the most successful agriculturists in North America.

The Hutterites are not totally egalitarian. Their society is ranked by age and gender: Members do not participate in the decision-making process until they are married, and women are considered intellectually and physically inferior to men. But the Hutterites reject the unequal distribution of wealth, as well as competition among members for status, prestige, or personal possessions. They minimize competition by renouncing ostentatious displays of wealth and by practicing collective consumption. There is little difference in dress, and adornment is usually frowned on. All the housing is plain and utilitarian. And, as in most Christian communes, they are careful to indoctrinate their children against competition. Children are taught to avoid seeking honors or placing themselves above others. They are taught never to envy others.

One way the Hutterites build commitment to the group is through frequent face-to-face interaction. Members eat together in a communal dining hall, work together, and meet frequently to discuss the affairs of the community. Almost every evening the entire community gathers for evening church service. While the Hutterites have no formal means of punishing those who violate group rules, they do practice a form of ostracism called *den Frieden nehmen,* "taking away the individual's peace of mind." An ostracized man is not allowed to talk to other members, including his own wife. He may also be assigned a separate room in which to sleep and may be required to eat alone.

In addition, the practice of "branching," or community division, functions not only to adjust community size, reduce friction, and settle other colonies but also to build internal commitment and reduce competition. Erasmus points out that social movements have difficulty maintaining long-range goals, especially as wealth accumulates. The Hutterites address this problem by dividing the communities, or branching, every 15 years. During this period, each community saves a portion of its earnings to purchase additional land, build houses and barns, and accumulate necessary machines and livestock to start a new colony. When the new physical facilities are complete, members of the community draw lots to determine which families will relocate. Branching provides each Hutterite community with a tangible goal. More "wealthy" colonies that delay branching are often disrupted by internal quarrels and become examples of the danger of failing to branch on schedule. Branching also has a built-in renewal factor; new communities reproduce the founding enthusiasm and ideals. If there is competition, it is between colonies, not individuals.

The Hutterites have resisted specialization, unlike other movements that have become more like industries producing goods such as silverware in the Oneida community in New York and furniture and woolens in the Amana Society colonies in Iowa. The Hutterites have also resisted hiring outside labor; instead they exchange labor among colonies and use technology to further agricultural production.

In sum, the Hutterites, by a collective effort, have created within the larger society a community without poverty, without economic classes, and with little or no crime, in which each person contributes to the common good without the promise of material reward. There are, however, some negatives. The Hutterites are a Bible-based religious community that teaches male supremacy and severely limits individual freedom. The question is whether such negatives outweigh the benefits of creating nonstratified communities. There is also the question of whether cooperative communities can serve as a model for the poor who are a part of the larger society. That is, does the establishment of closed, collective communities offer a solution to the endemic poverty of those at the bottom level of modern society, and does the success of the Hutterites suggest that it is within our means to build societies without poverty?

Conclusions

The problem underlying this chapter is why extremes of poverty and wealth exist in modern societies. The criteria customarily used to rank people in social hierarchies include wealth or income, occupation, ethnic group membership, personal appearance, race, gender, and age. The consequences of such ranking, especially in the creation of poverty and the gap between the rich and the poor, have raised some of the most challenging problems in modern societies.

There are two theories of social stratification that offer different explanations of why societies construct social hierarchies. In the integrative theory, it is assumed that stratification exists because of the need of a society to integrate the activities of its members and to ensure its smooth functioning. In the exploitative theory, it is assumed that stratification is due to the political dominance of one group over another for the exploitation of labor and resources.

People come to accept social hierarchies as natural because they believe that hierarchy is a biological principle. Some people are thought to be naturally more or less intelligent than others or otherwise more or less worthy. Females' biological functions, for example, have been described in terms that make women seem less worthy than men.

People at the lowest level of the social hierarchy, those who live in poverty, adapt to their conditions in various ways. Blacks in The Flats of a midwestern city adapted by building kinship ties, and Hispanic Americans in the Lower East Side of New York City adapted by building an underground economic system.

A few groups have demonstrated that it is possible to build egalitarian, nonstratified communities within a large industrial society. Perhaps the most successful in the United States has been the Hutterites, a religious group that emphasizes communal ownership of property and equal distribution of production, while rejecting competition, violence, and war.

References and Suggested Readings

INTRODUCTION: THE RATIONALE FOR SOCIAL INEQUALITY The epigraph comes from Robert Hertz, *Death and the Right Hand,* translated and edited by Claudia and Rodney Needham (Free Press, 1960). The quote by Thomas Belmonte is from *The Broken Fountain* (Columbia University Press, 1989).

HOW DO SOCIETIES RANK PEOPLE IN SOCIAL HIERARCHIES? One of the classic works on social hierarchy, especially as it relates to India's caste system, is Louis Dumont's *Homo Hierarchicus: An Essay on the Caste System*

(University of Chicago Press, 1970). Pierre L. van den Berghe and his associates produced a series of books on class and ethnicity in Europe, Africa, and South America. These include *Inequality in the Peruvian Andes: Class and Ethnicity in Cuzco*, with George P. Primov (University of Missouri Press, 1977); *South Africa: A Study in Conflict* (Wesleyan University Press, 1965); and *Race and Ethnicity* (Basic Books, 1970). A review of anthropological studies of social class is Raymond T. Smith's article, "Anthropology and the Concept of Social Class," in *Annual Review of Anthropology*, vol. 13 (1984), pp. 467–494. Ruth Sidel's analogy of the sinking of the *Titanic* and American society is in *Women and Children Last: Social Stratification in America* (Vantage, 1986). Statistics on poverty can be found in *Poverty in the United States: 1990*, U.S. Department of Commerce, Bureau of the Census, *Current Population Reports*, Series P–60, No. 175 (August 1991) and in the yearly editions of the *Statistical Abstract of the United States*, also issued by the Bureau of the Census. An excellent review of the literature on women's status is "Anthropological Studies of Women's Status Revisited, 1977–1987," by Carol C. Mukhopadhyay and Patricia J. Higgins, in *Annual Review of Anthropology*, vol. 17 (1988), pp. 461–495.

WHY DO SOCIETIES CONSTRUCT SOCIAL HIERARCHIES? For excerpts from Herbert Spencer's organic view of society, see Talcott Parsons et al., *Theories of Society*, vol. I (Free Press, 1961). Morton H. Fried explores some of the reasons for social stratification in *The Evolution of Political Society* (Random House, 1967).

HOW DO PEOPLE COME TO ACCEPT SOCIAL HIERARCHIES AS NATURAL? Stephen Jay Gould's examination of Morton's experiments on cranial capacity and intelligence is described in *The Mismeasure of Man* (W. W. Norton, 1981). An evaluation of the literature on differences in IQ scores, contrasting the hereditarian and environmentalist positions, is in John F. Longres, *Human Behavior in the Social Environment* (F. E. Peacock Publishers, 1990). Emily Martin's work on the social construction of female biology is represented by *The Woman in the Body: A Cultural Analysis of Reproduction* (Beacon Press, 1987). Hertz's analysis of the symbolic use of the human body to justify hierarchy can be found in *Death and the Right Hand* (cited above). A review of the ways in which reproductive biology affects the role of women is given in "The Politics of Reproduction," by Faye Ginsburg and Rayna Rapp, in *Annual Review of Anthropology*, vol. 20 (1991), pp. 311–343.

HOW DO PEOPLE LIVING IN POVERTY ADAPT TO THEIR CONDITION? Oscar Lewis's pioneering work on the lives of people in poverty is represented by *Five Families: Mexican Case Studies in the Culture of Poverty* (Basic Books, 1959). A critique of the culture-of-poverty concept can be found in Charles A. Valentine's work, *Culture and Poverty: Critique and Counter Proposals* (University of Chicago Press, 1968). Carol Stack's report of her The Flats study appears in *All Our Kin: Strategies for Survival in a Black Community* (Harper & Row, 1974). The research on how Hispanic Americans on the Lower East Side of Manhattan adapted to their socioeconomic situation is reported in the article by Jagna Wojcicka Sharff, "The Underground Economy of a Poor Neighborhood," in *Cities of the United States: Studies in Urban Anthropology*, edited by Leith Mullings (Columbia University Press, 1987).

CAN A NONSTRATIFIED COMMUNITY EXIST WITHIN A LARGER SOCIETY? The examination of attempts to build egalitarian societies is based primarily on Charles Erasmus, *In Search of the Common Good* (Free Press, 1977). The description of the Hutterites relies on John Hostetler's study, *Hutterite Society* (Johns Hopkins University Press, 1974). For additional work see Robert Moos and Robert Brownstein, *Environment and Utopia* (Plenum Press, 1977) and Kathleen Kinkade, *A Walden Two Experiment: The First Five Years of Twin Oaks Community* (William Morrow, 1973).

THE SOCIAL CONSTRUCTION OF VIOLENT CONFLICT

PROBLEM 7: HOW DO SOCIETIES GIVE MEANING TO AND JUSTIFY COLLECTIVE VIOLENCE?

Rosa had her breasts cut off. Then they cut into her chest and took out her heart. The men had their arms broken, their testicles cut off, and their eyes poked out. They were killed by slitting their throats, and pulling the tongue out through the slit.

Witness to the soldiers' attack (1984)

INTRODUCTION: *The Problem of Violent Conflict*

When the Spaniards invaded the New World in the sixteenth century, they met fierce resistance from the Carib. A warlike people, the Carib inhabited the northeast portion of South America around what is now Venezuela and Guyana. The neighbors of the Carib recognized their ferocity by calling them "sons of the tiger's teeth." And the Carib were cannibals. To prepare for war, a Carib chief would hold a feast at which women urged the dancing warriors to be fierce and avenge their dead. The dancing was intended to encourage the tiger spirit, *Kaikusi-yuma,* to take possession of the warriors, and when they went to war, it was the spirit of *Kaikusi-yuma* that killed, not them. A warrior could rid himself of the possession only after tasting the blood and flesh of a dead enemy.

From our perspective, the acts of the invading Spanish, like the acts of the Carib, were horrific. The Spanish invaders murdered and enslaved thousands of indigenous people, and the Carib devoured human flesh. But both the Europeans and the Carib considered their acts to be moral and proper; the Spaniards justified their killing and enslavement as the work of God, and the Carib defined their killing as the act of an animal possessing a human body. Both peoples constructed meanings for their acts that distanced them from the consequences of their violence. While we may condemn these acts, we live in a world in which governments construct systems of meaning that allow them to plan and contemplate the use of weapons that are much more deadly than the clubs, spears, crossbows, and primitive firearms of the Carib and Spaniards—weapons that would incinerate millions.

Purposeful, organized, and socially sanctioned combat involving killing, what most people call war or feud, seems to be an intrinsic feature of human societies. In fact, it is difficult to find societies that do not sanction violence for one reason or another. But why is collective violence so universally sanctioned? Some suggest that human beings have an innate instinct toward aggression, and the roots of war and collective violence lie somewhere in the biological mechanisms that animals and humans have in common. Violent conflict is regarded as a part of human nature. Others reject this explanation as simplistic; collective violence, they say, is above all a social construction whose roots are in the human mind, not in the genes. While there may be some innate aggressive impulse, only human beings are said to have the ability to choose whether or not to give meaningful form to that impulse.

The fact that human beings construct systems of meaning to justify violent conflict and to distance themselves from its consequences suggest that it has little to do with a natural aggressive impulse. Acts of collective violence, such as that described in the epigraph, are rationalized as purposeful, noble, or inevitable, not as evidence of wanton cruelty. The problem is to discover how societies construct meanings for violent conflict that mask its consequences and convince people that it is right and proper.

To evaluate this issue, the first question to be addressed is how societies create a bias in favor of collective violence. That is, what kinds of meanings are constructed to encourage people to commit violence against others? Then, if there are societies without collective violence, how do they create a bias against it? If violent conflict is not simply natural and inevitable but is socially constructed, it may be possible to learn from societies in which there is little if any violence. The question is, are there significant social, economic, or political differences between violent and peaceful societies? Next, the effects of violent conflict on societies can be examined to determine whether, as some maintain, engaging collectively in deadly quarrels may in the long run serve some useful purpose. Finally, since collective violence is sanctioned in American society, it is instructive to ask how we have created a bias toward violent conflict and constructed meanings that allow us to contemplate, plan for, and pursue the destruction of millions of peoples of other nations.

QUESTIONS

7.1   How do societies create a bias in favor of collective violence?
7.2   How do societies create a bias against violent conflict?
7.3   What are the economic, political, or social differences between peaceful and violent societies?
7.4   What are the effects of war on society?
7.5   How is the American bias toward collective violence created?

QUESTION 7.1 *How Do Societies Create a Bias in Favor of Collective Violence?*

One way societies create a bias toward collective violence is to reward it. Among the Native Americans of the Great Plains, for example, horses symbolized wealth, and in many groups a man's importance was measured by the number of horses he owned and gave to others as gifts. Native Americans captured some of the horses brought to North America by the Spaniards in the 1500s and acquired others in trade. Eventually, raiding other Native American groups for horses became a principal means for gaining wealth and status.

Horses, Warfare, and Rank among the Kiowa

The Kiowa, one of the most wide-ranging of the Plains Indians, obtained many of their horses by attacking other Native American groups with raiding parties of from 6 to 10 and occasionally as many as 30 men. The object of the raid was not only to secure as many of the enemy's horses as possible but also to demonstrate bravery. Among the Kiowa, rank was determined in two ways:

TABLE 7.1   KIOWA RANKING AND HONORS

Group I	Group II	Group III
1. Counting first coup	1. Killing an enemy	1. Dismounting, turning horse loose and fighting on foot
2. Charging an enemy while the party is in retreat, thus covering the retreat	2. Counting second coup	
	3. Receiving a wound in hand-to-hand combat	2. Counting third and fourth coup
3. Rescuing a comrade while the party is retreating before the enemy		3. Serving as raid leader
		4. Success in stealing horses
4. Charging the leading man of the enemy alone before the parties have met		5. Efficiency in war camp life

Source: Information from Bernard Mishkin, *Rank and Warfare among the Plains Indians* (Seattle: University of Washington Press, 1940).

by the number of horses a man possessed and by the honors accruing to him in warfare.

Kiowa society was divided into four ranks or grades. In the top rank were *ongop,* men who were generous, owned considerable wealth, and, most important, had distinguished themselves in war. In the second rank were *onde-igupa,* men who had property, especially horses, and were generous but had not yet distinguished themselves in war. The lower ranks of Kiowa society were occupied by *keen* or *dupom,* people who were poor, propertyless, or helpless.

To rise in status, a young Kiowa male needed to acquire a horse. Often he would begin his climb through the ranks of Kiowa society by borrowing a horse from a kinsperson to go on a raid, hoping to repay the loan with another horse he captured. With a horse of his own, he could participate in more raids, gradually obtaining enough horses to rise to the rank of *ondeig-upa,* or, as the Kiowa put it, "rise out of the bush of *keen.*" Several years of raiding might bring him 20 to 30 horses, at which point people would begin speaking of him with respect. To rise to the top rank of *ongop,* however, also required the accumulation of honors won in war. The Kiowa had a very elaborate system of battle honors divided into three groups of brave deeds, with Group I being the most honorific (see Table 7.1). The number of feathers a man wore in his headdress was a measure of his heroic exploits.

Bernard Mishkin estimates that approximately 10 percent of the men would rise to the top rank of Kiowa society by obtaining a significant number of horses and accumulating sufficient battle honors. In this way, the Kiowa rewarded aggressive behavior and bravery in battle.

Good Hosts among the Yanomamo

Another way societies create a bias in favor of collective violence is to make it necessary as a way of protecting valuable resources. A classic example is the Yanomamo of Venezuela. They live in villages of from 40 to 250 people and practice slash-and-burn (swidden) agriculture, subsisting primarily on the crops they grow in their gardens.

Intervillage warfare is endemic to the Yanomamo. Napoleon Chagnon, who has worked with the Yanomamo since 1964, reports that one village of 200 people was attacked 25 times and ten people were killed during a period of 15 months. The deaths represent a loss of 5 percent of the village population. Chagnon estimates that some 20 to 25 percent of all male deaths are the result of warfare.

For the Yanomamo, women and children are valuable resources. The men believe that to protect themselves and these resources, they must be fierce, and raiding another village is one way they demonstrate their ferocity. Raids may be conducted to avenge the death of a village member at the hands of an enemy village or as the result of an act of sorcery by an enemy. Raids may also be made to capture women or children; violence may take the form of inviting members of another village to a feast and, usually with the aid of allies from another village, killing the guests and abducting their women. Raiding by other villages also forces the Yanomamo to move fairly frequently and sometimes to take refuge from their enemies in the villages of their allies. This is risky, however, because host villages generally expect sexual access to the wives of their guests or expect unmarried female guests to marry men of their village. These expectations often lead to open hostilities between hosts and guests.

Expressions of hostility may be directed among village members as well. For example, men often vent anger and demonstrate their ferocity to others by beating their wives. A man who accuses another of cowardice or makes excessive demands for goods or women may challenge his opponent to a chest-pounding duel. The opponents take turns hitting each other in the chest as hard as they can, and the duel generally ends when one of them is too injured to continue. Fights with clubs are another form of settling disputes between two men, but they generally result in free-for-alls and occasionally are deadly.

This environment, in which each man strives to acquire females from others, encourages the adoption of an antagonistic stance toward others, the development of what the Yanomamo call *waiteri* (ferocity). The *waiteri complex,* as Chagnon calls it, is evidenced in ways other than direct conflict. The Yanomamo express it in their origin myth, which tells how the original people were created from the blood of the moon, which had been shot with an arrow by beings who believed that the moon was devouring their children's souls. The first Yanomamo born of the blood of the moon were exceptionally fierce and waged constant war on one another.

The Yanomamo also socialize male children to be aggressive and hostile. Boys are teased to strike tormentors and to bully girls. At one gathering of two villages attended by Chagnon, men were to satisfy their grievances against each other with a chest-pounding duel. Prior to the duel the men gathered all the boys between the ages of 8 and 15 and forced them to fight one another.

At first, says Chagnon, the boys were reluctant and tried to run away, but their parents dragged them back and insisted that they hit other boys. At the first blows the boys cried, but as the fight progressed, fear became rage, and they ended up pounding each other while they screamed and rolled in the dirt, to the cheers and admiration of their fathers.

Defending Honor in Kohistan

Other societies create a bias toward collective violence by making it part of a religious code of honor. Among the Kohistani in the mountains of northwest Pakistan, villagers follow a code that demands vengeance against any threat to a man's honor. When Lincoln Keiser worked in the village of Thull in 1984, defense of honor continually led to relationships of *dushmani,* or blood feud. The men of Thull view each other with guarded suspicion, and relationships of friendship can easily slip into *dushmani.* They believe that if another person wrongs them, they must retaliate, but the act of revenge should not exceed the original wrong. However, any unwarranted behavior toward a man's daughter, wife, or unmarried sister requires deadly retaliation. Even staring at these female relatives can mean death for the offender.

One of Keiser's friends related how a neighbor killed his brother Omar while he was bringing a basket of food to the neighbor's family, who Omar had heard had nothing to eat. "But why," asked Keiser, "would a man kill his neighbor who only tried to help him?" "Who knows?" the friend said, "But I will take vengeance." Keiser says he has no doubt he would. Looking into the incident, Keiser heard gossip that Omar was killed because he really went to the house to stare at his neighbor's wife and brought the food only as a trick. Keiser himself was ultimately forced to leave Thull because of a rumor that in taking a photograph of a goatherd he was actually trying to photograph the herd owner's wife.

The people of Thull are mostly farmers and herders. As followers of Islam, a religion that emphasizes peace and harmony, they have constructed a system of meaning in which taking vengeance is considered a religious act. Central to the beliefs of the people of Thull is the idea of *ghrairat,* a man's personal worth, integrity, or character. *Ghrairat* is given to men by God and can be lost only if they fail to protect it. Women's behavior is also a matter of *ghrairat* because men must control their women; any act of a woman, or a person toward a woman, that threatens to bring shame is a direct attack on the man's *ghrairat* and must be avenged. Women must never walk outside their father's or husband's house without an escort, must never speak to an unrelated man, and must always comport themselves with modesty, hiding and minimizing their sexuality. Men who allow their women freedom are *baghrairatman,* "men without personal integrity."

Defending *ghrairat,* however, is more than simply the concern of an individual. Because of the webs of kinship, friendship, and political ties, it often involves whole groups within the community in violence against one another. Men in Thull constantly ally themselves with others in groups that may be based on kinship or may represent political factions. A man seeking vengeance for a wrong may enlist the help of others with whom he is allied.

More important, an act of vengeance may be taken not only against the man who committed the wrong but also against a kinsperson or a member of his faction.

One example reported by Keiser illustrates the course of collective violence as a feud. Two young men, Mamad Said and Amin, were herding their goats in the mountains. In response to a friendly shove, Mamad Said playfully swung a stick at Amin, hitting him in the face and drawing blood. Amin went to his uncle, Shah Hajji Khan, who gathered some of his friends to avenge the injury by beating Mamad Said. But they were met by friends and relatives of Mamad Said, and, in the ensuing melee Shah Hajji Khan's group suffered greater injuries; his son almost lost his life from an axe blow to the head. Now, two insults needed to be avenged by Shah Hajji Khan—the original blow received by his nephew, and the beating inflicted on his son by friends and relatives of Mamad Said. Some two years later, Shah Hajji Khan hatched a plot to ambush Mamad Said, who escaped by hiding in an irrigation ditch. Mamad Said later died from tuberculosis, which might be expected to bring an end to the feud begun by his accidental blow to Amin's face. But his brother, Qai Afsal, claimed that Mamad Said had died from sickness he contracted while hiding in the irrigation ditch. In revenge he allegedly killed the son of a friend of Shah Hajji Khan who had helped avenge the injury to Amin. Qai Afsal was later shot in the stomach but survived.

As a consequence of such escalation of violence, the men of Thull habitually walk around armed, design their houses for defense against the gunfire of their neighbors, and spend most of their money on rifles and arms. A prized personal possession is a Russian-made AK–47 assault rifle.

EXERCISE 7.1

Examples of group-sanctioned violent conflict are readily available in reports in newspapers. To examine the justifications for such conflict, follow a daily newspaper for a couple of days and document the instances you find of group-sanctioned violence and the reasons attributed for it.

Status, protection or acquisition of valuable resources, and the defense of honor are embodied in the meanings of collective violence, not only in small-scale societies such as those of the Kiowa, Yanomamo, or Kohistani but in large-scale nation-states as well. "Remember the Alamo" was the rallying cry for Texans in their war against Mexico in 1847, and the American desire to avenge the Japanese attack on Pearl Harbor in 1941 was a powerful factor in mobilizing the American people in World War II.

In each of these examples, societies construct a bias in favor of collective violence. But this does not answer the question of why they do so. That is, people may be able to justify killing if they wish. But we know from anthropological research that violent conflict also can be given meanings that actively discourage its occurrence.

QUESTION 7.2 *How Do Societies Create a Bias Against Violent Conflict?*

Thomas Gregor suggests that, since war is so widespread in human societies, the task of the social scientist is not so much to explain war as it is to explain peace. Peaceful societies, he says, are difficult to find. By peaceful, he means a society that is not involved in internal collective violence and in which there is little interpersonal violence. A peaceful society has no special roles for warriors, and it places a positive value on nonaggressive behavior and the peaceful resolution of conflict. Societies that have been characterized as relatively peaceful include the !Kung, the Semai of West Malaysia, the Inuit, the Xinguano of the Amazon region in South America, and the Buid of the Philippines.

Characteristics of Peaceful Societies

Conflict over material resources is avoided in peaceful societies by a strong emphasis on sharing and cooperation. It is expected that everyone in the group has a legitimate claim to what the group possesses. Among the !Kung, the person whose arrow kills an animal is considered to be the owner of the game, and he is obligated to distribute it. The !Kung will share arrows, with the understanding that if they kill an animal with an arrow given to them by someone else, they will give the owner the game to distribute. This also distributes the responsibility for meat sharing and the glory (and perhaps the potential hostility) that accompanies meat distribution.

The Semai of West Malaysia are known for their nonaggressiveness and avoidance of physical conflict. The approximately 15,000 Semai live in small hamlets of less than 100 people each. According to Clayton Robarchek, Semai nonviolence is based on the notion of *pehunan,* a state of being in which a person is unsatisfied in regard to some need or want, such as food or sex. The Semai believe that to refuse a request and deny a person a need intensifies the danger to both the individual and the group; for that reason, the group is obligated to help. The idea of *pehunan* thus encompasses the conception of the community as nurturant care-givers. Rather than saying that it is each person's obligation to meet his or her own needs, the Semai believe that it is the obligation of all members of the community to help and give nurturance to others. Semai personal values stress affiliation, mutual aid, and the belief that violence is not a viable option for settling disputes.

Another way people in peaceful societies create a bias against violence is by condemning those who boast or make claims that can be interpreted as a challenge to others. Among the !Kung, for example, no one is praised for gathering food or making a kill, and people go out of their way to minimize their accomplishments. Those who make boastful claims are ridiculed. Richard Lee painfully learned this lesson when, to show his appreciation to the !Kung for the help they had given him with his research, he brought a fine ox to be slaughtered and distributed at a Christmas feast. The !Kung, much to Lee's chagrin, ridiculed the ox, claiming it was thin and unappetizing. Lee later realized that they were acting toward him as they would have to one of their own. They were letting him know that he wasn't as important as the gift and the killing of the ox made him think he was.

People in peaceful societies also avoid telling others what to do and carefully control their emotions in order to maintain goodwill. The Inuit, for example, fear people who do not demonstrate their goodwill by smiling or laughing, because someone who is unhappy may be hostile. The Inuit believe that strong thoughts can kill or cause illness, and they go to great pains to satisfy other people so that resentment does not build up. Jean Briggs, who lived among a group of Inuit, describes them as people who emphasize kindness and concern and never, under any circumstances, demonstrate anger or resentment. So great is their fear of causing conflict that they make requests indirectly to avoid being refused or embarrassing someone by making them refuse a request. And so great is the crime of losing one's temper that someone who does so may be ostracized from the group. Briggs herself was virtually ignored for months by her adopted family after she lost her temper with some Canadian sports fishermen who she thought were taking advantage of them.

Gregor notes that villagers in the Xingu basin of the Amazon maintain harmony by purposely sanctioning village monopolies in the production of certain goods such as shell belts, stone axes, salt, cotton, fish spears, and ceramic pots. In this way, each village has something that other villages need. The villages therefore maintain good relations, since to alienate another village might deprive one's own village members of a desired good. Moreover, trade is positively valued in itself. When villagers are asked why they don't make the goods they need themselves, they may reply that this could anger those who do make them. Or they may claim that they do not have the knowledge to produce the items, although when they are temporarily cut off from a supply, they seem to learn how to make or acquire them very quickly. Gregor says it is unlikely that any village could not produce the goods desired, since marriage between groups is common, and each village contains people with the skills of other villages.

Xinguanos place a strong negative value on aggression and things that symbolize aggression. Killing is wrong because it produces blood; even animal blood is considered defiling. Most game animals are considered inedible, and fish must be well cooked so there is no blood. The Xinguanos also hold strong negative stereotypes of aggressive groups. They consider non-Xingu Indians to be "wild Indians" who are violent; they beat their children, rape their women, and shoot arrows at white men's planes. The wild Indian has almost the status of an animal and represents everything a Xinguano doesn't want to be. When Xingu villages have been the object of aggression by others they have defended themselves, but successful warriors take no trophies and are given no special honor. In fact, they have to take special medicine to cleanse themselves of the defilement of the blood of their victims.

The Buid of the Philippines are also known for their nonviolence. For them, says Thomas Gibson, violence is an expression of everything they dislike. For example, they have no word for courage, and one of their most prestigious activities is the creation of poetry. The Buid believe that the outside world is filled with threatening spirits that prey upon people, and any intragroup hostility might weaken the group and expose them to these spirits.

Peaceful societies also minimize violence and conflict through ceremony. The !Kung believe that everyone has what they term their medicine or power. In the same way the Bantu tribes that live nearby have witchcraft and sorcery, and Europeans have pills and syringes, the !Kung have *n/um,* a substance that lies in the pit of the stomach. *N/um* has the capacity to keep people healthy and help cure people who are sick. Most important, *n/um* can be transferred from a person acting as a healer to others through the medium of the trance dance, the most common !Kung ceremony. The idea of the dance is for a person to "heat up" his or her *n/um* by dancing; as the person dances, the *n/um* in the stomach is vaporized and travels up the spinal cord into the brain, which causes the dancer to go into a trance. The dancer then goes from person to person, laying on hands and transfering power to those who are touched, thereby enabling them to ward off sickness and death. Anyone can be a healer among the !Kung; in a lifetime, each person is likely to serve as a healer at one time or another.

The trance dance has meanings that go beyond the power to heal, however. Some !Kung are thought to have special powers that allow them to see the ghosts of dead ancestors who hover around the fires, the ability to see distant scenes, to see through things, and, in special cases, to change themselves into lions and stalk the veldt in search of human prey. Trance dances are most frequent when large numbers of people come together—from about once a month in small groups up to four times a week in large camps—and during certain occasions such as the arrival of visitors to a camp, the presence of meat, or sickness. The congregation of large numbers of people, the presence of meat, and the arrival of new people are all occasions that in one way or another create the potential for interpersonal conflict. The fact that trance dances are more frequent during such times seems to indicate that they may serve to heal social conflict as well as individual maladies. By bringing people together in the ceremony, by the sharing of *n/um* and the ritual recognition of common threats, the trance dance unites people and serves to symbolize the relationship between group harmony and individual well-being.

In sum, peaceful societies create a bias against violence by sharing, valuing nonaggressive behavior, building relations of dependence between individuals and groups, and engaging in collective behaviors that promote harmony. They are not, of course, always successful, and even among some so-called peaceful societies, there is violence. For example, Lee collected accounts of 22 homicides among !Kung groups during a 35-year period from 1920 to 1955; however, he found little, if any, sanctioned group violence.

QUESTION 7.3 *What Are the Economic, Political, or Social Differences between Peaceful and Violent Societies?*

Thomas Hobbes, a seventeenth-century philosopher, proposed that human beings in their natural state, without government or laws, are driven by greed and the quest for gain. Without some common power to keep them in awe, Hobbes said, they live in a state of war, with every person against every other person. Here is one of the more famous passages from *Leviathan,* in which Hobbes describes his vision of life before civilization:

> Whatsoever therefore is consequent to a time of warre, where every man is enemy to every man; the same is consequent to a time, wherein men live without other security, than what their own strength and their own invention shall furnish them withall. In such a condition there is no place for Industry; because the fruit thereof is uncertain; and consequently no Culture of the Earth [agriculture]; no navigation, nor use of the commodities that may be imported by sea; no commodious Building; no Instruments of moving, and removing such things as require much force; no Knowledge of the face of the Earth; no account of Time; no Arts; no Letters; no Society; and which is worst of all, continual feare, and danger of violent death; And the life of man, solitary, poore, nasty, brutish, and short. (Hobbes 1881:94–96)

Hobbes saw human beings as having a natural inclination to be violent, an inclination that can only be controlled by some form of centralized authority. However, as anthropologists have discovered, societies with little formal government, such as the !Kung, Inuit, Buid, and Semai, are among the most peaceful in the world (see Question 7.2). These peaceful societies also are small in scale and get their living primarily by hunting and gathering or by slash-and-burn agriculture. Most are relatively isolated and lack formal mechanisms for resolving conflict once it begins. There are no courts, no police, no jails, and no formally sanctioned threats of violence, even against wrongdoers. Since there is little that people in these societies can do once violence begins, they go to great lengths to avoid it.

Had Hobbes known the Yanomamo, however, he might have found that his vision of a stateless society, "where every man is enemy to every man," had been verified. Their social and economic life closely resembles that of the Semai, and they live in virtually the same environment and are neighbors of the peaceful Xinguano. But the Yanomamo society creates attitudes favoring collective violence in order to protect its women and children (see Question 7.1), which suggests that Hobbes may have been correct, at least in part. In this case, the lack of any centralized control or formal mechanisms for putting an end to conflict results in unrestrained violence, rather than the avoidance of conflict.

The Need to Protect Resources and Honor

In societies without any form of centralized control and a bias favoring collective violence, such as those of the Yanomamo and the Kohistani (whose code of honor demands vengeance for any threat), individuals must protect their own resources through force. Because the Yanomamo, for example, do not effectively control intravillage conflict, men of their own as well as other villages are constantly seeking to seduce one another's wives. The men, individually or in groups, therefore must build a reputation for fierceness in order to protect themselves and their families. Failure to control conflict and the need for men to build a reputation for aggressiveness to protect their resources combine to produce a society that places a positive value on violent behavior.

The conditions that give rise to violent conflict among the Yanomamo are not unlike those that promote violence in street gangs in the United States. When Lincoln Keiser worked in the 1960s with the Vice Lords, a Chicago street gang (or "club," as they preferred to call themselves), he concluded that the boys joined gangs because alone they could not protect themselves from shakedowns or safeguard their interests in girls. Whereas the Yanomamo encourage *waiteri*—fierceness—the Vice Lords valued *heart*—a willingness to follow any suggestion regardless of personal risk. A Yanomamo demonstrates fierceness in chest-pounding duels, axe fights, and raids against enemy villages, and street gangs in Chicago confirmed heart in gang fights, or "gangbangs." They even formed alliances with one another against other gangs, similar to Yanomamo villages. The similarities in the dynamics and values of violent conflict among the Yanomamo and among street gangs in the United States illustrates how, under certain conditions, individuals form groups to protect themselves against other groups. To discourage attacks from others in the absence of protection from other agencies, these groups cultivate a reputation for violence.

The gang violence of Chicago of the late 1960s that Keiser wrote about has escalated since, and weapons more typical of Thull are being used. Alex Kotlowitz reports in *There Are No Children Here* that when the Vice Lords became one of three gang factions in Chicago in the early 1990s, they were making use of an arsenal that includes Uzis and grenades. Their purposes were similar, but the stakes were higher. Drugs had become the major source of contention among Chicago gangs (the head of one Vice Lord faction grossed $50,000 to $100,000 a week), and the violence that erupted over territory reflected the increased stakes and more massive firepower. Four members of the Vice Lords who came upon a rival gang member in the lobby of a housing project shot him five times with an Uzi, two sawed-off shotguns, and a .25 caliber automatic handgun to establish their dominance in the neighborhood.

The social and political conditions that characterize the societies of the Vice Lords and the Yanomamo are such that in each of them, individuals must mobilize and use force to protect or acquire desired resources. In neither case is there any effective centralized authority to guarantee the safety of resources or stop violence once it begins. There is a centralized force in Chicago—the police—but they rarely intervene in gang violence, because they are unwilling or do not have the resources to do so, or because local residents are afraid or reluctant to report violence.

The idea that violence may erupt because of a lack of centralized control to protect valued resources is evident also among the Kohistani in Thull. Good land is scarce, and ownership of land is often questioned because there is no central system of land recording or registration. Land is usually acquired by inheritance, but there is little to stop anyone from saying that some relative was wrongfully denied ownership of a particular piece of land in the past and claiming the land on that basis. Whether such a claim is won or lost may depend on which of the claimants has the greater influence or firepower. Even Keiser was suspected of potential land-grabbing while he was conducting fieldwork. He was accused of burying papers in the woods that he would later dig up and claim were old documents giving him title to the land. Since he must have political connections,

Urban gangs may engage in collective violence to protect their resources or honor. These Ching-a-Ling gang members in the South Bronx maintain that they provide the only means of protection for people in their neighborhood.

he would win. In Thull, also, an ideology that encourages collective violence may be attributable to a need to protect resources in the absence of any effective centralized authority.

Private Property and Rebellion

Another difference between violent and peaceful societies is the existence of private property. Among peaceful societies there is widespread sharing; that is, there is little notion of ownership. Resources are viewed as communal or as being part of the natural landscape. In societies that sanction collective violence, on the other hand, personal possessions are highly valued. The importance of horses for the Kiowa is one example where private ownership encouraged an ideology of violence.

Eric Wolf argues that the conversion of communal property into private property was characteristic of societies in which violent revolutions had occurred. Examining major revolutionary movements in Mexico, Russia, China, Algeria, and Vietnam, Wolf concluded that the imposition of capitalistic economies was a major factor in creating the conditions that led to peasant revolt. Capitalism transformed land into a commodity, a piece of private property that, like any other object in a capitalistic economy, could be bought or sold. Transforming land into a commodity created conditions in which peasant farmers, willingly or unwillingly, sold their lands. The result was the creation of a landless population that became the impetus for revolution.

Sexism and Violent Conflict

Gender roles also may differ in peaceful and violent societies. Among the !Kung, Buid, Xinguano, and Semai, men and women are relatively equal, and there is little institutionalized violence against women. In contrast, the Yanomamo and Kohistani (and the Vice Lords) are characterized by male dominance, and they all sanction violence against women. Several reasons have been advanced to support the link between sexist values and violent conflict. First, it is men that traditionally wage war, though women have filled certain positions in armed forces. Societies where women engage in armed combat are the exception rather than the rule. Even in a war of liberation such as the Sandanista rebellion in Nicaragua, where women took an active role in combat, they were banned from it once the Sandanistas gained power. Second, there is a strong cross-cultural link between patriarchy and violent conflict. After examining information on over 1,000 societies, William Tulio Divale and Marvin Harris concluded that the intensity of collective violence is significantly higher in societies characterized by a strong male bias—patrilocal residence, patrilineal descent, polygyny, postmarital sex restrictions on females, male secret societies, and men's houses. Finally, there is evidence that societies characterized by sexual violence against women tend to be more warlike and prone to collective violence. Peggy Sanday's study of 95 societies in which there was evidence of frequency of rape supports this conclusion. The question is, does a sexist ideology promote violent conflict, or does the incidence of violent conflict promote sexism?

Those who claim that sexism promotes violent conflict make that connection in various ways. Betty Reardon and Leslie Cagan suggest that societies that relegate women to an inferior position explicitly or implicitly sanction violence against women. Moreover, violence toward women serves as what they call a "primal" paradigm for violent warfare against other peoples. That is, once violence is allowed as a means of domination of one group such as women, it can serve as a model for dominance and violence against other groups.

For Peggy Sanday, as well as many others, both sexism and violent conflict have their roots in competition over scarce resources. She says women are generally associated with fertility and growth, while men are associated with aggression and destruction. During periods in which resources are not scarce, both males and females are valued equally. But when there is an imbalance between food supply or distribution and the need for food, or groups are competing for other resources, males become of greater value, females become objects to be controlled, and sexual violence becomes one way that men demonstrate their dominance. Among the cattle-herding people of eastern Africa, for example, raiding for cattle was common and sometimes led to violent conflict between groups. Violence was defined as a manly activity, and these societies placed great emphasis on masculinity and manliness. Manliness, however, was tested not only in battle but in male-female relations as well, for sex was a way of demonstrating strength. Among the Acoli, for example, a boy could demonstrate his strength against girls. Girls would frequently visit their boyfriends in their huts, but it took a strong boy to get a girl to lie on the bed and yield. A weak one had to *keng ki ngwece,* or "be content with the smell."

In sum, factors such as a lack of centralized control, competition over scarce resources, the existence of private property, and sexism may lead societies to construct an ideological bias toward violence.

QUESTION 7.4 *What Are the Effects of War on Society?*

Are there any beneficial effects of violent conflict? For example, biologists studying animal populations suggest that predators help the species they prey on by limiting population growth and eliminating the weak from the breeding population. Some anthropologists suggest that war may play a similar function for the human species, either by limiting population or by influencing the biological composition of the human species through the process of natural selection.

The Impact of War on Population

In a fascinating book entitled *The Statistics of Deadly Quarrels,* mathematician Lewis F. Richardson statistically examined the causes and effects of violent conflict between 1821 and 1945. During that period there were 282 wars that had battle fatalities of from 300 to 20 million people. If Richardson's estimate of the number of murders committed and the number of deaths from disease caused or spread because of war are included, deaths from deadly quarrels would account for about 10 percent of all deaths that occurred in that period.

Frank Livingstone has concluded, however, that, in spite of the enormity of the number of deaths inflicted by modern war, it seems to have had little appreciable effect on population growth. About 51 million people died as a result of World War II, including 9 percent of the Russian population and 5 percent of the German population. Yet this had almost no effect on their rates of population growth, for these two populations had recovered within a decade to the level they would have been at had there been no war. In the United States the effect of World War II on population was almost negligible; only about 0.2 percent was lost.

Violent conflict in small-scale societies may have had a much greater impact on their populations, as Livingstone points out. Among the Murngin of Australia about 28 percent of male deaths were due to war, and among the Enga and the Dani of New Guinea, about 25 percent of all male deaths came from violent conflict. Chagnon estimates a death rate due to fighting of 20 to 25 percent among the Yanomamo. Among the Blackfoot Indians of the American plains, there was a 50 percent deficit for males in the male–female ratio in 1805 and a 33 percent deficit in 1858, when horse raiding was still common. During the reservation period, after horse raiding was banned, the sex ratio approached 50–50. Livingstone notes, however, that it is hard to see where any of this has affected the biology of the species. The killing seems to have been more or less random. Moreover, since males were the most frequent victims, and, since the incidence of polygyny (more than one wife) increases in societies that suffer losses, the number of children born should remain more or less constant.

William Tulio Divale and Marvin Harris address the problems posed by Livingstone by proposing that violent conflict does indeed regulate population growth, but it does so not by killing grown men but by encouraging the killing of infant girls. The incidence of violent conflict, they reason, is strongly associated not only with a strong preference for male children but also with female infanticide or the benign neglect of female infants. Evidence of this can be found in direct reports of female infanticide or the skewed sex ratios of children under the age of 14. Societies characterized by violent conflict average 128 boys to 100 girls under 14, far higher than the normal ratio of 105 boys to 100 girls.

If war or violent conflict is frequent in a society, the society or group that raises the largest number of fierce, aggressive warriors will be at an advantage. Consequently, the existence of violent conflict encourages a strong preference for rearing male children, supports the ideological restrictions on the rearing of female children, and, in general, creates an ideology of male supremacy. Moreover, restricting the number of childbearing females in a population is a far more effective means of population control than killing adult males is. Thus, Divale and Harris conclude, war and violent conflict do encourage sexism, but only because they serve to promote selective population control.

The Evolution of the Nation-State

Anthropologists also suggest that violent conflict may encourage certain forms of political organization. Robert Carneiro argues, for example, that in the course of human history, violent conflict has been the primary agent that has transformed human societies from small-scale, autonomous communities into vast, complex nation-states. Carneiro reasons that war has served as a means to promote the consolidation of isolated, politically autonomous villages into chiefdoms of united villages and then into states. At first, war pits village against village, resulting in chiefdoms; then it pits chiefdom against chiefdom, resulting in states; and then it pits state against state. War began as the effort to oust a rival from a territory but soon evolved into an effort to subjugate and control an enemy. As the process continued, warfare became a mechanism for reducing the number of political units in the world. Carneiro predicts that if the number of political states continues to decline as it has in the past, by the year 2300 there should be only a single world state.

The rise of the Zulu state in Africa illustrates Carneiro's theory of how a group of largely separate political units is transformed into larger forms of state organization through violent conflict. The Zulu state took form in southeast Africa in the early nineteenth century. Prior to that time, the region was inhabited by small, sometimes warring groups. About 100,000 people lived in an area of some 80,000 square miles by practicing agriculture and cattle herding. While there were separate entities labeled tribes by Westerners, the largest political unit was the clan. Warriors from these clans raided each other for cattle, but there was no conquest for land.

Warfare increased between 1775 and 1800 as the population of southeast Africa increased. The strongest groups were those that could muster the most warriors and organize and discipline them effectively. The process of state formation whereby these separate groups combined into a larger political unit was begun by a leader of the Mtetwa tribe named Dingiswayo. He developed new ways to organize his troops and began to take control of the land of those he defeated. When he conquered an area he would appoint a person from the head family of that group to rule for him. Using new techniques of war and political control, he achieved dominance over a wide area. His reason for extending his control, according to one nineteenth-century writer, was to make peace among warring groups; Dingiswayo, it was said, "wished to do away with the incessant quarrels that occurred amongst the tribes, because no supreme head was over them to say who was right or who was wrong."

By the early 1800s, Dingiswayo had conquered and united some 30 different groups. He was aided by a young officer named Shaka Zulu, the son of the chief of the Zulu clan. When the Zulu chief died, Dingiswayo installed Shaka as the head of the clan, and when Dingiswayo was killed by a rival, Shaka took over the army and established Zulus as the dominant clan. By 1822 Shaka had defeated every rival and was master of all present-day Zululand and Natal.

Violence and Male Solidarity

In addition to controlling population and uniting tribal societies into large-scale states, violent conflict may also be valued as a means of promoting group solidarity. Male solidarity, for example, seems to be enhanced by collective violence. Societies in which there is frequent violence often have more men's clubs, men's sports teams, or special men's houses. But some assume that male solidarity, and the resulting domination of women, leads to increased collective violence, and others assume that increased male solidarity is itself the result of conflict. Ralph Holloway suggests that when the psychological attributes that allow human beings to create sentimental bonds between members of a group are turned outward, they promote violent conflict against nongroup members. That is, collective violence is simply the other side of group togetherness.

There is evidence to support the idea that societies that engage in war place a greater emphasis on male solidarity. There are all-male clubs or organizations such as men's clubs among the Plains Indians, and men's houses among tribes in New Guinea. In Frederic Thrasher's classic study of boys' gangs in Chicago in 1927, he concluded that fighting, gang encounters, outwitting enemies, raiding, robbing, defending the hangout, and attacking enemies was the type of activity that produced male solidarity. In fact, the gang does not solidify as a group unless there is conflict.

QUESTION 7.5 *How Is the American Bias toward Collective Violence Created?*

Is the ability to give violence such a wide range of meanings to justify it and even make it praiseworthy a factor in its wide acceptance among human societies? When the Spaniards and the Carib confronted each other in the sixteenth century with clubs, spears, crossbows, and primitive firearms, they professed noble reasons for their actions, and the consequences of their collective violence were minor compared to the consequences of ours. War today is fought with weapons whose destructive power is limited only by human imagination or technological expertise. Yet Americans seem as able as the Spaniards and the Carib were to distance themselves from the consequences of their acts.

To examine how Americans construct the meaning of collective violence, I will discuss how the meaning of the recent Gulf War was constructed to serve the purposes of government and then examine what one researcher discovered about the world of meaning of those who plan American nuclear strategy. My primary goal is to examine the meanings Americans give to violent conflict and how these meanings reveal certain realities but mask others.

Metaphors of War in the Persian Gulf Conflict

Linguist George Lakoff examined how the language, especially the metaphors, used by government officials and the mass media to describe and report the war in the Persian Gulf in 1990–1991 emphasized certain meanings but obscured others. The meaning of war for American military planners, says Lakoff, is based on a perspective first outlined by a Prussian general in the late nineteenth century, Carl von Clausewitz, who defined war as "politics pursued by other means." In other words, violence is simply another political tool governments have at their disposal in dealing with other governments. In American politics another layer of meaning has been superimposed on the "war = politics" equation. In many respects, politics is seen as an extension of business principles through which political questions come down to the question of whether gains from an action or policy would outweigh its acceptable costs. When these metaphors are extended to war, war also comes down to the question of whether its possible gains are worth its costs. And that is the way many Americans thought and spoke about the Gulf War.

During the debate in Congress preceding the war, senators and representatives spoke of how much we had to lose by taking or avoiding military action and made constant reference to the costs and gains of war. The argument was often put in Clausewitz's terms: War is justified if more is to be gained by going to war than by not going to war; war is not justified if the costs are too high. Largely absent from these congressional debates was consideration of the morality or immorality of the violence. This, says Lakoff, is not because the people who were debating whether or not to go to war are immoral, but because the Clausewitz metaphor allows war to be discussed only in pragmatic, not moral, terms. There was no debate over whether the metaphor was appropriate, only whether the cost of going to war was worth the gains. Few members of Congress spoke of the possibility of war as the *failure of diplomacy*. Few of them questioned the realities hidden by the use of the cost-benefit metaphor, such as *who* gained and *who* lost? Did rank-and-file members of the military forces, drawn disproportionately from minorities and the poor in America, have as much to gain as those who didn't fight? Did women have as much to gain as men?

The use of the cost-benefit metaphor, however, was only one layer of the constructed meaning of the Gulf War. Another metaphorical equation that helped distance people from the consequences of the war was the analogy made between ruler and state: "We have to get Saddam out of Kuwait" was the rallying cry. Americans went to war not against Iraq but against its ruler, Saddam Hussein; still, no one in America ever said "George Bush marched into Kuwait." For many Americans, equating Iraq with Saddam was crucial, for by portraying him as evil, the war was metaphorically transformed into a morality play or fairy tale in which the United States was the hero, Saddam was the villain, and the hero was left with no choice but to engage the villain in battle.

War was also equated with a game that can be won or lost, a game in which the goal is victory. Americans tend to view war as a competitive game such as chess or as a sport such as football or boxing. In the same way our sports language is filled with metaphors of war (see Question 1.5), our descriptions of war often resemble accounts of sporting events. Sports metaphors imply that in any conflict there is a clear winner and loser, and a clear end to the game that results in victory for one side and defeat for the other. And so, in the Gulf War, Americans went to war to win, and when it was over they celebrated their victory. It might be useful to ask whether, if we had defined war as the failure of diplomacy, we would have mourned the defeat of our diplomatic team or would have allowed them to lose at all.

EXERCISE 7.2

There is some suggestion of a link between militarism and competitive sports; that is, societies that are prone to collective violence are more likely to value games in which men aggressively compete against other men. Does this apply to American society? Which sports in America most closely resemble or promote the values of militarism and war? Does the language of these sports reflect militaristic values? Do gender roles reflect these values?

Lakoff's analysis of the various levels of meaning given the Gulf War does not argue with the judgment that Saddam Hussein was a ruthless leader, nor does it argue with the possible economic consequences of Iraq's invasion of Kuwait. His analysis simply portrays how this particular act of collective violence was justified, how it was given a meaning that allowed Americans to distance themselves from the reality of the death of hundreds of thousands of soldiers and civilians, and the exposure of millions of largely innocent adults and children to starvation and disease. More important, the applications of the various metaphors masked other realities. The reality of the situation as it was defined by millions of Arabs, for example, was almost completely ignored.

For the sake of the fairy-tale rescue scenario, Kuwait was portrayed by government agencies and the media as an innocent victim, "raped" by Saddam. Rarely mentioned by either the American government or the media were the grievances of Iraq against Kuwait. Kuwait had long been resented by Iraqis and Muslims in other Arab states. Capital rich but labor poor, Kuwait imported cheap labor from neighboring countries to do its least pleasant work. At the time of the invasion by Iraq, there were in Kuwait 400,000 citizens and 2.2 million foreign laborers who were denied rights of citizenry and treated as lesser beings. Kuwait was also undermining the Iraqi economy and drilling for oil in territory claimed by Iraq. In short, to the Iraqis and the people in many other Arab countries, Kuwait was badly miscast as a purely innocent victim. Lost in the scenario was also the fact that the "legitimate" government that Americans sought to reinstate in Kuwait was an oppressive monarchy. None of this, of course, justifies the horrors perpetrated on Kuwait by the Iraqi army. But it is part of what was hidden when Kuwait was cast as an innocent ingenue.

The Gulf War metaphors also hid the attempts of Arab countries to achieve dignity through unity. Most Arabs view Western countries from the perspective of a colonial past in which the West dominated the Arab world and defined political boundaries to suit its own convenience. These boundaries, many Arabs feel, created a few oil-rich states dominated by the West, such as Kuwait and Saudi Arabia, which in turn created an artificial gap between rich and poor. Poor Arabs see rich Arabs as rich only through political acts of the West. Oil wealth, they feel, should be shared by all Arabs as members of one big family.

Feeling weak and dominated is also common to the Arabs' perception of their relationship to Western nations. They view this weakness metaphorically in sexual terms, as emasculation. A proverb that was reported to be popular in Iraq during the war was, "It is better to be a cock for a day than a chicken for a year." In other words, it is better to be a strong male, if only for a short period, than to be a weak and defenseless female. One of the reasons Saddam gained support from the Arab world was that he was seen as standing up to the United States.

By their own choice of metaphors to conceptualize the Gulf War, were Americans able to construct meanings that hid from view certain realities? If these realities had been revealed, would they have significantly reduced the support the government received for this act of collective violence? What about the idea that America had achieved a great victory? Americans certainly *celebrated* a victory: parades, speeches, military heros, yellow ribbons were all part of the euphoria. But in the application of collective violence, what is victory, and what is won? After the military confrontation ceased, an oppressive government was reinstated in Kuwait, Saddam Hussein remained in power, and Arab nationalism was reinforced. As Lakoff observes, even the closest thing to a victory doesn't look very victorious in this case. In the debate over whether to go to war, very little had been said to clarify what a "victory" would be.

Americans celebrate what they defined as a victory in the Persian Gulf War of 1990–1991. Government agencies and the media helped give a positive meaning to the collective violence engaged in by U.S. armed forces.

The Language of Nuclear Destruction

Individual Americans' perceptions of the Gulf War, of course, are skewed by their social and political positions. As with any construction of meaning, social position is critical in constructing the meaning of collective violence. There is a potential for violence, however, that few people, regardless of their nationality, their political views, or their social position, can imagine as being beneficial—the potential for nuclear war. Nevertheless, certain officials have the responsibility to plan a national nuclear strategy. Since the ability to mask the consequences of violent conflict may be one of the reasons for its frequency, it is useful to examine how people manage to mask for themselves the consequences of planning what now would be the ultimate form of violence.

Carol Cohn spent one year studying the culture of a strategic studies institute, or "think tank," for government defense analysts who plan nuclear strategy. She began her study with the questions: How are people whose job it is to plan nuclear destruction able to do it? How can they think that way? One of her conclusions is that language is used to distance the planners from the consequences of the actions they are planning. The language they use obfuscates and reassembles reality in such a way that what is really being talked about—the fundamental business of war, which is destroying human creations and injuring and killing human beings—is somehow hidden from view behind metaphors and euphemisms.

During her first weeks at the center, as she listened to the participants (all men) talking matter-of-factly about nuclear destruction, she heard language that she labeled *technostrategic*. In this language there is reference to *clean bombs* (fusion bombs that release more energy than fission bombs, not as radiation but as explosive power), *penetration aids* (technology that helps missiles get through enemy defenses), *collateral damage* (human deaths), and *surgical strikes* (bombing that takes out only weapons or command centers). Domestic metaphors are common in technostrategic talk: missiles are based in *silos;* piles of nuclear weapons in a nuclear submarine are referred to as *Christmas tree farms;* bombs and missiles are referred as *reentry vehicles* or *RVs.* Massive bombing becomes *carpet bombing.* Cohn says that the domestic images not only distance the speakers from the grisly reality they are discussing. Calling the pattern in which a bomb falls a *footprint* seems to remove the speakers from any position of accountability for the acts they are contemplating.

Cohn's experience is similar to that of anthropologists who find themselves immersed in the reality of another culture. She discovered, for example, that the language and metaphors of those working at the institute seemed incapable of expressing certain realities. In the language of technostrategic, the aftermath of a nuclear attack is described in terms of practical problems such as the need to maintain communication in "a nuclear environment." The situation is said to be "bound to include EMP blackout, brute force damage to systems, a heavy jamming environment, and so on." In contrast is a description of the aftermath of the nuclear bombing of Hiroshima from the perspective of Hisako Matsubara, a survivor, who describes it in *Cranes at Dusk:*

> Everything was black, had vanished into the black dust, was destroyed. Only the flames that were beginning to lick their way up had any color. From the dust that was like fog, figures began to loom up, black, hairless, faceless. They screamed with voices that were no longer human. Their screams drowned out the groans rising everywhere from the rubble, groans that seemed to rise from the very earth itself. (quoted in Cohn 1987:708)

There is, says Cohn, no way of describing this experience with the language of technostrategic. The speaker is a victim; the speaker of technostrategic, on the other hand, in the first instance is preparing for the deployment of nuclear weapons. One of the consequences of technostrategic is that it removes the speakers from having to think about themselves as victims of nuclear war. This does not mean that defense analysts convince themselves that they would not be victims, but the language removes them from the point of view of a victim and provides them with that of the planner, the initiator of nuclear war.

Cohn also discovered that she could not use ordinary language to speak to the defense analysts. If she tried, they acted as if she were ignorant or simpleminded. To communicate at all, she had to use terms such as *subholocaust engagement* and *preemptive strikes.* The word *peace* was not a legitimate part of the vocabulary; to use it was to brand oneself as a softheaded activist. The closest she could come to *peace* in the language of technostrategic was *strategic stability.*

Cohn encountered descriptions of nuclear situations that made little sense until she realized that different realities were being discussed. For example, the following passage describes a nuclear exchange in a situation in which missiles with more than one warhead are mutually banned:

> The strategic stability of regime A (a scenario) is based on the fact that both sides are deprived of any incentive ever to strike first. Since it takes roughly two warheads to destroy the enemy silo, an attacker must expend two of his missiles to destroy one of the enemy's. A first strike disarms the attacker. The aggressor ends up worse than the aggressed. (quoted in Cohn 1987:710)

By what type of reasoning, asks Cohn, can a country that dropped a thousand nuclear bombs 10 to 100 times more powerful than the one dropped on Hiroshima end up "worse off" than the country it dropped the bombs on? This would be possible only if winning depends on who has the greatest number of weapons left. In other words, nuclear war would be a kind of game in which the object is to have more weapons at the end than the enemy has.

To an anthropologist, the fact that people are limited by their culture, their language, and their point of view is, of course, no surprise. All cultures give a characteristic meaning to violent conflict, whether it be viewed as the act of an animal in possession of a human body (like the tiger spirit of the Carib), the will of God, or a kind of game to determine winners and losers. The more serious implication of Cohn's observations is that the roles of nuclear planners as scientists and academics lend weight to their claim that their perspective is "objective" and therefore has greater truth value than other perspectives. Moreover, says Cohn, if one can speak to defense analysts only in the language of technostrategic, and if the language is constructed in such a way as to be incapable of expressing different realities, then there is no way for these analysts to appreciate or understand the other realities involving the use of nuclear weapons.

CONCLUSIONS

To examine how people give meaning to and justify collective violence, the first questions had to do with how societies create a bias in favor of or against collective violence. Violent conflict is justified in some societies as a way of achieving status or acquiring or protecting possessions, as a means of revenge, or as a necessary defense of personal honor or integrity. In peaceful societies, violence is avoided by widespread sharing of resources, building relations of dependence among groups, devaluing or discouraging aggressive behavior, or emphasizing collective behaviors that promote intra- and intergroup harmony.

There are economic, political, and social differences between peaceful and violent societies. One difference is the encouragement in violent societies of competition over resources that, because of a lack of central authority, requires individuals to protect their own property by violent means. The conversion of communal property to private property, which resulted in the disenfranchisement of peasant farmers, has been linked to revolution, and sexist ideologies in violent societies can promote violent behavior against other groups.

A question in examining the effects of war on society is whether there have been any beneficial effects that might explain the occurrence of violent conflict. Population does decline in war, especially in small-scale societies, but apparently not enough to exercise any control on population growth or to have any impact on the human species through biological selection. War, according to some, has served throughout human history to promote the centralization of authority and the growth of state-level political structures. While violent conflict may increase male solidarity, it also can promote greater violence against women.

Examples of how Americans create a bias toward collective violence by constructing the meanings of violent conflict are the media and official presentations of the war in the Persian Gulf and the justification of defense analysts for their planning of nuclear war. In both cases, the language of war is masked by speaking of it in other terms. In the case of the Gulf War, violent conflict became an extension of politics, or a fairy-tale rescue, or a sports event, all of which not only gave acceptable meanings to the conflict but also successfully masked alternative meanings. The language of defense analysts masks some of the realities of nuclear destruction, keeps them from viewing themselves as victims, and turns nuclear planning into a game.

REFERENCES AND SUGGESTED READINGS

INTRODUCTION: THE PROBLEM OF VIOLENT CONFLICT The opening quote is from an account of a witness to a Contra attack on a Nicaraguan village in 1984, as cited in Noam Chomsky's *Turning the Tide: U.S. Intervention in Central America and the Struggle for Peace* (South End Press, 1985). The account of Carib warfare is based on Neil Lancelot Whitehead's article, "The Snake Warriors—Sons of the Tiger's Teeth: A Descriptive Analysis of Carib Warfare, ca 1500–1820," in *The Anthropology of War,* edited by Jonathan Hass (Cambridge University Press, 1990). The definition of war relies on Clark McCauley's "Conference Overview," in *The Anthropology of War.* McCauley draws for his definition from a book compiled from a symposium on war held in 1966, War: *The Anthropology of Armed Conflict and Aggression,* edited by Morton Fried, Marvin Harris, and Robert Murphy (Natural History Press, 1967). Different views on the cultural or biological roots of war can be found in *Societies at Peace: Anthropological Perspectives,* edited by Signe Howell and Roy Willis (Routledge, 1989), and in Carol Greenhouse, "Cultural Perspectives on War," in *The Quest for Peace: Transcending Collective Violence and War among Societies, Cultures and States,* edited by R. Varynen (Sage Publications, 1987).

HOW DO SOCIETIES CREATE A BIAS IN FAVOR OF COLLECTIVE VIOLENCE? The account of Kiowa warfare and horse raiding is from Bernard Mishkin, *Rank and Warfare among the Plains Indians* (Seattle: The University of Washington Press, 1940). The account of the Yanomamo is based on Napoleon Chagnon's article, "Reproductive and Somatic Conflicts of Interest in the Genesis of Violence and Warfare among Tribesmen," in *The Anthropology of War,* cited above, and from Chagnon's *The Fierce People,* 3rd edition (Holt, Rinehart and Winston, 1983). The feud in Kohistan is described by Lincoln Keiser in *Friend by Day, Enemy by Night: Organized Vengeance in a Kohistani Community* (Holt, Rinehart and Winston, 1991). A classic work on violent protest is Eric Hobsbaum's *Primitive Rebels: Studies in Archaic Forms of Social Movement in the 19th and 20th Centuries* (Frederick A. Praeger, 1959).

HOW DO SOCIETIES CREATE A BIAS AGAINST VIOLENT CONFLICT? Thomas Gregor discusses peaceful societies in "Uneasy Peace: Intertribal Relations in Brazil's Upper Xingu," in *The Anthropology of War* (cited above). The discussion of the !Kung relies on Elizabeth Thomas, *The Harmless People* (Alfred A. Knopf, 1959), and Richard Lee, *The Dobe !Kung,* (Holt, Rinehart and Winston, 1984). The description of the Semai is based on Clayton Robarchek, "Motivations and Material Causes: On the Explanation of Conflict and War," in *The Anthropology of War.* Robarchek also discusses the Hobbesian image of man as it relates to the Semai in "Hobbesian and Rousseauan Images of Man: Autonomy and Individualism in a Peaceful Society," in *Societies at Peace: Anthropological Perspectives,* edited by Signe Howell and Roy Willis, cited above. The material on the Xinguanos comes from Thomas Gregor's article (see above). The description of the Inuit is derived from Jean Briggs, *Never in Anger* (Harvard University Press, 1970), and an account of the Buid can be found in Thomas Gibson, "Raiding, Trading and Tribal Autonomy in Insular Southeast Asia," in *The Anthropology of War.*

WHAT ARE THE DIFFERENCES BETWEEN PEACEFUL AND VIOLENT SOCIETIES? Two works cited above deal extensively with debates about the reasons for war—*War: The Anthropology of Armed Conflict and Aggression,* edited by Morton Fried, Marvin Harris, and Robert Murphy, and *The Anthropology of War,* edited by Jonathan Hass. The views of Thomas Hobbes are taken from *Leviathan,* first published in 1651 (Oxford University Press, 1881). *The Vice Lords: Warriors of the Streets* (Holt, Rinehart and Winston, 1969) contains Lincoln Keiser's account of Chicago street gangs in the 1960s. Alex Kotlowitz gives an account of the lives of two Chicago children growing up amid the violence of Chicago housing projects in *There Are No Children Here* (Anchor Books, 1991). Work on the anthropology of revolution can be found in Eric Wolf, *Peasant Wars of the Twentieth Century* (Harper & Row, 1969).

William Tulio Divale and Marvin Harris discuss the connection between male dominance and war in "Population, Warfare, and the Male Supremacist Complex," *American Anthropologist,* vol. 78 (1976), pp. 521–538. The feminist analysis of war is represented by Leslie Cagan, "Feminism and Militarism," in *Beyond Survival: New Directions for the Disarmament Movement,* edited by M. Albert and D. Dellinger (South End Press, 1983); Riane Eisler, *The Chalice and the Blade* (Harper & Row, 1987); and Betty Reardon, *Sexism and the War System* (Columbia University Teachers College Press, 1985). Peggy Sanday reports her study of rape and war in "The Socio-Cultural Context of Rape: A Cross-Cultural Study," *Journal of Social Issues,* vol. 37 (1981), pp. 5–27. A description of the Acoli appears in Dent Ocaya-Lakidi, "Manhood, Warriorhood and Sex in Eastern Africa," in *Journal of Asian and African Studies,* vol. 12 (1979), pp. 134–165.

WHAT ARE THE EFFECTS OF WAR ON SOCIETY? The figures on the number of people killed in modern war come from Lewis Richardson's classic work, *The Statistics of Deadly Quarrels* (Boxwood Press, 1960) and Quincy Wright's extensive work, *A Study of War* (University of Chicago Press, 1965). Frank B. Livingstone discusses "The Effects of Warfare on the Biology of the Human Species" in *War: The Anthropology of Armed Conflict and Aggression,* cited above. The connection between war and female infanticide is made in Divale and Harris's article, "Population, Warfare, and the Male Supremacist Complex," cited above.

Robert Carneiro's theories about the relationship between war and the development of the state can be found in his article, "Political Expansion as an Expression of the Principle of Competitive Exclusion," in *Origins of the State,* edited by Ronald Cohn and Elman Service (Institute for the Study of Human Issues, 1978), and more recently in his article, "Chiefdom-Level Warfare as Exemplified in Fiji and Cauca Valley," in *The Anthropology of War* (cited above). The description of the rise of the Zulu state comes from Elman Service's *Origins of the State and Civilization* (W. W. Norton, 1975). A discussion of war and human bonding can be found in Ralph Holloway, Jr., "Human Aggression: The Need for a Species-Specific Framework," in *War: The Anthropology of Armed Conflict and Aggression* (cited above). Frederic Thrasher's study of Chicago gangs is reported in *The Gang,* originally published in 1927 (University of Chicago Press, 1963). An excellent article on the relationship between sports and war is Richard G. Sipes, "War, Sports, and Aggression: An Empirical Test of Two Rival Theories," *American Anthropologist,* vol. 74 (1973), pp. 64–86.

HOW IS THE AMERICAN BIAS TOWARD COLLECTIVE VIOLENCE CREATED? George Lakoff discusses the 1991 War in the Persian Gulf in an article, "Metaphor and War: The Metaphor System Used to Justify War in the Gulf," distributed on Bitnet (electronic mail) by *XCULT-L.* Carol Cohn's article, "Sex and Death in the Rational World of Defense Intellectuals," appeared in *Signs,* vol. 12 (1987), pp. 687–718. For more on what Cohn calls "newspeak," see her article, "Decoding Military Newspeak," in *Ms,* 1991, no. 5. The description of the aftermath of the atomic bombing of Hiroshima comes from Hisako Matsubara, *Cranes at Dusk* (Dial Press, 1985).

CHAPTER 8

APPLICATIONS TO PROBLEMS OF CULTURAL DIVERSITY

We are inadequately prepared to deal with cultural diversity. Experts who go abroad technically well qualified to cut down infant deaths, improve nutrition, or increase food production are unequipped to understand how the problems with which they must deal are rooted in a foreign way of life. Guidebooks tell tourists precisely what monuments and buildings to visit, but stop short of explaining life-ways they will encounter abroad. If we want to learn, we must know what questions to ask and how to interpret our observations.

John J. Honigmann

INTRODUCTION: *The Problems of Cultural Diversity*

Cultural anthropology is about cultural diversity, whether it occurs from one country to another or in a single classroom. Human beings seem ill-equipped to deal with their cultural differences. The fact that different peoples assign different meanings to events, objects, individuals, and emotions is a source of considerable conflict, miscommunication, and misunderstanding. Anthropologists seek to explain this diversity, to help people understand one another better. In the process, they also apply their knowledge to social, economic, educational, and political problems created by diversity.

In this chapter I will give you the opportunity to work out solutions to problems drawn from actual instances in which anthropologists were asked to apply their knowledge or experience to specific situations in various societies. Each application, in its way, is related to a problem resulting from cultural diversity, specifically, differences in the meanings that different peoples give to their experiences. The promotion of mutual respect, tolerance, and understanding for cultural differences is one of the most important contributions cultural anthropology can make in today's world.

The five problems concern applications in health care, economic development, education, architecture, and law. For each problem, after a brief orientation to the application of anthropology to a general area, put yourself in the position of an anthropologist or a professional with a background in anthropology who has been asked to solve a specific problem in this area. As you read the background information on this problem, think how you might go about solving it. What kinds of questions would you need to ask, what kinds of information might you need, what practical advice would you offer? After writing down your proposed solution for the problem, compare it with the solution used by the anthropologist who actually worked on it, which is described in the final section.

These cases do not come near to exhausting the possible applications of anthropology to practical problems. Nevertheless, they clearly illustrate some of the ways experience in anthropology is used to address problems in diversity.

APPLICATION 8.1 *Anthropology in Health Care*

One example of the real practical problems that are due to cultural diversity is in the area of health care. Disease and illness are part of a cultural text; that is, the human propensity to give meaning to such experiences as death, status, and success also gives meaning to illness and disease. And the meaning given an illness will likely suggest a cure. In a society where people believe that all illness is spread in the air, they are not likely to be receptive to measures to stop waterborne diseases, for example. The differences in conceptions of disease understandably produce difficulties when health-care practitioners try to introduce innovations from one culture into another. Anthropologists, doctors, nurses, and health-care administrators with anthropological training have often been called upon to help with such problems.

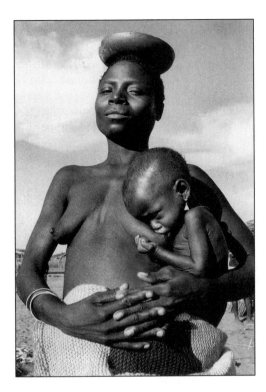

A mother in Mozambique attempts to care for her child in the customary way, with breast-feeding. Anthropologists are able to help peoples of diverse cultures deal with problems of childhood illness or malnutrition by providing their health-care workers with information or products developed for their use.

Health Care among the Swazi

THE PROBLEM Childhood diarrhea is the most serious of the waterborne parasitic infections that cause infant death in Swaziland in southeastern Africa. Suppose you have been asked by the government of Swaziland to help its health-care workers acquaint the Swazi with the Western explanation for the cause of childhood diarrhea and encourage parents to seek appropriate medical treatment for their children. For various reasons, the Swazi have not been receptive to the treatment that has been found to be most effective—oral rehydration therapy. This simple treatment replaces the fluids the child loses because of the diarrhea with an electrolyte solution to promote water retention. The solution contains potassium and sodium chloride, sodium citrate, and dextrose, not unlike Gatorade, and it is cheap, easily administered, and effective. Other treatment for viral diarrhea is to avoid all milk products and feed the baby breast milk, clear fluids, binding foods such as bananas, rice, cereal, and toast.

BACKGROUND OF THE PROBLEM The Swazi have their own system of cultural meanings concerning the causes of diarrhea. Generally they classify all diseases into two categories. Traditional diseases are believed to be caused by either sorcery (the deliberate use of spells and medicines) or the withdrawal of spiritual protection by ancestors angered by some act (see Question 2.4). Nontraditional diseases such as cholera, tuberculosis, and venereal disease were introduced by Europeans. Traditional healers are sought when the problem is thought to be caused by sorcery or ancestral displeasure, while Western clinics and doctors are sought when the disease is thought to be European.

The Swazi also believe that diseases are frequently carried in the air. Vapors from powerful medicines mixed carelessly or deliberately may cause illness, as can traces of vapors caused by lightning or thunder. An environment can be polluted by evil spirits that have been removed from a victim and seek to enter another person. Illness may be caused by poison hidden by an enemy in a place the intended victim is likely to pass by or touch, such as the entrance to a latrine or a toilet seat. Because of fear of this kind of illness, the Swazi are reluctant to build latrines.

The Swazi classify diarrhea as a traditional disease. If home remedies fail to cure children, their mothers usually take them to traditional healers who recognize three types of diarrhea, each with a recommended cure. *Umsheko,* the passing of loose, wet stools, is believed to be caused by such things as bad or insufficient food, cow's milk, powdered or spoiled milk, physical relocation of the child, or the flies that buzz around Swazi settlements. Healers use herbal medicines to treat the symptoms and recommend breast-feeding and certain foods such as sorghum and a porridge made of maize. The second type, *kuhabula,* is a more serious form that the Swazi believe is caused by invisible vapors to which the child may be deliberately or accidentally exposed. The child is treated with medicines and enemas to purify or drain out the bad air believed to be contributing to the illness. The third type of diarrhea is *umphezulu.* Babies are believed born with it because of some act of the mother; she may have passed through a place where lightning hit or where evil medicines were deliberately placed, or she did not keep her head covered during her pregnancy. A cure for this kind of diarrhea is to take the child to the place where the mother was infected and give the child an enema.

Some of these traditional curing techniques for diarrhea conflict with Western practice and belief. For example, dehydration is the most serious symptom of diarrhea, and giving the child an enema would aggravate rather than relieve the effects of the disease. Furthermore, since diarrhea is thought to be a traditional disease, mothers usually do not take their children to the clinics that could supply electrolyte fluids. Other beliefs and practices, such as breast-feeding the child and giving binding foods, medicinal teas, and other fluids, are consistent with Western practice and belief.

Western-educated government officials at first were biased against native healers. In fact, from 1894 to 1955, when Swaziland was controlled by the British, all "witch-doctoring" was considered illegal in Swaziland. While the government has since removed legal obstacles to the practice of traditional medicine, it is still considered "backward" by Western-educated government officials and health practitioners.

As an anthropologist, you know that asking the Swazi to give up or change their beliefs and practices would be futile, and they do have a long tradition of treating illness. Knowing what you do about traditional Swazi beliefs and practices and understanding the medical background of the problem, what kind of recommendations would you make to help the people of Swaziland cope with childhood intestinal problems?

AN ACTUAL SOLUTION When Edward C. Green was hired by the government of Swaziland to solve the problem, here's how he went about it. He recognized that the traditional healers must play a major role in any health program to prevent or cure diarrheal diseases. They are far more accessible than doctors; there is one healer per 100 people in Swaziland, but only one doctor per 10,000 people. Moreover, traditional healers are influential members of their communities whose opinions would be critical for the acceptance of new ways of treating illness.

Green also recognized that while the Swazi do not accept biomedical germ theory, they have many traditional concepts of health and disease that do coincide with Western beliefs. For example, Swazis believe that unseen agents can cause some disease. They say that these agents are spread through the air and are highly contagious; people are infected by "breathing" them into their bodies. Recent scientific experiments have revealed, in fact, that some stomach disorders are caused by airborne viruses. Green recommended building on the Swazi beliefs that recognize waterborne agents as a cause of diarrhea. He also recommended building on beliefs that are common to both Western and Swazi medical practices. Because the Swazi believe that fluids are necessary to keep up babies' strength, he proposed teaching traditional healers how to use oral rehydration therapy. If spells were believed needed to counteract the effects of sorcery or exposure to evil medicine, they could be used after rehydration.

By drawing on his training and experience as an anthropologist, Green was able to make concrete recommendations to enable health officials to translate the practices of one culture into those of another. Crossing the barrier of cultural difference thus could contribute to the prevention and treatment of disease.

APPLICATION 8.2 *Anthropology in Economic Development*

One of the first areas in which anthropological research was applied was economic development in Third World countries. Government planners trained in Western countries who wanted to introduce new agricultural techniques, technology, or crops often hired anthropologists to determine if farmers would accept these innovations, and, if not, what changes might be made to ensure their successful adoption. The anthropologists sometimes found it necessary to point out to these officials that the agricultural practices of peasant farmers that they considered inefficient or wasteful were, in fact, highly functional. More recently, anthropologists have been asked to direct such projects as reforestation or to help convince farmers of the need to conserve resources.

Growing Trees in Haiti

THE PROBLEM Suppose you had been asked by funding agencies in the United States in the 1980s to direct a reforestation program in the island republic of Haiti. After hundreds of years of tree-cutting to clear land for farming or to harvest lumber for sale, the land has been virtually deforested. There have been other attempts to convince peasant farmers to plant trees, if only to prevent soil erosion. The U.S. Agency for International Development (AID) gave millions of dollars in aid to the government of Haiti for this purpose, but the number of jobs it created seemed to outnumber the number of seedlings planted. Those that were planted were likely to be pulled out by the peasant farmers, or they might turn the reforestation projects into goat forage projects. Official threats against removing the trees and ecological messages urging conservation had little effect.

BACKGROUND OF THE PROBLEM   Haiti is the poorest nation in the Western hemisphere; 50 percent of its six million people were unemployed in 1987. It occupies the western third of the large island of Hispaniola, which it shares with the Dominican Republic. Haiti is the size of Maryland; about two-thirds of its land is mountainous, and much of the rest is semiarid. The third of the land that is arable is mostly divided into tiny plots owned by peasant farmers; there are an estimated 500,000 farms in this small area.

Haitian farmers initially resisted planting trees because they felt that the land taken for reforestation would reduce the arable land, scant as it is, on which they grow their food or cash crops. They could see no benefit in growing forests for ecological reasons or in covering their cropland with government-owned trees. The farmers' plots average only a hectare and a half (about four acres), and the traditional reforestation method was to cover whole areas with seedlings. Moreover, past efforts at channeling AID money to reforestation had often failed because the money was lost or misappropriated by the Haitian government bureaucracy.

Given all these problems, what steps could you, with your anthropological training, recommend to get farmers to plant and maintain trees?

AN ACTUAL SOLUTION   In the late 1970s, Gerald F. Murray made the mistake of jokingly telling a Haitian official working on reforestation that, based on his ethnographic research with Haitian farmers, he could get more seedlings planted with a jeep and $50,000 than they would with their multimillion-dollar program. To his surprise, two years later they took him up on it, giving him a jeep and $4 million to direct a four-year reforestation effort, beginning in 1980. They asked him how many seedlings he would get planted and how many farmers he would convince to participate. When his initial estimate of two thousand farmers and one million trees was considered too small, he raised it to six thousand farmers and three million trees. The question, of course, was how would he do it.

The first thing Murray did was to reorient the whole project from serving environmental and ecological purposes to introducing a new cash crop—trees—to the farmers. He proposed that the seedlings, rather than being owned by the government, were to be given to the farmers. They were told that when the trees matured they could cut them down and sell the lumber or the charcoal produced by burning the roots. Moreover, the trees would take up only a small amount of farmland and would not interfere with the growing of other crops, but they could bring in more money than the farmers' entire annual income from other crops. Murray located fast-growing, lumber-producing trees that matured quickly, in about four years. He suggested a planting pattern in which the trees would be planted along the borders of fields rather than being planted in blocs, which would allow tree-growing to be mixed with other crops. Finally, realizing that government bureaucracies might endanger the program, he set up a network in which local representatives were to take delivery of and distribute the seedlings.

The results were dramatic. By the end of the fourth year of the project, 75,000 Haitian farmers had planted 20 million trees. The project was so successful that farmers who had not signed up for the project were stealing seedlings from their neighbors and planting them on their land. There were also unexpected results; the farmers were not cutting their trees when they matured. Partly this may have been due to their pride in owning the trees, but they also viewed the trees as a bank account to be drawn on if their other crops failed.

Murray's account of the project is one of the most entertaining descriptions of applied anthropology you are likely to find, and I recommend that you read the original for additional information on problems and results. It is an excellent illustration of how anthropological method and theory can be used to assist economic development.

APPLICATION 8.3 *Anthropology in Education*

The manner in which people communicate to others, and the verbal and non-verbal messages they send, can differ significantly from society to society. They may unintentionally convey entirely inappropriate messages about who they think they are and who they think someone else is. Even a smile in the wrong place at the wrong time can convey unintended meanings. Laray Barna reports how a Japanese student, newly arrived in the United States, was confused by the smiles he received from American girls he didn't know. At first he assumed that the smiles constituted an invitation to a close relationship. Finally he realized that, as he put it, "they have no interest for me; it means only a kind of greeting to a foreigner. If someone smiles at a stranger in Japan, especially a girl, she can assume he is either a sexual maniac or an impolite person."

Helaine K. Minkus, who applies anthropology in workshops she conducts for American students studying abroad and for foreign students studying in the United States, found that the friendly, open behavior of Americans creates predictable difficulties for foreign students. They appreciate the friendliness but are often disappointed when they discover that it is not an invitation to a close, intimate relationship. The cultural conflict is over the meaning of friendship; most Americans combine a close core of friends with a wide circle of acquaintances. They make a concerted effort to maintain close friends but devote little attention to those who form the wider circle. Even standard greeting rituals such as "How are you?" are often misinterpreted by foreign students as genuine inquiries into their state of health.

Other American customs also confuse foreign students. Our efforts to impress others with our success of proficiency make little sense to those who were taught to be modest and self-deprecating. Most students from China or Japan expect authority figures to behave accordingly and tell them what to do; they are often surprised at the informality of American teachers. Foreign students who come from cultures where people fear appearing greedy may refuse an initial offer of refreshments, expecting to be able to accept on the second or third offer; as Minkus points out, they often leave American homes hungry after refusing the first and only offer of food.

Interacting with people whose cultures assign different meanings to behaviors, events, objects, and emotions can be an unsettling experience. However, intercultural interaction is a necessity in today's world. Diplomacy, business, education, recreation, and tourism are just a few of the areas in which misunderstandings arising from cultural diversity must be overcome. One of the questions anthropologists address is how knowledge of other cultures can foster intercultural understanding and communication. An area in which the need for this knowledge and understanding is increasingly evident is the problems posed by cultural diversity in American schools and colleges.

Intercultural Understanding in American Schools

THE PROBLEM   Suppose you are a school administrator in an urban school district that may include students and families from Asian American, Afro-American, Hispanic American, Euro-American, and Native American cultural backgrounds. Problems have been reported in relations among students and between students and teachers that you think might be due to the difficulty of communication among people of diverse cultures. You have been asked to develop a series of workshops for the students, teachers, and administrators in the district to foster better intercultural understanding and communication in the schools.

BACKGROUND OF THE PROBLEM   The United States has a multicultural society that places an emphasis on maintaining cultural diversity. Because the schools include students from a variety of cultural backgrounds, almost every American school or college and classroom, from the primary level through the graduate level, has its own cultural mix and consequently its own potential for miscommunication and misunderstanding. Differences in patterns of family interaction, language spoken at home, attitudes toward authority, and educational standards must be accommodated. Moreover, the cultural background of the teacher often differs from that of some of the students.

Some cultural groups, such as Asian Americans, firmly link education with success. These parents strongly encourage their children to excel in school, and teachers are likely to view them as model students. Students from cultures that do not see education as essential to the good life may be disdainful of it, and teachers may view them as problem students. Other conflicts can occur in the values of teachers and parents toward education. Teachers may view education as a vehicle of change and personal improvement, while families and the community may view it as a vehicle of cultural maintenance. Parents may want their children to speak standard American English or the minority dialect or a native language. They may want them to be obedient or to question authority. They may want their children to go away to college or to remain at home and find a job.

In the light of these problems of the diverse cultures prevalent in a multicultural society such as the United States, what kinds of problems in intercultural understanding and communication should your school workshops address?

AN ACTUAL SOLUTION Richard Ammann applies anthropology in conducting cross-cultural workshops for teachers, students, and administrators in American schools, as well as for businesspeople working abroad. He makes five points about his workshops for educators that might apply to any cross-cultural training experience. Ammann points out that some potential cultural conflicts are common to many environments, but some are unique to the school setting.

The first two points apply generally. People need to become acquainted with the rules, values, and communication patterns of their own culture. In order to appreciate and understand other cultures, they must be aware that they too are cultural animals. People also need to understand how the meanings they give to their experiences affect their views of other peoples and how they interact with them.

The next three points apply specifically to educators. Teachers and administrators need to be familiar with classroom situations that highlight cultural differences and the kinds of miscommunication and misunderstandings that can occur in these situations. They need to learn techniques and strategies to use in communicating and interacting with students from cultural backgrounds different from their own, and how to share them with students to help them get along with one another.

As Ammann points out, training in cross-cultural sensitivity such as he offers in his workshops is not the only solution to the problems of cultural misunderstandings that can develop in educational settings. Anthropologists and people with anthropological training are in increasing demand by schools and colleges to help solve problems in diversity among students and between them and faculties and administrators.

APPLICATION 8.4 *Anthropology in Architecture*

Space is a cultural construction that is often taken for granted. People in different cultures have different ideas about space. Westerners, for example, tend to view it as a void filled with objects, but in other societies there is no such thing as empty space. A space is always filled with something, even if that thing is spiritual in nature. In some societies, people like to maintain some physical distance from others and are uncomfortable if someone stands closer to them than a couple of feet; in other societies, people converse with their faces inches apart.

Edward T. Hall was a pioneer in exploring how different societies construct different ideas about space and how people and things are distributed within it. In his book *The Hidden Dimension,* he describes the different ways people think of space and movement and the difficulties that could arise when they are unaware of such differences.

Cultural differences in ideas about space have various practical consequences, not the least of which has to do with architecture. Housing styles vary considerably from culture to culture, as does the arrangement of living space. In some societies, the living area is one large open space; in others, such as ours, the living area is partitioned into smaller units to protect privacy and convey ownership. In some societies, the cooking area of a house is the main gathering point; in others, the preference is to have rooms reserved for social gatherings. Anthropology is applied in the architectural design of houses to make them conform to the space requirements of the people who will inhabit them.

Designing Homes Apache Style

THE PROBLEM Suppose you have been hired as an architectural consultant to help with a government-funded project to build a new village for the Tonto Apache in central Arizona. The builders want to avoid the problems encountered by other architects who had designed and built new Native American communities based on a Euro-American design, only to find that the residents were so uncomfortable with their new houses that they moved back into their old ones. Your problem is to consult with the Apache about their living space needs and convey their ideas to the architects so they can be accommodated in the housing design.

BACKGROUND OF THE PROBLEM Like the traditional Apache wickiup, the existing Tonto Apache homes have a sleeping area and another large space used for all daytime activities. What Euro-Americans define as shy behavior in the Apache is more a function of their definition of appropriate social behavior (see Question 3.3). Apache like to enter a social interaction slowly, assessing it in steps and making decisions about whether to interact further. They prefer open spaces so they can view the entire social setting and still maintain enough distance that verbal interaction is unnecessary. Eating together is a major social activity for the Apache, especially if they haven't seen one another for a time. Hosts always offer food, and guests never refuse. The women cook for many people at once, and during the summer most cooking is done outdoors.

Traditionally, when Apaches died their shelters were burned; even simple homes were torn down.

Once you are aware of such special requirements for Apache dwellings, what would you recommend to the architects about the design of new homes for them?

AN ACTUAL SOLUTION The problem you face is exactly the one faced by anthropologist George S. Esber, Jr., who made a number of recommendations to the architects. While privacy was desired for sleeping areas, there should be as few partitions as possible in the homes so people could visit yet maintain some social distance. The cooking area and the visiting space should be in full view to accommodate the roles of food preparation and visiting. Portable wood stoves that could be moved outdoors should be used, and instead of standard-size sinks, larger sinks and cupboards should be installed to meet the cooking demands in Apache homes.

There wasn't too much Esber could do about the destruction of homes after a death. One suggestion was that surviving family members could stay with relatives or friends while others redecorated the home to give it a new appearance.

When Esber returned to the community after it was built, he found the Apache genuinely enthusiastic about their new homes.

APPLICATION 8.5 *Anthropology in Law*

All societies have some means of resolving conflict, as well as a customary legal system that maps out rules for proper and improper behavior and penalties for violation of these rules. However, as indigenous peoples begin to be absorbed into nation-states, or as countries become independent and develop or adopt national legal systems, there is often a conflict between the new legal systems or means of resolving conflicts on the one hand and customary methods of conflict resolution on the other. In some societies of New Guinea, for example, it is customary for homicide cases to be settled by a compensatory payment made by the group whose member committed the homicide to members of the victim's family or clan. How could this system of conflict resolution be reconciled with a Western judicial system that focuses on the punishment of the perpetrator rather than compensation to the victim?

Writing Law in New Guinea

THE PROBLEM In 1972, Papua New Guinea became an independent nation of three and one-half million people, speaking some 750 mutually unintelligible languages, and living under a combination of a Western legal system that had been imposed by Australia and almost 1,000 different customary or traditional legal systems. How could a national legal system be developed that took into account so many diverse legal principles? To solve the problem, the new government of Papua New Guinea established a Law Reform Commission to make recommendations to the parliament. Suppose you had been hired as an anthropologist to direct the Customary Law Project.

BACKGROUND OF THE PROBLEM The problems of reconciling customary law with the legal system that had been imposed by Australia on Papua New Guinea can be illustrated with the impact of legal change on the Abelam. One Abelam man had been jailed because he buried his deceased mother inside her house, when custom required a corpse to be laid to rest in the house in which the person had worked and slept, covered with only a thin layer of soil. The house would then be abandoned and eventually collapse around the burial site. Australian officials wanted this practice discontinued because they felt it constituted a health hazard. Another legal problem was polygamy. While most Abelam marriages were monogamous, some men had more than one wife. One elderly man with two wives expressed concern when he discovered that he was breaking the law, but he explained that he could never choose one wife over the other because he loved both.

There was also the problem of homicide compensation. Such conflicts in Papua New Guinea were customarily resolved by payments of some sort to the aggrieved survivors. The payment, which was supposed to be proportionate to the act that caused the conflict, implied acceptance of responsibility by the donor and willingness to end the dispute by the recipient. These arrangements were not recognized under state law, and the use of customary law changed as indigenous people came into contact with Western society. Some cases involved huge groups of people and claims of large compensatory payments. For example, when a man driving a truck struck and killed a man from another province, members of the clan of the victim demanded hundreds of thousands of *kina* (currency equivalent to the Australian dollar) in compensation from the driver's whole province.

As director of the Customary Law Project, in what ways would you have helped legal practitioners and identified problems for the legislators who were to draft legislation to reconcile customary law with a national legal system?

AN ACTUAL SOLUTION Richard Scaglion, an anthropologist working with the Abelam, was hired to address this problem. He began by conducting bibliographical research on studies that had been done on different groups in New Guinea, most of it conducted by anthropologists. He discovered a lack of specific legal case studies, that is, instances of conflict with descriptions of how the conflict was resolved, along with a statement of the legal principles from which a dispute was settled. His next step was to set up a system for gathering information about customary law in New Guinea. He selected and trained students from the University of Papua New Guinea to work in their home areas gathering information. Some 600 extended case studies of conflict resolution were collected, and a computer retrieval system was designed to allow lawyers, judges, and lawmakers to scan and use the material in their work. The results of his work were also disseminated in publications directed to members of the legal profession and to other applied anthropologists working in the area of legal development in the Pacific.

As a result of Scaglion's work, lawyers in Papua New Guinea were able to find customary precedent cases to use in arguing the cases of clients before the courts. For example, he helped one attorney who needed information about customary divorce practices in a particular area, and investigated issues related to domestic violence and women's access to justice in rural Papua New Guinea. He was able to identify problem areas for legislators and to draft legislation to resolve those problems. Because some men had reason to be concerned about the legal consequences of bigamy, a family law bill was drafted to recognize customary marriages as legal and to allow polygamous marriages under certain conditions. Domestic violence was becoming a problem because of changing patterns of residence. Traditionally, after marriage a woman went to live with her husband's family, but her own family would be nearby, and if she was abused by her husband she could return to her own family. To obtain employment in developing areas, however, families often had to move to other parts of the country, and wives could not return home easily. Lawmakers needed to be made aware of these changes in problem areas.

Legislation was prepared that recognized the exchange of wealth and services as a means of resolving conflicts involving death, injuries, and property damage. It sought to regulate payments by specifying the amount of compensation to be paid in specific circumstances. Scaglion solicited opinions from other anthropologists on the draft bill to ensure that its provisions did not conflict with the customary law of the groups with which they were working. For example, Andrew Strathern noted that the draft bill might unintentionally set limits on the competitive ceremonial exchange, or *moka,* of the Melpa (see Question 5.5). As a result of Strathern's information, a revised version of the legislation was prepared.

REFERENCES AND SUGGESTED READINGS

INTRODUCTION: THE PROBLEMS OF CULTURAL DIVERSITY The opening quote is from John J. Honigmann, *Understanding Culture* (Harper & Row, 1963), pp. 1–2. A general review of applied anthropology can be found in the article by Erve Chambers, "Applied Anthropology in the Post-Vietnam Era: Anticipations and Ironies," in *Annual Review of Anthropology,* vol. 16 (1987), pp. 309–337.

ANTHROPOLOGY IN HEALTH CARE Edward C. Green describes his work in "Traditional Healers and Childhood Diarrheal Disease in Swaziland: The Interface of Anthropology and Health Education," *Social Science and Medicine,* vol. 20 (1985), pp. 277–285, and in his article, "Anthropology in the Context of a Water-Borne Disease Control Project," in *Practicing Development Anthropology* (Westview Press, 1986). Jeannine Coreil reports on her similar work in "Innovation among Haitian Healers: The Adoption of Oral Rehydration Therapy," *Human Organization,* vol. 47 (1988), pp. 48–56. For those interested in how anthropology has been used in the nursing profession, see the article by Molly C. Dougherty and Toni Tripp-Reimer, "The Interface of Nursing and Anthropology," in *Annual Review of Anthropology,* vol. 14 (1985), pp. 219–241, and the special issue of *Practicing Anthropology* on nursing, vol. 10, no. 2 (1988).

ANTHROPOLOGY IN ECONOMIC DEVELOPMENT Gerald F. Murray describes the role of anthropology in Haitian reforestation projects in "The Domestication of Wood in Haiti: A Case Study in Applied Evolution," in *Anthropological Praxis: Translating Knowledge into Action,* edited by Robert M. Wulff and Shirley J. Fiske (Westview Press, 1987). The article is reprinted in *Applying Cultural Anthropology: An Introductory Reader,* edited by Aaron Podolefsky and Peter J. Brown (Mayfield Publishing, 1991). The role of anthropologists working in economic development is discussed by Allan Hoben in "Anthropologists and Development," in *Annual Review of Anthropology,* vol. 11 (1982), pp. 349–375.

ANTHROPOLOGY IN EDUCATION The experience of the Japanese student with smiling American women is reported by Laray M. Barna in "Stumbling Blocks in Intercultural Communication," in *Intercultural Communication: A Reader,* 4th edition, edited by Larry A. Samovar and Richard E. Porter (Wadsworth Press, 1985). Helaine K. Minkus describes her workshops for students in "Cross-Cultural Issues for Foreign Students," *Practicing Anthropology,* vol. 9, no. 3 (1987), and Richard Ammann reports in his work with students, teachers, and administrators in the same issue. Catherine Pelissier provides a review of the work done by anthropologists in education in "The Anthropology of Teaching and Learning," in *Annual Review of Anthropology,* vol. 20 (1991), pp. 75–95.

ANTHROPOLOGY IN ARCHITECTURE   Edward T. Hall's ideas on how people and objects are distributed in space in different societies can be found in *The Hidden Dimensions* (Doubleday, 1966). George S. Esber describes his work with the Apache in "Designing Apache Homes with Apache," in *Anthropological Praxis: Translating Knowledge into Action,* cited above.

ANTHROPOLOGY IN LAW   Richard Scaglion describes his work on the Customary Law Project in "Customary Law Development in Papua New Guinea," in *Anthropological Praxis: Translating Knowledge into Action.* Thomas Weaver discusses the role of anthropology in public policy in "Anthropology as a Policy Science: Part II, Development and Training," *Human Organization,* vol. 44 (1985), pp. 197–205. A review of the literature on anthropology and public policy can be found in "Anthropology, Administration, and Public Policy," by Robert E. Hinshaw, in *Annual Review of Anthropology,* vol. 9 (1980), pp. 497–522.

balanced reciprocity: The term suggested by Marshall D. Sahlins for a form of exchange in which items of equal or near-equal value are exchanged on the spot.

bilateral kinship: A system in which individuals trace their descent through both parents.

brideservice: The requirement that when a couple marries the groom must work for the bride's parents for some specified period of time.

bridewealth (brideprice): The valuables that a groom or his family is expected or obligated to present to the bride's family.

caste: A system of social stratification based on assignment at birth to the ranked social or occupational groups of parents. There is no mobility from one caste to another, and intermarriage may be forbidden.

clan: A unilineal descent group whose members claim descent from a common ancestor.

cultural anthropology: One of the four major subfields of anthropology, the others being physical or biological anthropology, archaeology, and linguistics. Cultural anthropology seeks to explain the varieties of human belief and behavior and make sense of the meanings that different peoples ascribe to their experiences.

cultural text: A way of thinking about culture as a text of significant symbols—words, gestures, drawings, natural objects—that carries meaning.

culture: The system of meanings about the nature of experience that are shared by a people and and passed on from one generation to another.

culture change: The change in meanings that a people ascribe to experience and changes in their way of life.

culture of poverty: A phrase coined by Oscar Lewis to describe the life-style and worldview of people who inhabit urban and rural slums.

division of labor: A work system characterized by division of tasks and specialization of occupations.

domain of experience: An area of human experience (e.g., business, war, science, family life) from which people borrow meaning to apply to other areas.

dowry: The goods and valuables a bride's family supplies to the groom's family or to the couple.

egocentric: A view of the self that defines each person as a replica of all humanity, the locus of motivations and drives, capable of acting independently from others.

ethnocentric fallacy: The mistaken notion that the beliefs and behaviors of other cultures can be judged from the perspective of one's own.

ethnocentrism: The tendency to judge the beliefs and behaviors of other cultures from the perspective of one's own.

ethnographic method: The immersion of researchers in the lives and cultures of the peoples they are trying to understand in order to comprehend the meanings these peoples ascribe to their existence.

ethnographic present: Use of the present tense to describe a culture, although the description may refer to situations that existed in the past.

exogamy: A rule that requires marriage to someone outside one's own group.

exploitative theory of social stratification: A theory based on the assumption that social stratification and hierarchy exist because one group of individuals seeks to take advantage of another group for economic purposes.

extended family: A family group based on blood relations of three or more generations.

family of orientation: The family group that consists of a father, a mother, the self, and siblings.

family of procreation: The family group that consists of a husband, a wife, and their children.

generalized reciprocity: A form of exchange in which persons share what they have with others but expect them to reciprocate later.

holistic: A view of the self in which the individual cannot be conceived of as existing separately from society or apart from his or her status or role.

identity struggle: A term coined by Anthony F. C. Wallace and Raymond D. Fogelson to characterize interaction in which there is a discrepancy between the identity a person claims to possess and the identity attributed to that person by others.

ideology of class: A set of beliefs characteristic of stratified societies that justifies the division of a society into groups with differential rights and privileges as being natural and right.

impartible inheritance: A form of inheritance in which family property is passed undivided to one heir.

incest taboo: A rule that prohibits sexual relations among certain categories of kin, such as brothers or sisters, mothers or fathers, or, in some cases, cousins.

individualistic: A view of the self in which the individual is primarily responsible for his or her own actions.

integrative theory of social stratification: A theory based on the assumption that social hierarchy is necessary for the smooth functioning of society.

interpersonal theory of disease: A view of disease in which it is assumed that illness is caused by tensions or conflicts in social relations.

irrigation agriculture: A form of cultivation in which water is used to deliver nutrients to growing plants.

key metaphors: Metaphors that dominate the meanings that people in a specific culture attribute to their experience.

key scenarios: A term coined by Sherry Ortner to identify dominant stories or myths that portray the values and beliefs of a specific society.

matrilineage: A kinship group that is formed by tracing descent in the female line.

matrilineal kinship: A system of descent in which persons are related to their kin through the mother only.

means of production: The materials, such as land, machines, or tools, that people need to produce things.

metaphor: A figure of speech in which linguistic expressions are taken from one area of experience and applied to another.

myth: A story or narrative that portrays the meanings people give to their experience.

negative identity: The attribution of personal characteristics believed to be undesirable.

negative reciprocity: A form of exchange in which the object is to get something for nothing or to make a profit.

nuclear family: The family group consisting of father, mother, and their own or adopted children.

partible inheritance: A form of inheritance in which the goods or property of a family is divided among the heirs.

participant observation: The active participation of a researcher or observer in the lives of those being studied.

patrilineage: A kinship group that is formed by tracing descent in the male line.

patrilineal kinship: A system of descent in which persons are related to their kin through the father only.

phallocentrism: A term coined by Peggy Sanday to describe the deployment of the penis as a symbol of masculine social power and dominance.

plow agriculture: A form of cultivation in which fields must be plowed to remove weeds and grasses prior to planting.

political or social repression: The use of force by a ruling group to maintain political, economic, or social control over other groups.

polyandry: A form of marriage in which a woman is permitted to have more than one husband.

polygamy: A form of marriage in which a person is permitted to have more than one spouse.

polygyny: A form of marriage in which a man is permitted to have more than one wife.

population density: The number of people in a given geographic area.

positive identity: The attribution to people of personal characteristics believed to be desirable.

principle of reciprocity: The social principle that giving a gift creates social ties with the person receiving it, who eventually is obliged to reciprocate.

progress: The idea that human history is the story of a steady advance from a life dependent on the whims of nature to a life of control and domination over natural forces.

relativism: The attempt to understand the beliefs and behaviors of other cultures in terms of the culture in which they are found.

relativistic fallacy: The idea that it is impossible to make moral judgments about the beliefs and behaviors of members of other cultures.

revitalization movements: The term suggested by Anthony F. C. Wallace for attempts by a people to construct a more satisfying culture.

rites of passage: The term suggested by Arnold van Gennep for rituals that mark a person's passage from one identity or status to another.

ritual: A dramatic rendering or social portrayal of meanings shared by a specific body of people in a way that makes them seem correct and proper (see **symbolic action**).

Sapir-Whorf hypothesis: The idea that there is an explicit link between the grammar of a language and the culture of the people who speak that language.

secondary elaboration: A term suggested by E. E. Evans-Pritchard for attempts by people to explain away inconsistencies or contradictions in their beliefs.

sedentary: A style of living characterized by permanent or semipermanent settlements.

selective perception: The tendency of people to see and recognize only those things they expect to see or those that confirm their view of the world.

slash-and-burn or **swidden agriculture:** A form of cultivation in which forests are cleared by burning trees and brush and crops are planted among the ashes of the cleared ground.

social class: A system of social stratification based on income or possession of wealth and resources. Individual social mobility is possible in a class system.

social identities: Views that people have of their own and others' positions in society. Individuals seek confirmation from others that they occupy the positions on the social landscape that they claim to occupy.

sociocentric: A view of the self that is context-dependent; there is no intrinsic self that can possess enduring qualities.

state: A form of society characterized by a hierarchical ranking of people and centralized political control.

surplus value of labor: The term suggested by Karl Marx and Friedrich Engels for the portion of a person's labor that is retained as profit by those who control the means of production.

symbolic action: The activities—including ritual, myth, art, dance, and music— that dramatically depict the meanings shared by a specific body of people.

violent revolution: The term suggested by Karl Marx and Friedrich Engels for the necessary response of workers to their repression by the ruling class.

B I B L I O G R A P H Y

Adams, John W. 1973. *The Gitksan Potlatch: Population Flux, Resource Owner-ship and Reciprocity.* Toronto: Holt, Rinehart and Winston of Canada.

Alford, Richard D. 1988. *Naming and Identity: A Cross-Cultural Study of Per-sonal Naming Practices.* New Haven, CT: HRAF Press.

Ammann, Richard. 1987. "Cross-Cultural Training Workshops for Educators." *Practicing Anthropology* 9:8.

Angeloni, Elvio. 1990. *Anthropology 90/91.* Guilford, CT: Dushkin Publishing.

Anonymous. 1816. *Testimonies of the Life, Character, Revelations and Doctrines of Our Ever Blessed Mother Ann Lee . . . .* New York: J. Tallcott & J. Deming.

Arens, William. 1976. "Professional Football: An American Symbol and Ritual." In *The American Dimension: Cultural Myths and Social Realities.* Edited by William Arens and Susan P. Montague. Port Washington, NY: Alfred Publishing.

Barna, Laray M. 1985. "Stumbling Blocks in Intercultural Communication." In *Intercultural Communication: A Reader,* 4th edition. Edited by Larry A. Sam-ovar and Richard E. Porter. Belmont, CA: Wadsworth Press.

Barnes, Barry. 1974. *Scientific Knowledge and Sociological Theory.* London: Routledge & Kegan Paul.

Basso, Keith H. 1979. *Portraits of "The Whiteman": Linguistic Play and Cul-tural Symbols among the Western Apache.* New York: Cambridge University Press.

Bean, Susan. 1976. "Soap Operas: Sagas of American Kinship." In *The American Dimension: Cultural Myths and Social Realities.* Edited by William Arens and Susan P. Montague. Port Washington, NY: Alfred Publishing.

Bellah, Robert, Richard Madsen, William M. Sullivan, Ann Swidler, and Steven M. Tipton. 1984. *Habits of the Heart.* Berkeley: University of California Press.

Belmonte, Thomas. 1989. *The Broken Fountain.* New York: Columbia University Press.

Benedict, Ruth. 1934. *Patterns of Culture.* New York: Houghton Mifflin.

Boas, Franz. 1966. *Kwakiutl Ethnography.* Edited by Helen Codere. Chicago: University of Chicago Press.

Boas, Franz, and George Hunt. 1905. *Kwakiutl Texts.* Memoir of the American Museum of Natural History, vol. 5.

Bodley, John H. 1985. *Anthropology and Contemporary Problems,* 2nd edition. Palo Alto, CA: Mayfield Publishing.

Bohannan, Laura. 1966. "Shakespeare in the Bush." *Natural History Magazine,* August/September.

Bohannan, Paul, editor. 1970. *Divorce and After.* New York: Doubleday.

Briggs, Jean. 1970. *Never in Anger.* Cambridge, MA: Harvard University Press.

Cagan, Leslie. 1983. "Feminism and Militarism." In *Beyond Survival: New Direc-tions for the Disarmament Movement.* Edited by M. Albert and D. Dellinger. Boston: South End Press.

Cairns, Ed. 1982. "Intergroup Conflict in Northern Ireland." In *Social Identity and Intergroup Relations.* Edited by Henri Tajfel. New York: Cambridge Uni-versity Press.

Campbell, Joseph. 1949. *The Hero with a Thousand Faces.* Princeton, NJ: Princeton University Press.

Campion, Nardi Reeder. 1990. *Mother Ann Lee: Morning Star of the Shakers.* Hanover, NH: University Press of New England.

Carneiro, Robert. 1978. "Political Expansion as an Expression of the Principle of Competitive Exclusion." In *Origins of the State.* Edited by Ronald Cohn and Elman Service. Philadelphia: Institute for the Study of Human Issues.

Carneiro, Robert. 1979. "Slash-and-Burn Cultivation among the Kuikuru and Its Implication for Cultural Development in the Amazon Basin." In *The Evolution of Horticultural Systems in Native South America: Causes and Consequences, Anthropologica Supplement 2.* Edited by J. Wilbert. Caracas, Venezuela.

Carneiro, Robert. 1990. "Chiefdom-Level Warfare as Exemplified in Fiji and Cauca Valley." In *The Anthropology of War.* Edited by Jonathan Hass. New York: Cambridge University Press.

Carroll, John B. 1956. *Language, Thought, and Reality: Selected Writings of Benjamin Lee Whorf.* New York: John Wiley & Sons.

Cathcart, Dolores, and Robert Cathcart. 1985. "Japanese Social Experience and Concept of Groups." In *Intercultural Communication: A Reader, 4th edition.* Edited by Larry A. Samovar and Richard E. Porter. Belmont, CA: Wadsworth Publishing.

Chagnon, Napoleon. 1983. *The Fierce People,* 3rd edition. New York: Holt, Rinehart and Winston.

Chagnon, Napoleon. 1990. "Reproductive and Somatic Conflicts of Interest in the Genesis of Violence and Warfare among Tribesmen." In *The Anthropology of War.* Edited by Jonathan Hass. New York: Cambridge University Press.

Chambers, Erve. 1987. "Applied Anthropology in the Post-Vietnam Era: Anticipations and Ironies." In *Annual Review of Anthropology,* vol. 16, pp. 309–337. Palo Alto, CA: Annual Reviews.

Chomsky, Noam. 1985. *Turning the Tide: U.S. Intervention in Central America and the Struggle for Peace.* Boston: South End Press.

Clay, Jason W. 1984. "Yahgan and Ona—The Road to Extinction." *Cultural Survival Quarterly* 8:5–8.

Cohen, Mark. 1977. *The Food Crisis in Prehistory.* New Haven, CT: Yale University Press.

Cohen, Mark. 1989. *Health and the Rise of Civilization.* New Haven, CT: Yale University Press.

Cohn, Carol. 1987. "Sex and Death in the Rational World of Defense Intellectuals." *Signs* 12:687–718.

Cohn, Carol. 1991. "Decoding Military Newspeak." *Ms. magazine,* no. 5.

Collier, Jane E., and Michelle Rosaldo. 1981. "Politics and Gender in Simple Societies." In *Sexual Meanings: The Cultural Construction of Gender and Sexuality.* Edited by Sherry B. Ortner and Harriet Whitehead. New York: Cambridge University Press.

Coreil, Jeannine. 1988. "Innovation among Haitian Healers: The Adoption of Oral Rehydration Therapy." *Human Organization* 47:48–56.

Cowell, Daniel David. 1985/86. "Funerals, Family, and Forefathers: A View of Italian-American Funeral Practices." *Omega* 16:69–85.

Crick, Malcolm R. 1982. "Anthropology of Knowledge." In *Annual Review of Anthropology,* vol. 11, pp. 287–313. Palo Alto, CA: Annual Reviews.

Culler, Jonathan. 1977. "In Pursuit of Signs." *Daedalus* 106:95–112.

Davis, D. L., and R. G. Whitten. 1987. "The Cross-Cultural Study of Human Sexuality." In *Annual Review of Anthropology,* vol. 16, pp. 69–98. Palo Alto, CA: Annual Reviews.

Devita, Philip, editor. 1990. *The Humbled Anthropologist: Tales from the Pacific.* Belmont, CA: Wadsworth Publishing.

Devita, Philip, editor. 1991. *The Naked Anthropologist: Tales from around the World.* Belmont, CA: Wadsworth Publishing.

Devita, Philip, and James Armstrong, editors. 1992. *Distant Mirrors: America as a Foreign Culture.* Belmont, CA: Wadsworth Publishing.

Divale, William Tulio, and Marvin Harris. 1976. "Population, Warfare, and the Male Supremacist Complex." *American Anthropologist* 78:521–538.

Dougherty, Molly C., and Toni Tripp-Reimer. 1985. "The Interface of Nursing and Anthropology." In *Annual Review of Anthropology,* vol. 14, pp. 219–241. Palo Alto, CA: Annual Reviews.

Douglas, Mary. 1966. *Purity and Danger.* New York: Frederick A. Praeger.

Drèze, Jean, and Amartya Sen. 1991. *Hunger and Public Action.* New York: Cambridge University Press.

Dumont, Louis. 1970. *Homo Hierarchicus: An Essay on the Caste System.* Chicago: University of Chicago Press.

Durham, William H. 1990. "Advances in Evolutionary Culture Theory." In *Annual Review of Anthropology,* vol. 19, pp. 187–210. Palo Alto, CA: Annual Reviews.

Dwyer-Schick, Susan. 1991. "Some Consequences of a Fieldworker's Gender for Doing Cross-Cultural Research." In *The Naked Anthropologist: Tales from around the World.* Edited by Philip Devita. Belmont, CA: Wadsworth Publishing.

Eisler, Riane. 1987. *The Chalice and the Blade.* New York: Harper & Row.

Erasmus, Charles. 1977. *In Search of the Common Good.* Glencoe, IL: Free Press.

Esber, George S. 1987. "Designing Apache Homes with Apache." In *Anthropological Praxis: Translating Knowledge into Action.* Edited by Robert M. Wulff and Shirley J. Fiske. Boulder, CO: Westview Press.

Evans-Pritchard, E. E. 1937. *Witchcraft, Oracles and Magic among the Azande.* London: Oxford University Press.

Fei, Hsiao-Tung. 1939. *Peasant Life in China: A Field Study of Country Life in the Yangtze Valley.* London: Routledge & Kegan Paul.

Fernandez, James W. 1978. "African Religious Movements." In *Annual Review of Anthropology,* vol. 7, pp. 195–234. Palo Alto, CA: Annual Reviews.

Foley, Douglas E. 1990. *Learning Capitalist Culture: Deep in the Heart of Tejas.* Philadelphia: University of Pennsylvania Press.

Fried, Morton H. 1967. *The Evolution of Political Society.* New York: Random House.

Fried, Morton, Marvin Harris, and Robert Murphy. 1967. *War: The Anthropology of Armed Conflict and Aggression.* Garden City, NY: Natural History Press.

Geertz, Clifford. 1972. "Deep Play: Notes on the Balinese Cockfight." *Daedalus* 101:1–37.

Geertz, Clifford. 1973. "The Impact of Culture on the Concept of Man." In *The Interpretation of Cultures.* New York: Basic Books.

Gibson, Thomas. 1990. "Raiding, Trading and Tribal Autonomy in Insular Southeast Asia." In *The Anthropology of War.* Edited by Jonathan Hass. New York: Cambridge University Press.

Gilmore, David D. 1990. *Manhood in the Making: Cultural Concepts of Masculinity.* New Haven, CT: Yale University Press.

Ginsburg, Faye, and Rayna Rapp. 1991. "The Politics of Reproduction." In *Annual Review of Anthropology,* vol. 20, pp. 311–343. Palo Alto, CA: Annual Reviews.

Goffman, Erving. 1959. *The Presentation of Self in Everyday Life.* New York: Doubleday.

Gould, Stephen Jay. 1981. *The Mismeasure of Man.* New York: W. W. Norton.

Green, Edward C. 1985. "Traditional Healers and Childhood Diarrheal Disease in Swaziland: The Interface of Anthropology and Health Education." *Social Science and Medicine* 20:277–285.

Green, Edward C. 1986. "Anthropology in the Context of a Water-Borne Disease Control Project." In *Practicing Development Anthropology.* Boulder, CO: Westview Press.

Greenhouse, Carol. 1987. "Cultural Perspectives on War." In *The Quest for Peace: Transcending Collective Violence and War among Societies, Cultures and States.* Edited by R. Varynen. Beverly Hills, CA: Sage Publications.

Gregor, Thomas. 1990. "Uneasy Peace: Intertribal Relations in Brazil's Upper Xingu." In *The Anthropology of War.* Edited by Jonathan Hass. New York: Cambridge University Press.

Hall, Edgar T. 1966. *The Hidden Dimension.* Garden City, NY: Doubleday.

Harris, Marvin. 1977. *Cannibals and Kings: The Origins of Culture.* New York: Vintage Books.

Hayden, Dolores. 1981. *Seven American Utopias: The Architecture of Communitarian Socialism, 1790–1975.* Cambridge, MA: MIT Press.

Henle, Paul. 1958. *Language, Thought and Experience.* Ann Arbor: The University of Michigan Press.

Hertz, Robert. 1960. *Death and the Right Hand.* Translated and edited by Claudia and Rodney Needham. Glencoe, IL: Free Press. (originally published 1909)

Hinshaw, Robert E. "Anthropology, Administration, and Public Policy." In *Annual Review of Anthropology,* vol. 9, pp. 497–522. Palo Alto, CA: Annual Reviews.

Hobbes, Thomas. 1881. *Leviathan.* London: Oxford University Press. (originally published 1651)

Hoben, Allan. 1982. "Anthropologists and Development." In *Annual Review of Anthropology,* vol. 11, pp. 349–375. Palo Alto, CA: Annual Reviews.

Hobsbaum, Eric. 1959. *Primitive Rebels: Studies in Archaic Forms of Social Movement in the 19th and 20th Centuries.* New York: Frederick A. Praeger.

Holloway, Ralph L., Jr. 1968. "Human Aggression: The Need for a Species-Specific Framework." In *War: The Anthropology of Armed Conflict and Aggression.* Edited by Morton Fried, Marvin Harris, and Robert Murphy. Garden City, NY: Natural History Press.

Honigmann, John J. 1963. *Understanding Culture.* New York: Harper & Row.

Honigmann, John J. 1976. *The Development of Anthropological Ideas.* Homewood, IL: Dorsey Press.

Hostetler, John. 1974. *Hutterite Society.* Baltimore: Johns Hopkins University Press.

House, James S., Karl R. Landis, and Debra Umberson. 1988. "Social Relationships and Health." *Science* 241:540–545.

Hsu, Francis L. K. 1967. *Under the Ancestor's Shadow.* New York: Anchor Books.

Inhorn, Marcia C., and Peter J. Brown. 1990. "The Anthropology of Infectious Disease." In *Annual Review of Anthropology,* vol. 19, pp. 89–117. Palo Alto, CA: Annual Reviews.

Kearney, Michael. 1991. "A Very Bad Disease of the Arms." In *The Naked Anthropologist: Tales from around the World.* Edited by Philip Devita. Belmont, CA: Wadsworth Publishing.

Keesing, Roger. 1991. "Not a Real Fish: The Ethnographer as Inside Outsider." In *The Naked Anthropologist: Tales from around the World.* Edited by Philip Devita. Belmont, CA: Wadsworth Publishing.

Kehoe, Alice. 1989. *The Ghost Dance: Ethnohistory and Revitalization.* New York: Holt, Rinehart and Winston.

Keiser, Lincoln. 1969. *The Vice Lords: Warriors of the Streets.* New York: Holt, Rinehart and Winston.

Keiser, Lincoln. 1991. *Friend by Day, Enemy by Night: Organized Vengeance in a Kohistani Community.* New York: Holt, Rinehart and Winston.

Kelly, John D., and Martha Kaplan. 1990. "History, Structure, and Ritual." In *Annual Review of Anthropology,* vol. 19, pp. 119–150. Palo Alto, CA: Annual Reviews.

Kets de Vries, Manfred, and Danny Miller. 1987. "Interpreting Organizational Texts." *Journal of Management Studies* 24:233–247.

Kiefer, Christie. 1976. "The Danchi Zoku and the Evolution of the Metropolitan Mind." In *Japan: The Paradox of Progress.* Edited by Lewis Austin, with the assistance of Adrienne Suddard and Nancy Remington. New Haven, CT: Yale University Press.

Kinkade, Kathleen. 1973. *A Walden Two Experiment: The First Five Years of Twin Oaks Community.* New York: William Morrow.

Kotlowitz, Alex. 1991. *There Are No Children Here.* New York: Anchor Books.

Kottak, Conrad Phillip. 1990. *Prime Time Society: An Anthropological Analysis of Television and Culture.* Belmont, CA: Wadsworth Publishing.

Kroeber, Alfred L. 1948. *Anthropology.* New York: Harcourt, Brace.

Kuhn, Thomas. 1957. *The Copernican Revolution: Planetary Astronomy in the Development of Western Thought.* Cambridge, MA: Harvard University Press.

Lakoff, George. 1991. "Metaphor and War: The Metaphor System Used to Justify War in the Gulf." Distributed on Bitnet (electronic mail) by *Xcult-l@psuvm.*

Lakoff, George, and Mark Johnson. 1980. *Metaphors We Live By.* Chicago: University of Chicago Press.

Lappe, Frances Moore, and Joseph Collins. 1977. *Food First: Beyond the Myth of Scarcity.* New York: Random House.

Leach, Edmund. 1979. "Anthropological Aspects of Language: Animal Categories and Verbal Abuse." In *Reader in Comparative Religion,* 4th edition. Edited by William Lessa and Evon Z. Vogt. New York: Harper & Row.

Lee, Richard. 1969. "Eating Christmas in the Kalihari." *Natural History Magazine,* December.

Lee, Richard. 1984. *The Dobe !Kung.* New York: Holt, Rinehart and Winston.

Levi-Strauss, Claude. 1974. *Tristé Tropiques.* New York: Atheneum Publishers.

Lewis, Oscar. 1959. *Five Families: Mexican Case Studies in the Culture of Poverty.* New York: Basic Books.

Linden, Eugene. 1991. "Lost Tribes, Lost Knowledge." *Time* magazine, September 23.

Livingstone, Frank B. 1968. "The Effects of Warfare on the Biology of the Human Species." In *War: The Anthropology of Armed Conflict and Aggression.* Edited by Morton Fried, Marvin Harris, and Robert Murphy. Garden City, NY: Natural History Press.

Longres, John F. 1990. *Human Behavior in the Social Environment.* Itasca, IL: F. E. Peacock Publishers.

Malinowski, Bronislaw. 1929. *The Sexual Life of Savages in North-Western Melanesia.* New York: Halcyon House.

Malinowski, Bronislaw. 1961. *Argonauts of the Western Pacific.* New York: E. P. Dutton. (originally published 1922)

Mandelbaum, David G. 1949. *Selected Writings of Edward Sapir in Language, Culture, and Personality.* Berkeley: University of California Press.

Marshall, John. 1984. "Death Blow to the Bushmen." *Cultural Survival Quarterly* 8:13–17.

Marshall, Lorna. 1976. *The !Kung of Nyae Nyae.* Cambridge, MA: Harvard University Press.

Martin, Emily. 1987. *The Woman in the Body: A Cultural Analysis of Reproduction.* Boston: Beacon Press.

Marwick, Max. 1965. *Sorcery in Its Social Setting.* Manchester, England: University of Manchester Press.

Matsubara, Hisako. 1985. *Cranes at Dusk.* New York: Dial Press.

Mauss, Marcel. 1967. *The Gift: Forms and Functions of Exchange in Archaic Societies.* Translated by Ian Cunnison. New York: W. W. Norton. (originally published 1925)

McCauley, Clark. 1990. "Conference Overview." In *The Anthropology of War.* Edited by Jonathan Hass. New York: Cambridge University Press.

McElroy, Ann, and Patricia Townsend. 1979. *Medical Anthropology.* North Scituate, MA: Duxbury Press.

Mead, Margaret. 1963. *Sex and Temperament in Three Primitive Societies.* New York: Dell Publishing. (originally published 1935)

Minkus, Helaine K. 1987. "Cross-Cultural Issues for Foreign Students." *Practicing Anthropology* 9:9.

Mishkin, Bernard. 1940. *Rank and Warfare among the Plains Indians.* Monograph no. 3, American Ethnological Society. Seattle: University of Washington Press.

Moffat, Michael. 1990. *Growing Up in New Jersey.* New Brunswick, NJ: Rutgers University Press.

Montague, Susan P., and William Morais. 1976. "Football Games and Rock Concerts: The Ritual Enactment of American Success Models." In *The American Dimension: Cultural Myths and Social Realities.* Edited by William Arens and Susan P. Montague. Port Washington, NY: Alfred Publishing.

Mooney, James. 1965. *The Ghost Dance Religion and the Sioux Outbreak of 1890.* Chicago: University of Chicago Press.

Moos, Robert, and Robert Brownstein. 1977. *Environment and Utopia.* New York: Plenum Publishing.

Morgan, Lewis Henry. 1964. *Ancient Society.* Cambridge, MA: Belknap Press. (originally published 1877)

Mukhopadhyay, Carol C., and Patricia J. Higgins. 1988. "Anthropological Studies of Women's Status Revisited: 1977–1987." In *Annual Review of Anthropology,* vol. 17, pp. 461–495. Palo Alto, CA: Annual Reviews.

Murray, Gerald F. 1987. "The Domestication of Wood in Haiti: A Case Study in Applied Evolution." In *Anthropological Praxis: Translating Knowledge into Action.* Edited by Robert M. Wulff and Shirley J. Fiske. Boulder, CO: Westview Press. Reprinted in *Applying Cultural Anthropology: An Introductory Reader.* Edited by Aaron Podolefsky and Peter J. Brown. Mountain View, CA: Mayfield Publishing, 1991.

Myer, Fred R. 1988. "Critical Trends in the Study of Hunters-Gatherers." In *Annual Review of Anthropology,* vol. 17, pp. 261–282. Palo Alto, CA: Annual Reviews.

Neider, Charles. 1966. *The Complete Travel Books of Mark Twain.* New York: Doubleday.

Nordhoff, Charles. 1966. *The Communistic Societies of the United States.* New York: Dover Publications. (originally published 1875)

Ocaya-Lakidi, Dent. 1979. "Manhood, Warriorhood and Sex in Eastern Africa." *Journal of Asian and African Studies* 12:134–165.

Oldfield-Hayes, Rose. 1975. "Female Genital Mutilation, Fertility Control, Women's Roles, and the Patrilineage in Modern Sudan: A Functional Analysis." *American Ethnologist* 2:617–633.

Palgi, Phyllis, and Henry Abramovitch. 1984. "Death: A Cross-Cultural Perspective." In *Annual Review of Anthropology,* vol. 13, pp. 385–417. Palo Alto, CA: Annual Reviews.

Parsons, Talcott, Edward Shils, Kaspar D. Naegele, and Jesse R. Pitts. 1961. *Theories of Society.* Glencoe, IL: Free Press.

Pasternak, Burton. 1976. *Introduction to Kinship and Social Organization.* Englewood Cliffs, NJ: Prentice-Hall.

Paulos, John Allen. 1980. *Mathematics and Humor.* Chicago: University of Chicago Press.

Payne, David. 1989. "The Wizard of Oz: Therapeutic Rhetoric in a Contemporary Media Ritual." *Quarterly Journal of Speech* 75:25–39.

Pelissier, Catherine. "The Anthropology of Teaching and Learning." In *Annual Review of Anthropology,* vol. 20, pp. 75–95. Palo Alto, CA: Annual Reviews.

Philips, Susan U. 1980. "Sex Differences and Language." In *Annual Review of Anthropology,* vol. 9, pp. 523–544. Palo Alto, CA: Annual Reviews.

Pitcher, George. 1965. "Wittgenstein, Nonsense and Lewis Carroll." *Massachusetts Review* 6:591–611.

Read, Kenneth E. 1965. *The High Valley.* New York: Columbia University Press.

Reardon, Betty. 1985. *Sexism and the War System.* New York: Columbia University Teachers College Press.

Richardson, Lewis. 1960. *The Statistics of Deadly Quarrels.* Pacific Grove, CA: Boxwood Press.

Ridington, Robin. 1968. "The Medicine Fight: An Instrument of Political Process among the Beaver Indians." *American Anthropologist* 70:1152–1160.

Rindos, David. 1984. *The Origins of Agriculture.* New York: Academic Press.

Robarchek, Clayton. 1990. "Motivations and Material Causes: On the Explanation of Conflict and War." In *The Anthropology of War.* Edited by Jonathan Hass. New York: Cambridge University Press.

Rosaldo, Michele, and Jane Monnig Atkinson. 1975. "Man the Hunter and Woman: Metaphors for the Sexes in Ilongot Magical Spells." In *The Interpretation of Symbolism.* New York: John Wiley & Sons.

Rosaldo, Renato. 1989. *Culture and Truth: The Remaking of Social Analysis.* Boston: Beacon Press.

Roy, Ramashray. 1985. *Self and Society: A Study in Gandhian Thought.* Beverly Hills, CA: Sage Publications.

Rubel, Arthur. 1964. "The Epidemiology of a Folk Illness: *Susto* in Hispanic America." *Ethnology* 3:268–283.

Saitoti, Tepilit Ole. 1986. *The Worlds of a Maasai Warrior.* New York: Random House.

Sanday, Peggy Reeves. 1981. "The Socio-Cultural Context of Rape: A Cross-Cultural Study." *Journal of Social Issues* 37:5–27.

Sanday, Peggy Reeves. 1990. *Fraternity Gang Rape: Sex, Brotherhood, and Privilege on Campus.* New York: New York University Press.

Scaglion, Richard. 1987. "Customary Law Development in Papua New Guinea." In *Anthropological Praxis: Translating Knowledge into Action.* Edited by Robert M. Wulff and Shirley J. Fiske. Boulder, CO: Westview Press.

Scaglion, Richard. 1990. "Ethnocentrism and the Abelam." In *The Humbled Anthropologist: Tales from the Pacific.* Edited by Philip Devita. Belmont, CA: Wadsworth Publishing.

Schieffelin, Bambi B., and Elinor Ochs. 1986. "Language Socialization." In *Annual Review of Anthropology,* vol. 15, pp. 163–191. Palo Alto, CA: Annual Reviews.

Schrire, Carmel. 1984. "Wild Surmises on Savage Thoughts." In *Past and Present in Hunter Gatherer Studies.* Edited by Carmel Schrire. New York: Academic Press.

Schwartz, Gary, and Don Merten. 1968. "Social Identity and Expressive Symbols." *American Anthropologist* 70:1117–1131.

Service, Elman. 1975. *Origins of the State and Civilization*. New York: W. W. Norton.

Sharff, Jagna Wojcicka. 1987. "The Underground Economy of a Poor Neighborhood." In *Cities of the United States: Studies in Urban Anthropology*. Edited by Leith Mullings. New York: Columbia University Press.

Shipton, Parker. 1990. "African Famines and Food Security." In *Annual Review of Anthropology,* vol. 19, pp. 353–394. Palo Alto, CA: Annual Reviews.

Shweder, Richard A., and Edmund J. Bourne. 1984. "Does the Concept of the Person Vary Cross-Culturally?" In *Cultural Conceptions of Mental Health and Therapy*. Edited by A. J. Marsella and G. M. White. Boston: D. Reidel Publishing.

Sidel, Ruth. 1986. *Women and Children Last: Social Stratification in America*. New York: Penguin Books.

Sipes, Richard G. 1973. "War, Sports, and Aggression: An Empirical Test of Two Rival Theories." *American Anthropologist* 74:64–86.

Smith, Arthur H. 1970. *Village Life in China*. Boston: Little, Brown.

Smith, Raymond T. 1984. "Anthropology and the Concept of Social Class." In *Annual Review of Anthropology,* vol. 13, pp. 467–494. Palo Alto, CA: Annual Reviews.

Smith, Robert J. 1983. *Japanese Society: Tradition, Self and the Social Order.* New York: Cambridge University Press.

Spindler, George, and Louise Spindler. 1983. "Anthropologists View American Culture." In *Annual Review of Anthropology,* vol. 12, pp. 49–78. Palo Alto, CA: Annual Reviews.

Stack, Carol B. 1974. *All Our Kin: Strategies for Survival in a Black Community.* New York: Harper & Row.

Stone, Lawrence. 1977. *The Family, Sex and Marriage in England 1500–1800.* New York: Harper & Row.

Strathern, Andrew. 1971. *The Rope of Moka: Big Men and Ceremonial Exchange in Mount Hagen New Guinea*. London: Cambridge University Press.

Thomas, Elizabeth. 1959. *The Harmless People*. New York: Alfred A. Knopf.

Thrasher, Frederic. 1963. *The Gang*. Chicago: University of Chicago Press. (originally published 1927)

Trice, Harrison M., and Janice M. Beyer. 1984. "Studying Organizational Cultures through Rites and Ceremonials." *Academy of Management Review* 9:653–669.

Turner, Victor. 1967. *The Forest of Symbols: Aspects of Ndembu Ritual*. Ithaca, NY: Cornell University Press.

U.S. Department of Commerce, Bureau of the Census. 1991. *Poverty in the United States: 1990*. Current Population Reports, Series P–60. No. 175 (August).

Valentine, Charles A. 1968. *Culture and Poverty: Critique and Counter Proposals*. Chicago: University of Chicago Press.

van den Berghe, Pierre L. 1965. *South Africa: A Study in Conflict*. Middletown, CT: Wesleyan University Press.

van den Berghe, Pierre L. 1970. *Race and Ethnicity*. New York: Basic Books.

van den Berghe, Pierre L., and George P. Primov. 1977. *Inequality in the Peruvian Andes: Class and Ethnicity in Cuzco*. Columbia: University of Missouri Press.

van Gennep, Arnold. 1960. *The Rites of Passage*. Translated by Monica B. Vizedom and Gabrielle L. Chaffe. Chicago: University of Chicago Press. (originally published 1906)

Wagner, Roy. 1984. "Ritual as Communication: Order, Meaning, and Secrecy in Melanesian Initiation Rites." In *Annual Review of Anthropology*, vol. 13, pp. 143–155. Palo Alto, CA: Annual Reviews.

Walens, Stanley. 1981. *Feasting with Cannibals: An Essay on Kwakiutl Cosmology*. Princeton, NJ: Princeton University Press.

Wallace, Anthony F. C. 1966. *Religion: An Anthropological View*. New York: Random House.

Wallace, Anthony F. C., and Raymond D. Fogelson. 1965. "The Identity Struggle." In *Intensive Family Therapy*. Edited by I. Boszormenyi-Nagy and J. L. Framo. New York: Harper & Row.

Weaver, Thomas. 1985. "Anthropology as a Policy Science: Part II, Development and Training." *Human Organization* 44:197–205.

Weiner, Annette B. 1976. *Women of Value, Men of Renown*. Austin: University of Texas Press.

Weiner, Annette B. 1988. *The Trobrianders of Papua New Guinea*. New York: Holt, Rinehart and Winston.

White, Leslie. 1949. *The Science of Culture*. New York: Farrar, Straus and Giroux.

White, Leslie. 1959. *The Evolution of Culture*. New York: McGraw-Hill.

Whitehead, Harriet. 1981. "The Bow and the Burden Strap: A New Look at Institutionalized Homosexuality in Native North America." In *Sexual Meanings: The Cultural Construction of Gender and Sexuality*. Edited by Sherry B. Ortner and Harriet Whitehead. New York: Cambridge University Press.

Whitehead, Neil Lancelot. 1990. "The Snake Warriors—Sons of the Tiger's Teeth: A Descriptive Analysis of Carib Warfare, ca 1500–1820." In *The Anthropology of War*. Edited by Jonathan Hass. New York: Cambridge University Press.

Williams, Walter L. 1986. *The Spirit and the Flesh: Sexual Diversity in American Indian Culture*. Boston: Beacon Press.

Wilmsen, Edwin N., and James R. Denbow. 1990. "Paradigmatic History of San-speaking Peoples and Current Attempts at Revision." *Current Anthropology* 31:489–512.

Wolf, Eric. 1966. *Peasants*. Englewood Cliffs, NJ: Prentice-Hall.

Wolf, Eric. 1969. *Peasant Wars of the Twentieth Century*. New York: Harper & Row.

Wolf, Eric. 1982. *Europe and the People without History*. Berkeley: University of California Press.

Wolf, Margery. 1968. *The House of Lim*. Englewood Cliffs, NJ: Prentice-Hall.

Woodburn, James. 1968. "An Introduction to Hadza Ecology." In *Man the Hunter*. Edited by Richard Lee and Irven DeVore, with the assistance of Jill Nash. Chicago: Aldine Publishing.

Worsley, Peter. 1982. "Non-Western Medical Systems." In *Annual Review of Anthropology*, vol. 11, pp. 315–348. Palo Alto, CA: Annual Reviews.

Wright, Quincy. 1965. *A Study of War*. Chicago: University of Chicago Press.

Yanagisako, Sylvia Junko. 1979. "Family and Household: The Analysis of Domestic Groups." In *Annual Review of Anthropology*, vol. 8, pp. 161–205. Palo Alto, CA: Annual Reviews.

Young, Allan. 1982. "The Anthropologies of Illness and Sickness." In *Annual Review of Anthropology*, vol. 11, pp. 257–285. Palo Alto, CA: Annual Reviews.

N A M E   I N D E X

215

Cultural Anthropology

Designed by Lesiak/Crampton Design, Inc., Chicago, Illinois
Edited by Gloria Reardon, Belvidere, Illinois
Production supervision by Kim Vander Steen, Palatine, Illinois
Composition by Point West, Inc., Carol Stream, Illinois
Printed and bound by Arcata Graphics, Kingsport, Tennessee
Paper, Finch Opaque
The text is set in Garamond; display in Caslon